Molecular Computing

Molecular Computing

edited by Tanya Sienko, Andrew Adamatzky, Nicholas Rambidi, and
Michael Conrad

The MIT Press
Cambridge, Massachusetts
London, England

This book was set in Times New Roman on 3B2 by Asco Typesetters, Hong Kong, and was printed and bound in the United States of America.

Library of Congress Cataloging-in-Publication Data

Molecular computing / edited by Tanya Sienko ... [et al.].
   p. cm.
 Includes bibliographical references and index.
 ISBN 0-262-19487-2 (hc. : alk. paper)
 1. Molecular computers. I. Sienko, Tanya.
QA76.887.M65 2003
621.391—dc21   2002044409

10 9 8 7 6 5 4 3 2 1

Dedicated to the memory of Michael Conrad, who died during the preparation of this book

Contents

Michael Conrad
1941–2000

In Memoriam

Professor Michael Conrad, one of the editors of this book, passed away on December 28, 2000 after a battle with lymphoma. Michael was truly a giant figure in the fields of non–von Neumann, biologically oriented information processing. His efforts were fundamental and manifold.

In the mid-1980s, I took an interest in solving problems of high computational complexity. As a first step, I prepared a paper wherein I tried to formulate approaches based on information processing by biomolecular and simple biological entities. I sent it to the *Journal of Molecular Structure*. Shortly thereafter, I received a very professional and friendly referee's report. The referee did not want to remain anonymous. Professor Michael Conrad from Wayne University was the referee for my paper. We met later in Moscow, and during the following years, I remained in close contact with Michael—the recognized leader in the field—and had the opportunity to discuss with him general principles of molecular and chemical-based computing. Michael's fundamental pioneering ideas lie at the foundation of this field.

Michael received an AB in biology from Harvard University in 1963 and a PhD in biophysics from Stanford University in 1969. He was a postdoctoral fellow at the Center for Theoretical Studies at the University of Miami and a postdoctoral scholar in the Department of Mathematics at the University of California at Berkeley. He spent three years at the Institute of Information Processing at the University of Tubingen in Germany. In 1979, he moved to the position of professor of computer science at Wayne State University in Detroit, Michigan after holding associate professorships in the Biology Department at the City College of New York and in the Department of Computer and Communication Sciences at the University of Michigan.

He wrote more than two hundred scientific publications on such topics as molecular information processing, enzyme and membrane dynamics, computational modeling of complex biological systems, neuromolecular networks and brain models, evolutionary programming, adaptability theory, and comparative analysis of information processing in organisms and machines. His pioneering works—"Molecular information processing in the central nervous system" (1974), "On design principles for a molecular computer" (1985), and "The brain-machine disanalogy" (1989), are the fundamental basis of contemporary molecular and chemical-based information processing.

Michael's high standards and friendly psychological background were an inspiration for his students. Without exception, they will tell of their special relationship with Michael, his unending support and tireless devotion to them, even after their graduation.

Michael was a versatile and gifted person. He was keen on modern painting. And his rare moments of relaxation were devoted to this flame. He was a good friend and a loving husband and father.

We miss him greatly, but he has shown us an example to follow.

Nicholas G. Rambidi

Introduction: What Is Molecular Computing?

The history of technology is also the history of ideas. Sometimes ideas that have become stale and rigid continue to hold sway and hamper scientific and technological innovation. The difficulty is that once a certain set of concepts and images are set into place, the influence of these concepts may take on a life and power of their own—far beyond what its creators intended—guiding and shaping further development downstream until it becomes inconceivable to think of a certain technology as having taken any other track.

The standard paradigm of digital computing with its division into "hardware" and "software" is a case in point. The division has been recruited to explain (among other things) the relationship between brain and mind, where the human mind is nothing more than the software that happens to be running on the "wetware" that is the human brain. In fact, the strong version of the Church-Turing thesis would state that all processes in nature are digitally duplicable, within reason, using a set of rules of the Turing form. Turing restated this with his famous Turing test, wherein he assumed it would be possible to program a digital computer in such a way that its responses would be indistinguishable from those of a human, claiming that such a machine had just as much right to be called intelligent as the human did. Here, the specifically biological properties of the brain would not be essential in any way to its information processing capabilities.

The authors of this book take a different view. We believe that the great power of the human brain and other similar biological organisms—feats of recognition, immense parallel processing abilities—are due to the fact that we do not operate according to the digital information/hardware split, nor are we Turing machines. Although systems in nature may be describable by mathematical maps that are Turing computable, there is no claim that the amount of time and space required satisfies real-time constraints imposed by the environment, or that they are even computable given all the time, space, and energy available in the universe. Nor is there evidence that actual biological intelligences work this way. Humans and other biological organisms do not have little zeros and ones encoded in our systems, nor do we operate according to digital algorithmic principles. Enzymes in our bodies perform marvelous feats of recognition—being able to recognize one particular protein out of the myriad we have running around and break it in half—yet none of this is done according to any digital program encoded somewhere or stored tables of discrete rules. We (and other biological organisms) work according to what we call in this book *molecular computing*. As Michael and Deborah Conrad have argued (Conrad and Conrad 1997), biological organisms process information in a matter that exploits physical-dynamical features (including quantum effects) that are computationally costly in terms of the number of digital switching operations required—if able to be done at all. It is the physical characteristics of material systems—whether they be relatively simple chemical systems or material in biological cells—that allow highly complex information processing to occur. It is the feats of this paradigm that we wish to explore.

Molecular computers are information processing systems in which individual molecules play a crucial functional role. Artificial information processing systems fabricated from molecular materials might emulate biology or follow de novo architectural principles. Much work has already been done on shrinking the level of circuits and switches found in conventional silicon architecture down to the atomic level, using molecular wires, switches, and the Coulomb effect and "nano-islands" to allow the encoding of a bit in the presence or absence of one electron. With conductive polymers and the discovery of molecules such as the rotaxanes—which have bistable states and can theoretically encode information—much progress has already been completed and will undoubtedly lead to new "conventional computing" devices. But we should remind ourselves again that this is not how biological organisms process information.

The two biggest scientific developments in the second half of the twentieth century have been computer science and molecular biology. The existing parallels between these fields must have stimulated many investigators with wondering whether a deeper link should in fact be made, using analogies from one in an attempt to provoke advances in the other. One example would be the replication and transcription of DNA, which forcibly reminds one of various tape-writing and tape-reading operations in a digital computer. This analogy can be misleading: The transcription of DNA produces a protein, which in its unfolded form is a long line of amino acids bound to a polypeptide backbone. It then, under the influence of the surrounding cell medium and a nonzero temperature, somehow folds up to produce a three-dimensional protein held together by various weak interactions (van der Waals, proton hopping, etc.) The "information" can be argued to be in various different places: somewhat in the original chain, in the folding-up process, and in the final structure of the protein. In any case, the "encoding" of the information relies heavily on actual physical molecules, how they interact with each other and their environment, which includes a heat bath and the molecules of the surrounding medium. By comparison, the tape-reading/tape-writing aspect of computer programs is more or less irrelevant—a program is nothing more than pure information and could conceivably be encoded into the machine in various different ways. In fact, that conventional computers up to now have been able to ignore the effects of thermal noise and the atomic nature of the material is what has allowed the existence of software in the first place.

The present interest in biocomputing is due to many factors. The first impetus arises from electronics. Limits are extended year after year, yet at some point the size, speed, and power dissipation of switches based on silicon or other conventional materials will run into the deadlocks set by the basic laws of physics. Already the "leakiness" of quantum effects between nano-sized wires that are nanometers apart has sparked interest in somehow harnessing the power (quantum cellular automata, etc.) of quantum mechanical devices. The second impetus is that although conventional computer science has been extremely successful, a number of critical problems in information processing have persisted stubbornly beyond reach: pattern recognition, learning, and parallelism being three examples of where biological systems still remain far advanced beyond their silicon mimics.

Most frustrating is the fact that although integrated circuit technology has managed to squeeze ever more lines onto a chip, all but a small portion of the silicon is unused at any given time. Paradoxically, packing twice as many silicon switches into a given volume—increasing the number of components—decreases the fraction of actual active material. Because of this, it is doubtful that future computers will be able to do any better than present-day computers when it comes to problems of high complexity.

To harness the dormant computing power in a system it is, in general, necessary to give up conventional programmability. Conrad (1990) has expanded this notion into the trade-off principle:

A computing system cannot have all of the following three properties: structural programmability, high computational efficiency, and high evolutionary adaptability. Structural programmability and high computational efficiency are always mutually exclusive. Structural programmability and evolutionary adaptability are mutually exclusive in the region of maximum effective computational efficiency (which is always less than or equal to the computational efficiency).

Programmability versus evolvability. In order for a system to evolve toward higher efficiency, it is necessary for it to be able to change and adapt to circumstances. It is everyone's experience that a single change in a computer program usually leads to major changes in the execution sequence, and rarely with a resulting program that works! Redundancies can be introduced to confer fault tolerance, but in that case, any changes in function are prevented. A computer program can be considered a fragile system—small changes in it "break" it, and thus it cannot be considered a useable system for evolving. Variation and selection are efficient as a method of adaptation only if a potentially useful alternate can be produced through a single structural alteration. As any programmer knows, to his chagrin, something as simple as a bit swap or a misplaced character regularly renders a program completely unusable—in fact, often unable to be compiled. By comparison, in biological systems, enzymes usually have their shapes and functions only slightly altered by a point mutation. "Programming" occurs at the level of the amino acid sequence, but it can be considered as at least one step removed from the "running program" aspect of the enzyme, because shape and function emerge from this sequence through a continuous dynamical folding process. It is this intermediate step, the continuous dynamical process of protein folding, that allows the likelihood that single mutations will still lead to functionally acceptable forms of the enzyme, and this is critically important for maintaining a nonnegligible rate of evolution.

Programmability versus efficiency.   Individual components usually are not optimized for the task they are doing. If components could always evolve to specifically suit the task at hand, networks could learn to use their resources in parallel. If one had a computer composed of N particles, there are theoretically N^2 interactions that could be carried out simultaneously, thus producing incredible parallelism. Unfortunately, for a system to exhibit formal computational behavior, constraints must be introduced to suppress a large fraction of the interactions.

Much has been made of the supposed thermodynamic limits of computing. Bennett and Landauer (Bennett 1973; Landauer 1982) have shown that physical realizations of formal computation processes can, in principle, proceed with arbitrarily low dissipation when speed, reliability, and required memory space are not important considerations. Thermodynamic costs can be traded for other costs that can be restated in terms of components, reliability, and speed. If a machine is structurally programmable, these other costs are high, and hence the costs of adding more components or accepting less speed and reliability in order to reduce the dissipation would soon outweigh the advantages. If the system foregoes structural programmability, the balance changes. This is a probable explanation for the relatively low energy dissipation found in biological computing.

Efficiency versus complexity.   Here, the question is: How much bang does one get for one's buck with different types of problems and different types of computers? With a polynomial-time class of problem, the resources may increase with the degree of the problem size. For an exponential-time class problem, the resources required increase at least exponentially with problem size, say as 2^n. In the explosive 2^n case, a 10^{10}-fold increase in resources allows an additive increase in problem size of only 33. The dramatically different capabilities of biological organisms and von Neumann machines are largely due to the fact that the former are capable of solving much larger problems in the polynomial-time class. This may be because of the different mechanisms being used (see chapter 4 of this volume). Also, systems that opt for efficiency and evolutionary adaptability would be better suited to coupling increases in computation resources to increases in problem size.

The biologically motivated molecular computer engineer is not trying to solve the origin-of-life problem or to create "living computers." The more-than-sufficient objective is to exploit the characteristic properties of biological macromolecules to produce devices that perform useful information processing functions.

Looking at how biological organisms process information, one is struck by certain aspects:

. The ubiquitousness of proteins and a "two-step process" of transcription

. A very high degree of parallelism

. A high degree of complexity

Ignoring for the present the question as to whether proteins are the ultimate optimal mechanism or whether nature (and evolution) simply used what was available, it should be pointed out that a very important aspect is the dependence of biological systems for their "information processing" capabilities on what is known as *molecular recognition*. Molecules bind together weakly with other molecules—not as tightly as one finds in normal covalent bonding, but not so weakly that discrimination cannot be made between different molecules. This recognition is, at base, a quantum effect and is one of the mechanisms by which parallelism is introduced into the system.

Assume a potential surface with many valleys, one of which corresponds to the desired solution of a problem (i.e., the lowest energy state). In the absence of external perturbation (e.g., thermal agitation), a classical system would never make the transition from an incorrect potential well to the correct one. A microscopic (quantum) system, with particles such as electrons, would inevitably find the proper well by virtue of barrier penetration. But to actually exploit this for problem solving, it is necessary to "put a handle on the electron," or in more technical terms, embed the microsystem in a macroscopic architecture where the output state is obvious. Macromolecules—such as proteins—are an intermediate-size architecture that is too large to undergo barrier penetration per se, but its pattern-matching motions may in large part be controlled by the electronic wave function. When a protein is "recognized" by an enzyme, we are seeing the results of a many-valued parallel exploration of phase space made possible by quantum mechanics and carried up to the macroscale. Equivalently, the difficult problem of pattern recognition has been turned into the physical process of minimizing the free energy of the protein-enzyme complex, a natural occurrence in the physical universe.

This book has been written in an attempt to elucidate many of the issues surrounding the above ideas and their application to molecular computing systems. We have tried to organize the chapters in such a way that the flow is from most abstract and most basic to more and more complex or applied systems.

The following chapter (chapter 1) is by Michael Conrad and Klaus-Peter Zauner. Their chapter covers and expands on several of the issues mentioned above, analyzing the uses of proteins and other such molecules from an information processing point of view. Included are analyses of relevant molecular properties and the necessity of the macro-micro-interface. The authors then move into a description of a prototype system, complete with a recipe for how to build it. Finally, chapter 1 ends with descriptions of experimental systems and what has been accomplished so far.

Chapter 2 is by Jean-Marie Lehn and Tanya Sienko. As has already been mentioned, molecular recognition is what underlies many of these biological systems, running from the "information processing" aspects of enzymes to the aspects of self-recognition, self-assembly, and self-organizing systems. After a short explanation of what molecular recognition is and how to design systems to do it well, the authors work from the simplest types of self-recognition up to the most complex, along with a few comments on information transfer and how concepts of molecular recognition may be used.

The next two chapters, chapters 3 and 4, can be said to constitute the reaction-diffusion part of the book. The chemical components of the media themselves are not all that complex, yet the resultant activity can be extremely complex and lend itself to parallel information processing of certain tasks. Andrew Adamatzky (chapter 3) has contributed a chapter on the theory of computation in nonlinear media. The first part covers a theory of excitable and diffusive processors. Adamatzky then moves to an explanation of and samples of such systems with specialized processors. The chapter ends with a long section on universal processors, with a detailed explanation of the example of collision gates in DNA and monomolecular arrays. Chapter 4, by Nicholas Rambidi, goes further, with descriptions of physical reaction-diffusion systems found in chemical media, the theory of how to build a computer based on such, along with a large number of experimental examples.

At this point, we move back to more biologically oriented systems, and specifically to DNA computing. Carlo Maley (chapter 5) has kindly contributed a review chapter covering present work to date as well as comments on where the field will probably advance in the future, including all the pros and cons of the field.

Chapter 6 has been contributed by Duane Marcy, Bryan Vought, and Robert Birge, and covers bioelectronics and protein-based optical computing. The main focus of this chapter is on the possibilities inherent in biorhodopsin, as well as comments on how optical/biological computing would differ from semiconductor-based systems.

Finally, continuing our trend, we end up with a chapter on the present status of biosensors, contributed by Satoshi Sasaki and Isao Karube (chapter 7). Karube almost single-handedly invented the field many years ago, fusing electronics and micromachines together with biological films or organisms whose reaction (at the molecular level) could be read out (i.e., used) to provide a trigger signal to the micromachine/electronics. Japan remains the country most advanced in this field. We hope our readers will enjoy this review article, which covers a wide range of biosensors and what they can do.

Some final comments should be made about what we have not included in this book: We have not included articles on quantum computing because we feel this discipline lies outside the scope of what we wish to address. Nor, except in a tangential way, have we touched on the field of molecular electronics, where the attempt has been to shrink circuits down even further, to the level of say, a nanotube or a molecular wire. We have also stayed away from neural networks, feeling that there are sufficient books extant to satisfy any seeker of knowledge in that area.

What we have tried to do is sketch out, even if only lightly, certain areas and topics that have remained obscure to most computer scientists and that we feel have great potential for the future. Molecular computing and the non–von Neumann paradigms for information processing remain a vast area in which only a few explorers have left their footprints. We hope that this book is only the first of many guides into this new field.

References

Bennett, C. H. 1973. Logical reversibility of computation. *IBM J. Res. Dev.* 17: 525–532.

Conrad, M. 1990. *Molecular Computing*, issue of *Advances in Computers*, Vol. 31. New York: Academic Press.

Conrad, M., and D. Conrad. 1997. Of maps and territories: A three point landing on the mind-body problem. In *Matter Matters*, ed. P. Arhem, H. Liljenstrom, and U. Svedin, 107–137. New York: Springer-Verlag.

Landauer, R. 1982. Uncertainty principle and minimal energy dissipation in the computer. *Int. J. Theor. Phys.* 21: 283–297.

Molecular Computing

1 Conformation-Based Computing: A Rationale and a Recipe

Michael Conrad and Klaus-Peter Zauner

1.1 Objectives

Biological systems possess enviable information processing abilities, which are rooted in the self-organization of context-sensitive building blocks. Molecular computing can utilize this principle. Our objective in the present chapter is to show that this opens up a realm of information processing that is inaccessible to programmable machines. Our second objective is to present a tabletop prototype that illustrates a methodology for pursuing this direction.

Algorithmic complexity theory provides a framework for elucidating the comparative capabilities of programmable and nonprogrammable systems. Programmable architectures are amenable to a more compressible description, concomitant to the fact that they must conform to a simple user manual. To implement complex input-output behavior, it is necessary to supply a complex program. The programmer therefore must be the source of complexity. Biomolecular architectures are sharply different: Complexity is inherent. The capabilities are constructed by orchestrating a repertoire of complex components through an adaptive process. The number of functions that can be implemented is limited by the time available for adaptation and may not be larger than that in programmable systems. In this chapter, we will argue that the complexity of the actual achievable behavior is greater.

John von Neumann (1951) referred to such noncompressible complexity in a discussion of the visual cortex:

It is not at all certain that in this domain a real object might not constitute the simplest description of itself, that is, any attempt to describe it by the usual literary or formal-logical method may lead to something less manageable and more involved.   (1951, 24)

In our case, the real objects are proteins. We will show that it is possible to utilize the conformational dynamics of proteins to process input signal patterns—though at this stage not in a manner that transcends formal description.

1.2 Algorithmic Complexity Rationale

Digital computers are commonly referred to as general purpose machines. The seeming implication is that with sufficient memory and operating speed it should be possible to implement any computable process on such a machine. The concept of computation universality, originally expressed in terms of the Turing model of computation, captures this idea. For the present purposes, the Turing formalism can be equated to a digital machine with no a priori limit on available memory and time. Such an idealized machine would be capable of computing any computable function. Realizable machines are, of course, finite. The memory available may not be sufficient to perform the desired computation; or the computation might require an unacceptable span of time. Here we are especially concerned with a further limitation: The size of the program that can be presented to the machine is also subject to practical restrictions.

The above distinction, between limits on processing capacity and program size, has an important implication. Even if processing speed and memory space could be increased indefinitely, a large class of information processing tasks would still be inaccessible. The programs, or maps describing the input-output behavior of the system, can be too large to practically specify.

Let us take as a computer any system that, starting from a state that encodes a problem description, will change to a state interpretable as the solution of the problem. The limited precision and limited dynamic range of the computer's components, together with the requirement of a finite response time, restrict any computer to a finite set of discernible inputs and a finite repertoire of outputs.

A deterministic computer is a physical realization of a function that takes an input signal pattern as argument and returns as the value the associated output signal pattern. To make the computer perform a desired task, it is necessary to specify the appropriate function. The specification may be provided explicitly by programming or, in the case of an adaptable system, implicitly through training. In either case, the specification has to select the desired system behavior from the set of potential behaviors.

Consider a deterministic computer that is supposed to respond to each n-bit input pattern with an appropriate m-bit output pattern. The function that maps the input into output can, in principle (and for small values of n also in practice), be described by a table. The table would have 2^n rows, one for every possible input, and each row would contain the pattern that the computer should output in response to this input. Programming a computer requires that the table it should implement be communicated to it.

The amount of information necessary to specify the input-output map is given by the number of bits needed to select one specific table from the set of all possible tables. There are 2^n rows corresponding to the possible inputs in the table, and any one of the 2^m possible outputs may be assigned to each row. This gives rise to $2^{(m2^n)}$ possible tables. Selecting an arbitrary table from this set requires a specification that is $\log_2[2^{(m2^n)}] = m2^n$ bits long (Ashby 1968). The important implication is this: Even for input patterns of very moderate size, it will almost always be impossible to program a computer to perform a map arbitrarily selected from the set of possible maps. For example, consider a pattern of the size of a single character on a computer screen, say 10×10 black and white pixels ($n = 100$ bits), and suppose we want to classify such tiny images according to whether or not they contain a certain feature (meaning that $m = 1$ bit). This could require a program 10^{20} gigabytes in length.

On the surface, it might seem that for any particular job required, it should be possible to devise an appropriate program of practical size. The following considerations from algorithmic complexity theory reveal that programming a "general" purpose computer is in fact practical only in very special situations.

In the example considered above, every row of the table that describes the classification of the 10×10 pixel images has a 1-bit entry indicating the presence or absence of the feature. The content of the table corresponds to a binary string of length equal to the number of rows in the table. Chaitin (1966) asked the question: How long would a program need to be in order to generate such a sequence? For our purpose, we can take the ability to generate the contents of the table as equivalent to the capacity to implement the input-output map described by the table. Some classifications have short programs. If we want each input image to be classified according to whether it is all black, then all but one row in the table will contain the same bit. A program much shorter than the explicit table will be sufficient to generate the table. This corresponds to the fact that the table is highly compressible—the program being a compressed description of the table. The algorithmic complexity of the table is defined as the length, up to an additive constant, of the shortest program required to generate it (Li and Vitányi 1997). The additive constant reflects differences in machine architecture that, from a practical point of view, can have an immense impact as the constant becomes large (Kampis 1991).

For most tables, no significant compression is possible, as can be seen from a simple counting argument (Chaitin 1974). Under the assumption that (due to the capacity of the machine or its programmers) the longest practical program is limited to a length of b bits, there exist only 2^b distinct programs. The fraction η of tables describing n bit inputs mapped to m bit outputs, which can be compressed to a b-bit-long specification, is therefore at most

$$\eta = 2^{(b-m2^n)}$$

Furthermore, this maximum value of η can only be achieved if the machine architecture is not degenerate in the sense that two or more distinct programs yield identical input-output behavior.

The above equation shows that, in practice, only a very small fraction of the conceivable information processing tasks can be implemented by programming a putatively general-purpose computer. However, the compressibility of the tables is relative to the machine architecture on which they are specified. Different architectures can bring different input-output behaviors within reach of practical specifications. An extreme example would be a machine specifically constructed to solve a single large problem instance (Zauner and Conrad 1996).

Every realizable information processing machine can only implement a small subset of the possible input-output transforms and is therefore a special-purpose device (Zauner and Conrad 2001). The common computers, often naively assumed to be general purpose, are in fact specialized devices that have been designed to implement the narrow class of highly compressible input-output maps.

1.3   Trade-Off Principle

The comparative limits of programmable and nonprogrammable architectures can be stated in terms of a trade-off principle: Programmability, efficiency, and evolutionary adaptability are incompatible. A system, to achieve high programmability, must trade off efficiency and evolvability.

A computing system is programmable if the initial state and a chosen set of formally defined state transition rules can be explicitly invoked. The programmer communicates the intended relations among the system states to the system, which in turn interprets the rules in rigid adherence to a finite user manual. If the programmability is bound into the material structure of the system, we will refer to it as structural. Material physical systems generally have self-organizing dynamics, hence a will of their own that is incompatible with prescriptive programmability. The computer designer must quench these self-organizing aspects in order to achieve a physical realization of a formal system. Information processing systems, however, do not need to be programmable; functionality can be molded through adaptive procedures.

We can phrase the programmability-efficiency trade-off in terms of interactions. To be as generous as possible, let us make the assumption that elementary particles can serve as active components in a computing system and the system contains n such particles. The potential function of the system can call on as many as n^2 interactions. If the system is structurally programmable, the input-output behavior of components should remain the same as more components are added. This is only possible if the components have a fixed number of possible inputs. Thus the number of allowable interactions scales as Cn, where C is a constant. The fraction of interactions available for problem solving falls off as C/n as the number of components increases. If the system is run in a serial mode, therefore in an effectively programmable mode, the falloff is even faster (i.e., as K/n^2, where K is the number of components that can be active at any given time). If quantum features are pertinent to the system's problem solving, interference effects among the possible states of the particles must also be considered, further increasing the disparity between the potential complexity of natural systems and systems configured to be structurally programmable. The assumption that single particles could act in accordance with a finite user manual is of course quite unreasonable. As the number of particles per component decreases, it becomes increasingly likely that the system will self-organize in a way that escapes a simple user manual description (Conrad 1995).

The trade-off principle is intimately connected to the compression issues considered in section 1.2. The salient point is that all structurally programmable architectures must have a highly compressible description in order to conform to formal rules specified in a simple user manual. Constructing a formal component calls for a large number of particles, because this requires quenching of self-organizing characteristics that deviate from the user manual. A large number of such formal and hence low-complexity components is needed to build a system with complex behavior. Efficiency in terms of the necessary number of particles will therefore be low. In short, to make a heavyweight architecture out of lightweight components, the system must be large.

The conflict between structural programmability and evolutionary adaptability can also be understood in terms of compression. In a program that is a highly compressed description of the system's behavior, a change in any single bit will, in general, have radical effects on the behavior of the modified program. The program ordinarily describes an input-output table that is much larger than the program. Any bit modification in the program will, in general, alter many bits in the input-output table. Of course, the uncompressed input-output table can always be changed gradually (bit by bit). But it is only possible to act on this table through modifications of the program—hence the gradualism requirement for evolutionary adaptability cannot, in general, be satisfied. If biological systems were amenable to a highly compressed description, they would a fortiori be unsuitable for evolutionary adaptation.

The trade-off principle does not assert that structural programmability absolutely precludes evolutionary adaptability. Biological systems in nature are clearly highly evolvable. In principle, it should be possible to use a structurally programmable machine to simulate the structure-function plasticity that allows for this evolvability. As long as mutations are restricted to the virtual level, rather than to the program as encoded in the state of the base machine, it would be possible to duplicate the requisite evolvability. But this comes at a computational cost; the computational work required to simulate plastic structure-function relations puts a severe practical limit on the degree of evolvability that can be retained. In effect, the simulation program is a decompression of some highly compressed program that could do the same job as the simulated system. The decompression, if appropriately introduced, reduces the fragility of the program.

The decompression has an equivalent in the interaction picture. Redundancy in the number of components and interactions among them serves to buffer the effect of mutation on features of the system critical for function (Conrad 1979). This is not an entirely general fact; it is restricted to a subclass of systems with self-organizing dynamics. Protein folding, in particular, fits this picture. As the length of the amino acid chain increases or as more amino acids with similar properties are available for substitutions, the chance that a mutation will be acceptable increases. Without self-organization, the introduction of redundancy would only yield fault tolerance, not the topological distortability necessary for transformation of function (Conrad 1983).

The structure-function relations that enable high efficiency and high evolvability require context-sensitive components. This sensitivity of the components' behavior to their environment is in sharp contrast to the precisely defined and therefore context-free components of structurally programmable systems. Nevertheless, networks of context-free components run in a parallel mode can also exhibit self-organization, as in the case of artificial neural networks. The self-organization, however, causes a loss of effective programmability. With the main advantage of rigidly defined components lost, there is no reason to restrict the architecture of the network to context-free components. Instead, context-sensitive components that open the path to high efficiency and high evolvability can be employed.

The trade-off principle suggests that there are two sharply different modes of computing: the high programmability mode versus the high efficiency, high adaptability mode. Biological systems, because they are the products of evolution, must operate in the latter. The remainder of this chapter will focus on initial concrete steps in the direction of artificial systems that operate in the biological mode.

1.4   Pertinent Molecular Properties

The trade-off principle asserts that systems with nonprogrammable structure-function relations are capable of implementing transforms that are too complex to embody in general-purpose (programmable) architectures. The physical dynamics of such systems, suitably interpreted, effectuates the computation. Conceivably many types of physical dynamics could be utilized in this manner. Macromolecules afford a particularly powerful combination of properties (see table 1.1).

The main property is folded shape. This requires long, nonconjugated polymers (because rotation around single bonds is necessary). Carbon, the atom of life, sup-

Table 1.1
Computationally important properties of macromolecules

Property	Draws on	Confers
Folded shape	Long flexible chains, weak bonding, rotation around single bonds	Specificity, self-assembly
Conformational dynamics	Folded shape	Milieu sensitivity, allosteric control
Well-defined ground state	Individual molecules (not statistical ensembles)	Precisely duplicatable nonlinearity, specific shape
Brownian motion	Specific shape, low mass, heat bath	Cost-free search
High evolvability	Combinatorial variety, high dimensionality	Diverse repertoire of specialized functions
Specificity with speed	Defined shape, Brownian motion	Low dissipation pattern recognition
Supramolecular structure	Self-assembly, free energy minimization	Rich, extended 3-D architecture
Diverse specificities	Building block principle, heat bath, folded shape	Heterogeneous organization, dynamic complexity

ports this requirement. Silicon, the only competitor for carbon in this respect, is rather inferior (Henderson 1913; Conrad 1994b).

The C-C bond energy is about the same as for bonds with H or O. The energy required to break the Si-Si bond is only about half as much as the energy required to break Si-H and Si-O bonds. The number of carbon-based structures that are possible is accordingly much greater than is possible with silicon (Sidgwick 1950; Edsall and Wyman 1958). The longer chains possible with carbon allow for a greater variety of folded shapes.

The well-known lock-key metaphor (Fischer 1894) for enzyme-substrate recognition is based on this fact of folded shape. Proteins must be big enough to have significant shape features (not true for individual atoms) but small enough to scan each other's shapes through diffusion (which we can refer to as *Brownian search*). The shape fitting is in reality dynamic; conformational motions are critical to the rate of complex formation and (in the case of catalysis) complex decomposition. The conformational motions are sensitive to a variety of milieu features (e.g., temperature, ions, control molecules). The prototype device that we will shortly turn to utilizes this context selectivity for signal pattern recognition.

As in all chemical reactions, thermal fluctuation (heat motion) is sine qua non. The term *Brownian search*, used above, is intended to suggest its computational significance. Recall the discussion of complexity: Complexity must either be provided in a program fed to a system from the outside or it must have self-organizing dynamics, therefore nonprogrammable structure-function relations. Protein folding and complex formation are prime examples. The heat bath is a potent source of complexity. The amino acid sequence draws on thermal fluctuations to explore itself in the folding process. The folded structure draws on thermal fluctuations to explore molecules with which it interacts in the complex formation process. In general, physical self-organization is based either on energy minimization or entropy maximization. The randomness of the heat bath is an essential ingredient in both cases. If entropy maximization is the controlling feature, the fluctuations allow the system to assume a greater number of structural forms. If energy minimization dominates, thermal energy must be given up to the heat bath in an irreversible way. From the point of view of algorithmic complexity theory, the complexity of a pattern or process increases as the size of the shortest program required to generate it increases—that is, as its description becomes less compressible. Of all phenomena considered in physics, perhaps the heat bath has the most incompressible description.

The combinatorial variety of carbon compounds is another powerful virtue. The number of possible amino acid or nucleotide sequences is hyperastronomically large. The important point is that the notion of a general-purpose system takes on a new guise. Conventional electronic machines are constructed from simple standard building blocks—for example, NAND gates. Biological systems, in contrast, are built from an extremely large variety of macromolecular species, each capable of performing a specific complex transform. Cells and organisms with different input-output behaviors arise through adaptive processes that modify the proteins in the repertoire or that express these proteins in different combinations.

The high evolvability of proteins is requisite for the efficacy of the adaptation process. Again, folding is the key feature, because it allows for structure-function malleability. As noted in section 1.3, there is an intimate connection between evolvability and complexity. If protein folding could be described by an extremely compressed program, therefore a simple process from the algorithmic complexity point of view, then the structure-function relations would approach programmability and would be fragile. Most mutations would be cataclysmic. Evolutionary considerations thus imply that folding and (chemical) complex formation are complex processes in the algorithmic sense. At the same time, the introduction of redundant amino acids in the sequence and the utilization of amino acids with high replaceability serve to buffer the effect of mutation on conformational features critical for function (Conrad and Volkenstein 1981).

Sometimes the argument is put forward that biological molecules are insufficiently reliable for computing. The opposite is actually the case. Single molecules have definite ground states, as opposed to the macroscopic switches from which conventional computers are built. The latter are built from statistical aggregates of particles and are therefore subject to erosion. The reliability issue is rather subtle, because it is clear that with solid-state components, it is possible to perform many repetitive operations and to do so rapidly. But if we want to build a reliable information processing system out of nonlinear base components, the capability for reproducing the nonlinearity in a highly precise manner is absolutely critical. This is infeasible with conventional electronic or other macroscopic components, simply because it is impossible to exactly duplicate a statistical aggregate of particles, let alone preserve their nonlinear characteristics on an operational time scale. The discrete amino acid sequences that determine the function of proteins can be precisely specified. This is sufficient, at least for a large class of sequences, to uniquely determine the folded shape and the set of available conformational states. The shape (or conformation), of course, changes when the protein interacts with its environment, but the existence of a ground state and, more generally, discrete energy levels confer precision that is unobtainable with macroscopic processing elements.

1.5   Example: Protein Solubility as a Language

As a preliminary step, let us consider a transformation that is easy to implement with macromolecules but difficult with programmable machines. Practically speaking, any ab initio calculation of the properties of even a small cluster of particles outpaces programmable computational capabilities. For the present purpose, however, we would like to consider an example of a problem that typically arises in computer science—namely, the problem of deciding whether or not a sequence of symbols belongs to a given set of sequences. Such sets are considered in formal language theory. The question is whether it is possible to construct a machine, subject to given constraints, that can recognize the language. For example, the constraint might be that the machine is a finite automaton (as are actual computers).

Consider a language L in which the elements are protein sequences that satisfy a certain property (Davidson and Sauer 1994; Prijambada et al. 1996; Yamauchi et al. 1998). The alphabet of such a language would be a set of amino acids—for instance, the twenty amino acids that are the predominant building blocks of natural proteins. We can choose solubility S in water as the property that has to be satisfied by a sequence p composed of the amino acids that constitute the alphabet (Σ). The conditions c of the process must be fixed (e.g., temperature, pressure, pH, and cosolutes; Laidler and Bunting 1973; Cacace, Landau, and Ramsden 1997). Formally, we can write

$$L = \{p \in \Sigma^*: S_c(p) > x, |p| \leq w\}$$

where L denotes the language, x is a fixed solubility threshold ($mass_{protein}/mass_{solvent}$), and we assume that length ($|p|$) of the sequence of amino acids does not exceed some constant w. The important point is that S_c is a physical and not a formal condition.

In principle, a computer of sufficient size and speed should be able to answer the question whether a given sequence p is a member of L. In practice, however, performing physics calculations to answer the membership question for the above language by implementing formal rules is not efficient. To decide the membership of a sequence in this language, the properties of the (possibly folded) amino acid sequence need to be known, thus the language encodes the protein-folding problem. Calling on calculational methods of physics to solve this problem is clearly daunting; however, it is also possible to decide the membership by actually synthesizing the protein with the sequence in question and measuring its solubility. The synthesis and measurement procedure could be automated. The resulting machine can easily decide for any particular sequence presented to it whether it belongs to L, in effect performing a computation that may well exceed the practical capabilities of presently available general-purpose machines.

1.6   Macro-Micro Interface

Language-recognition problems of the type considered above can be viewed as pattern-recognition problems. The patterns might be computer codes that have to be compiled. Or they might be objects in the world—say, chairs. If all (and only) chairs were marked with a standard printed "C," then it would be easy for a digital computer to say "yes" whenever it is presented with a chair and "no" whenever it is presented with some other object. Without such preprocessing, however, no existing computer program can do this job. The morphology of chairs is too ambiguous and variable. The required program, though it might exist, is too complex to express in a reasonably compressed way, even assuming that we knew how to write it at all. Yet humans perform this transformation with relative ease.

The protein solubility example was intended to show that molecules can be used to perform transformations that are refractory to programmable machines. But of course that example is far from using this power to address any problem of interest. To do so, the molecular level needs to be connected to the external world and the transformation needs to be adapted into a useful function.

We will return to the adaptation issue in section 1.9. Here, it is pertinent to consider the general requirements for input and output (Conrad 1984, 1990). In biological cells, the signals that represent the patterns to be recognized could come from either the internal milieu or the environment. The former case is pertinent to regulation and the latter to perception-action activities. Three levels of scale are involved: macro, meso, and micro. The signals from the environment are generally macroscopic on some dimension of scale (energy, mass, dissipation, time, space) or represent features of the world that are macroscopic. The nerve impulse, for example, is a macroscopic signal. Signals inside the cells (say, diffusion of substances) can be either macroscopic or mesoscopic. The signals constitute the milieu patterns, or context, to which proteins and other biological macromolecules respond. Because these molecules must be sufficiently large to have significant shape features (and shape dynamics), they can be classified as mesoscopic. But the nuclear coordinates couple with the electronic coordinates, so that we also have to think in unambiguously microscopic terms (Conrad 1994a). In short, we have downward flow of influence from the macro to the meso to the micro.

This downward flow is complemented by an upward flow, triggered by the response of the macromolecule or macromolecular aggregate—say, a catalytic response in the case of an enzyme or a mechanical response in the case of a contractile unit. For the present purpose, it is sufficient to think in terms of enzymes. The chemical changes produced in the milieu link the activity of different enzymes. The linking chemicals can be thought of as signals, either because they provide context or because they serve as common intermediates. The communication between the processing macromolecules is thus essentially at a mesoscopic level. Macromolecules can also communicate through direct conformational interactions, in which case the signal energies are in the micro domain. Biological cells are replete with receptors that convert signals representing macro features of the external environment to internal signals that can be brought into the web of meso- and microlevel processing.

The amount of computational work performed at the meso- and the microlevels should be as great as possible, due to the thermodynamic cost of producing macroscopic signals. Enzymes, as catalysts, are thermodynamically reversible; their pattern-recognition work is free, driven only by the heat bath. The dissipation in a typical biochemical reaction can range from 10 to 100 kT. A nerve impulse might cost 10^5 to 10^{10} kT, depending on the size of the neuron. To the extent that processing is kept as close as possible to the microlevel, the amount of information processing obtainable is vastly enhanced.

Macro-micro communication links are essential for any computational system that utilizes the activity of individual molecules, as opposed to systems that employ only statistical aggregates of particles. The signal processing activities of the medium can itself have significant nonlinear dynamics (see chapters 3 and 4 of this volume). The whole medium, not just the controlling macromolecules, can then contribute to the input-output transform. But the controlling macromolecular components are critical, because the recognition-action events would otherwise be slow and difficult to mold for different functionalities. The addition of new signal substances and macromolecular species to the medium need not and in general does not yield an additive response. This nonlinear component interaction is where the potential for performing powerful context-sensitive transforms resides.

1.7 Prototype System

Recall (from section 1.4) that protein molecules are flexible chains of amino acids. Many sequences will curl up into a compact three-dimensional shape (cf., e.g., White, Handler, and Smith 1968; Stryer 1988). The folded shape is stabilized by electrostatic interactions among its atoms, but possesses at the same time a defined agility that enables it to assume numerous conformational states. Under given physiological conditions, a subset of these states is favored (Frauenfelder, Park, and Young 1988; Freire 1998). A change in physiochemical context can induce a switch to a different favored state. This prevalent protein behavior has two points of significance for novel information processing devices. The first is that proteins have substantial freedom to select the specific stimuli to which they respond and to associate these with a response in an essentially arbitrary way. The intricate conformational dynamics constitutes the second point, because this allows the protein to fuse information in a complex nonlinear fashion that would require large numbers of conventional components to duplicate.

The nonlinear conformational dynamics harbors the computational resource we seek to exploit but at the same time precludes direct engineering of a prototype system. An alternating sequence of exploratory and selective steps can be used instead to sculpt desired functionality. In general, there are three levels open to exploration: the coding of the input signals, the amino acid sequence and operational conditions that control the protein's capacity to fuse input signals, and the choice and interpretation of the output (figure 1.1). The output could, for example, be mediated by fluorescence probes attached to the protein. If the protein is an enzyme, however, its catalytic activity is most often critically dependent on conformational state and therefore provides a sensitive probe for conformation change. Changes in physiochemical context that alter the preferred conformational state of the enzyme will hence modulate the speed of the reaction catalyzed by the enzyme.

Enzymes that catalyze reactions involving NAD (nicotinamide adenine dinucleotide) are particularly convenient in this regard, because the oxidized form and the

Milieu signals

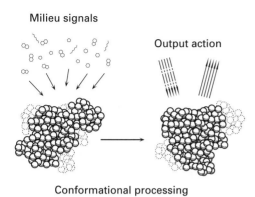

Output action

Conformational processing

Figure 1.1
Schematic illustration of signal fusion mediated by conformational dynamics.

reduced form of NAD have quite different absorbance in the ultraviolet (UV) range. Changes in the concentration of NADH can therefore be observed with little effort by a spectrophotometer.

We used an easy-to-tend enzyme, malate dehydrogenase (MDH), which participates in the citric-acid cycle and is widely available. MDH catalyzes the oxidation of malate to oxalacetate while reducing NAD^+ to NADH. For our purposes, we can view MDH as an implementation of a function that takes selected features of its physiochemical milieu as arguments and maps these into absorbance values. Different compositions of the reaction milieu are thereby grouped by MDH into classes of UV absorbance levels (Zauner and Conrad 2000). The aim is to associate input signals with milieu features in a way that results in a useful classification.

The number of potential milieu factors that could conceivably be used to encode input signals is virtually boundless and of course not limited to chemicals of known physiological significance. Only in exceptional cases can mechanistic kinetic models predict the outcome of a specific signal encoding. Furthermore, the cases where mechanistic models apply are likely to be of limited interest from a computational point of view, because the possibility of formulating such models indicates the realm of low-complexity behavior. Instead, empirical models of factor interactions mediated by the protein are employed to discover signal encodings that yield interesting response characteristics.

Sampling the protein's performance under different milieu conditions allows for the construction of a response surface for a small number of the potentially operative factors (Box and Draper 1987; Cornell 1990). Figure 1.2 shows such a response surface for MDH with respect to changes in the $MgCl_2$ and $CaCl_2$ concentration.

Table 1.2
Exclusive-or logic function

Input 1	0	1	0	1
Input 2	0	0	1	1
Output	0	1	1	0

The response surface, once established, can be used to analyze various signal encodings. Different encoding schemes are evaluated according to a performance measure. For pattern classification tasks, the minimum difference in the response to signal patterns that should be grouped into separate classes can serve as the performance measure, to be referred to as signal strength. Only encodings yielding a positive signal strength allow for the implementation of the desired function; in general, an encoding that maximizes signal strength is advantageous.

As a concrete example, consider the exclusive-or (XOR) operation (table 1.2). This can be viewed as a simple arithmetic operation adding two bits without carry. It is also the simplest pattern classification problem that is not linearly separable. For this reason, it is used as a benchmark for learning in natural and artificial systems (Griffith et al. 1968; Minsky and Papert 1969; Ellacott and Bose 1996). The XOR operation groups patterns into one output category when both input signals are the same and into another when the signals are different. The signal strength Δs for the XOR operation can therefore be expressed as

$$\Delta s = \mathrm{Min}[r(01), r(10)] - \mathrm{Max}[r(00), r(11)]$$

where the function r denotes the response to the signal pattern (e.g., $00, 01, \ldots$, etc.).

With this performance measure, we can ask which signal encoding best adapts the enzymatic system to the desired input-output behavior—here the XOR operation. The empirical response surface shown in figure 1.2 is used as the response function r. The question is how much $MgCl_2$ and $CaCl_2$ should be used for the input signals to maximize the signal strength Δs. Several encoding methods are possible. For example, $MgCl_2$ can be used as the signal carrier on one input line and $CaCl_2$ as carrier for the other input line. The XOR operation, however, is commutative and hence there is no need to encode the signals arriving from different input lines by different carrier substances. It is therefore possible, for example, to encode 1-signals independent of the input line by a mixture of $MgCl_2$ and $CaCl_2$ and 0-signals by a different mixture or the absence of ions. For encodings that use the same carrier substance for both input lines, only signal encodings up to half the concentration range covered by the response surface can be evaluated, because the carrier substances are additive

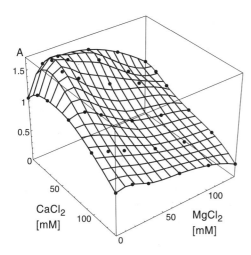

Figure 1.2
Empirical response surface of MDH with respect to $CaCl_2$ and $MgCl_2$. The dots are at concentrations where measurements were made. The surface is obtained by interpolation. (Reprinted with permission from *Biotechnol. Prog.* 2001, 17, 553–559. © 2001 American Chemical Society/AIChE.)

with respect to their contribution to the reaction milieu. Signal strengths for different encoding methods are shown in figure 1.3 as functions of the $MgCl_2$ and $CaCl_2$ concentrations used to represent the signals.

The areas of positive signal strength in figure 1.3 suggest that an enzymatic XOR based on MDH is feasible. To realize such a device, and more generally to explore enzymes as active components for the implementation of pattern classifiers, we constructed the experimental setup shown in figure 1.4. Small piston pumps, each composed of a 3 cm^3 syringe and two one-way valves, deliver input signals from reservoirs to a mixing chamber. The two signal solutions, one representing 0-signals and the other 1-signals, contain the same amount of L-malate, a substrate in the reaction catalyzed by MDH. In addition, the solution representing the 1-signal contains $MgCl_2$, while 0-signals are represented by the absence of $MgCl_2$. By injecting a defined amount of MDH/NAD$^+$ solution into the mixing chamber, a reaction is initiated. The reaction progresses while the mixture is pumped to a spectrophotometer and the absorbance of the NADH produced during the transit time is recorded as the output response.

Figure 1.5 illustrates the details of an improved version of the prototype in which the spectrophotometer cuvette (Cv) serves as the mixing chamber, thus permitting shorter response times and increased reliability. The injection of the enzyme solution

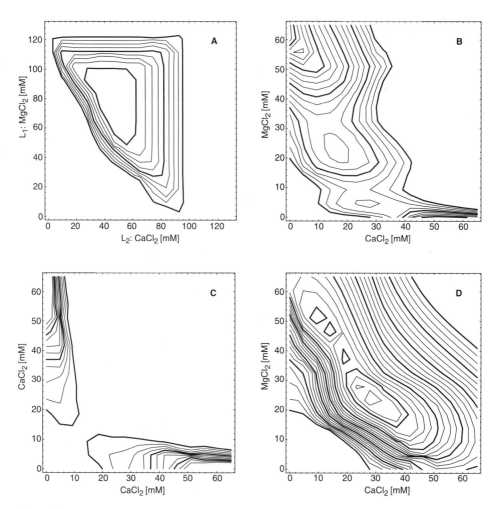

Figure 1.3

Signal strengths for the XOR operation under different signal encoding schemes. The contour lines indicate areas of positive signal strengths, therefore concentrations that make the XOR feasible. Bold contour lines indicate an increase in signal strength of 0.1, the outermost line being 0. (*A*) Input line 1 releases $MgCl_2$ when a 1-signal arrives on this line. Input line 2 releases $CaCl_2$ under the same condition. When the input is 0 no ions are released. Encoding the input lines by different signal substances makes it possible to utilize the whole concentration range of the response surface. (*B*) Here both signal lines are encoded the same way, with $MgCl_2$ representing the 1-signal and $CaCl_2$ representing the 0-signal. (*C*) Input lines 1 and 2 have the same encoding. The 0- and 1-signals are both encoded with $CaCl_2$ concentrations that consequently must be different in order to obtain a positive signal strength. The symmetry of the graph reflects the symmetry of the XOR operation with respect to negation of the input signals (cf. table 1.2). (*D*) In this case the 1-signal is encoded by a mixture of $MgCl_2$ and $CaCl_2$ for both signal lines. The 0-signal is encoded by the absence of these ions. (Reprinted in part with permission from *Biotechnol. Prog.* 2001, 17, 553–559. © 2001 American Chemical Society/AIChE.)

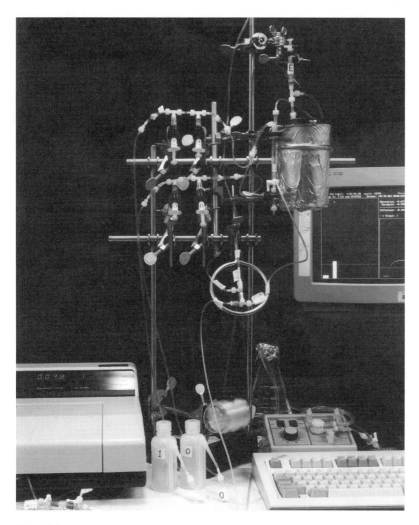

Figure 1.4
Experimental setup for first version of the tabletop XOR module. (© 2001 Zauner.)

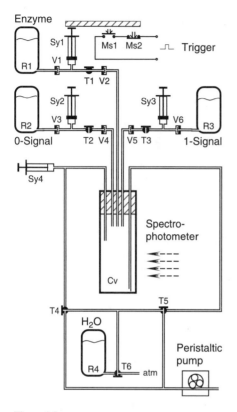

Figure 1.5
Flow diagram for direct injection version of the XOR module. Figure 1.4 shows an earlier version utilizing a mixing chamber separate from the cuvette. (Reprinted with permission from *Biotechnol. Prog.* 2001, 17, 553–559. © 2001 American Chemical Society/AIChE.)

(R1/Sy1) activates microswitches (Ms1, Ms2) that provide a trigger signal for the timing of the measurement used as the output response. A syringe (Sy4) takes up the air displaced when the cuvette (Cv) is filled. Several T-valves (T4–T6), a water reservoir (R4) and a peristaltic pump serve to clear the system between consecutive signal-processing cycles.

The XOR was also implemented with the improved setup (figure 1.5). The device was required to classify 135 consecutively presented 2-bit input patterns. The response time (i.e., the time period from injecting the enzyme/NAD solution until the output measurement is taken) was set to 10 sec. All 135 input patterns gave rise to response levels that permit correct classification by a single thresholding operation (figure 1.6). The choice of 10 sec is due to the limits of our tabletop instrumentation,

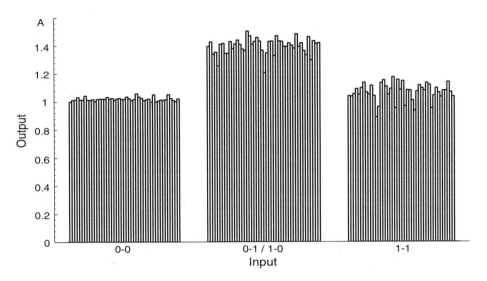

Figure 1.6
Experimental run illustrating repeated operation of the XOR module. The absorbance output separates the 01/10 inputs from the 00 and 11 inputs.

not to the underlying process. The prototype demonstrates that enzymes can be used to transform pattern classifications that are not linearly separable into simpler (linearly separable) problems. Of more importance, it points to the feasibility of developing novel computational systems that operate on the basis of high-complexity conformational processors.

1.8   Multienzyme Response Surfaces: A Simulated Example

The XOR demonstration points to the possibility of using networks of enzymes to create computationally richer response surfaces. This would only be of interest if the response of the individual components of the network interact in a nonlinear fashion. Placing multiple enzyme species in a common milieu can then lead to a response surface that is quite different from the summation of the surfaces yielded by the enzymes taken in isolation.

We have developed a software simulation tool to investigate the interaction of conformational, kinetic (reaction-diffusion), structural, and dynamic (force) interactions of protein networks in three-dimensional space that for the present purposes can be used to illustrate this nonadditivity (Zauner 1996; Zauner and Conrad 1997).

Recipe

Materials

UV-spectrophotometer ($\lambda = 339$ nm); analytic scale; adjustable micropipettes (200 μl, 1 ml); pH meter; timer.

   Malate dehydrogenase from porcine heart, as ammonium sulfate suspension (store refrigerated); NAD^+ (oxidized β-nicotinamide adenine dinucleotide), as free acid (store refrigerated or frozen); l-malic acid, as free acid; $MgCl_2$ as magnesium chloride hexahydrate ($MgCl_2 \cdot 6H_2O$); MOPS (3-[N-morpholino]propanesulfonic acid); glycine (aminoacetic acid), as free acid; 10 N HCl and 10 N NaOH (for pH adjustment); pure (distilled) H_2O. (Below, "water" always refers to pure H_2O.)

Method

1. Basis Solution for signals (120 mM glycine, 7.5 mM l-malic acid, 1 l): Dissolve 9 g glycine in about 950 ml water. Add 1 g l-malic acid and allow to dissolve while stirring. Adjust to pH 10.5 with 10 N NaOH. Fill with water to a final volume of 1000 ml.

2. $MgCl_2$ Solution (4 M $MgCl_2$, 50 ml): Dissolve 40.66 g $MgCl_2 \cdot 6H_2O$ in 15 ml hot water. Let the solution cool to room temperature. Fill with water to 50 ml.

3. Signal solutions: Add 5 ml of water to 100 ml of the signal basis solution (1). The resulting solution is used for 0-signals. Add 5 ml of the $MgCl_2$ solution (2) to 100 ml of the signal basis solution (1). The resulting solution is used for 1-signals.

4. Enzyme solution (MDH/NAD^+, 10 ml): Dissolve 20.93 g MOPS in about 300 ml water, then fill up to 475 ml. Adjust pH to 7.4 with 10 N NaOH. Fill up with water to a final volume of 500 ml. This is the 0.2 M MOPS buffer. Weigh 36 mg of NAD^+ into a test tube that can hold 10 ml fluid and is wide enough to access with the 1 ml micropipette. Add 10 ml of the 0.2 M MOPS buffer and shake to dissolve the NAD^+. Add about 20 μl malate dehydrogenase suspension and shake. If the response time for the signal processing is found to be too slow, more of the enzyme suspension can be added to the solution.

5. The volume of the signal solutions and the reaction solution may need to be adjusted for the particular spectrophotometer used. The minimum volume required to cover the beam path can be determined by marking the beam at $\lambda \approx 540$ nm on a white piece of paper fixed to the cuvette. If this volume is larger than 2.1 ml, the volume for the signals and the enzyme solution (6 and 8) should be adjusted proportionally.

6. The input signal pattern is composed of two 0.8 ml portions taken in any combination from the two signal solutions (3). The signal solutions are pipetted into a cuvette.

7. Set the spectrophotometer to continuously record absorbance at $\lambda = 339$ nm.

8. To start the processing, pipette 0.5 ml of the enzyme solution (4) into the cuvette containing the signal solutions (6). A timer is started and the cuvette content is mixed (e.g., by inverting the sealed cuvette or by stirring when the enzyme solution is added).

9. Record the progress of the reaction for various combinations of the input signals by repeating steps 6 through 8. Choose a response time that will separate 00 and 11 input patterns from 01 and 10 inputs and determine the threshold level from the corresponding absorbance values.

10. Signals can now be processed using the time and threshold determined in the calibration step (9).

Note: The above protocol can serve as a starting point to explore other signaling substances. It is quite robust and could easily be adapted (e.g., replacing the micropipettes with disposable syringes) for classroom use.

The basic concept of the simulator is as follows. The simulation space, a three-dimensional lattice, contains two classes of components: macrocomponents and microcomponents. The former represent proteins, and the latter represent milieu substances—that is, metabolites on which the proteins act catalytically, as well as control molecules and ions that trigger conformational changes. The microcomponents are represented by the integer number present in each unit cell. Each catalytic or diffusional event is associated with an integer increment or decrement of this number.

The macrocomponents are represented in the simulation space by dodecahedra, each consisting of up to twelve coupled finite-state automata that model active protein domains. Recognition, binding, control, and catalytic properties are assigned to the states of these domains. The state transitions of the domains correspond to conformational changes. Transition probabilities depend on the local milieu, and therefore on the microcomponents present in the location of the dodecahedra and on adjacent macrocomponents. The local milieu can change through reaction (catalyzed by macrocomponents) and by diffusion. The whole system forms a loop encompassing context, conformation, and action. Milieu molecules and adjacent macrocomponents provide the context in which enzymes function. This influences conformation. Conformation controls action, including catalysis and structure formation. Catalysis and structure formation in turn control context, and so on (figure 1.7).

For illustrative purposes, we consider two toy reactions running separately and then consider the response of the combined reaction. The first reaction, catalyzed by enzyme e_1, is

$$A + B \overset{e_1}{\longleftrightarrow} C + D$$

We assume that e_1 has ten conformational states that differ in the catalytic activity that they confer. The transition probabilities and activity associated with the different states are illustrated in figure 1.8. R and S in the figure denote substances used as milieu signals. The product D is chosen as output signal. The response surface of e_1 with respect to R and S, illustrated in figure 1.9, shows that even a relatively small number of conformational states can yield a nontrivial surface.

For the second reaction, catalyzed by enzyme e_2, we take

$$A + E \overset{e_2}{\longleftrightarrow} F + 2D$$

Here we assume that e_2 has only four conformational states. As shown in the state transition diagram (figure 1.10), the enzyme is sensitive to the same two signaling substances, R and S, as e_1. The response surface is shown in figure 1.11.

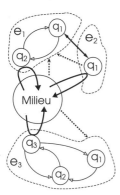

Figure 1.7
Schematic of interactions supported by the CKSD simulator (for simplicity limited to a three enzyme system). The enzymes (labeled by e_1, e_2, and e_3) have from one to three states (labeled by the q_i). States represent conformations. Arrows connecting states represent conformational transitions. These are typically influenced by the milieu components (dashed arrows) and also may be influenced by direct interactions between two enzymes (dashed arrow from e_2 to e_1). Specific conformational states catalyze milieu reactions (indicated by bent arrows). Enzymes in complementary conformational states may self-assemble to form quaternary structures (indicated by the double arrow between e_1 and e_2). Note that the transitions of distant enzymes may be coupled through their catalytic effect on the milieu.

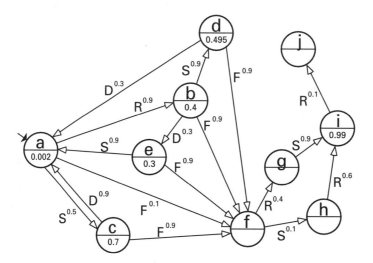

Figure 1.8
Conformational transition used to simulate enzyme e_1. The diagram is not based on any actual enzyme. The numbers below the state name indicate the relative catalytic activity of the state. Capital letters on the transitions refer to metabolites and signal molecules. The transition probabilities in the presence of these molecules is specified by superscripts.

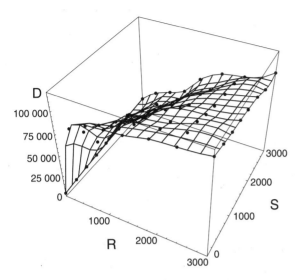

Figure 1.9
Simulated response surface for enzyme e_1 with respect to signaling substances R and S. The product D is used as the output value. The values in the diagram show the actual number of molecules present in the simulation space. The latter contained 200 e_1 enzymes distributed on a $61 \times 61 \times 21$ lattice.

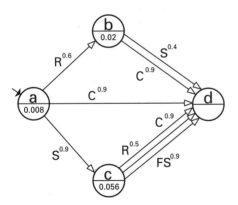

Figure 1.10
Conformational transition diagram for enzyme e_2. See caption of figure 1.8 for explanation.

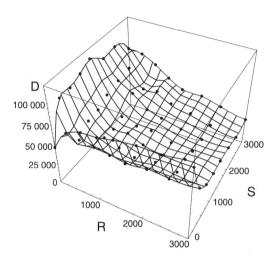

Figure 1.11
Simulated response surface for enzyme e_2. The space contained 300 e_2 enzymes; cf. figure 1.9.

Now suppose that both enzymes are introduced into the reactor. As can be seen from the reaction schemes above, e_1 and e_2 will then compete for substrate A and both will contribute to the output signal D. Furthermore, they affect each other's conformational transitions via the products C, D, and F (see figures 1.8 and 1.10). The resulting response surface is shown in figure 1.12. The response obtained by combining the enzymes cannot be easily predicted from knowledge of the response of the individual enzymes. This nonadditivity precludes the possibility of using a simpler user manual to anticipate the effect of adding components on the input-output map of the system. From our point of view, this means that it should be possible to build up molecular signal-processing modules that can implement transforms that cannot be achieved by linking the processing components in a context-independent way. The joint system self-organizes into a de novo transform.

1.9   Architectures and Adaptive Procedures

The tabletop prototype discussed in the previous section can be thought of as an extreme abstraction of the recognition-action dynamics of a biological cell. The cell is crudely pictured as a mixing chamber. The syringes roughly correspond to receptors that serve to introduce signaling substances into the chamber. The enzyme is the primary processing component, acting on the medium to trigger an output signal that could potentially control an action.

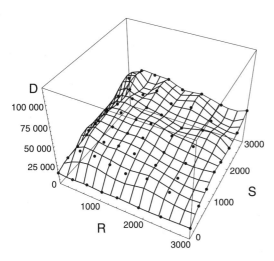

Figure 1.12
Combined response surface resulting from interaction between enzymes e_1 and e_2.

As noted above, more enzymes and signaling substances could be added. Alternative designs are possible—for example, designs with enzymes that are embedded in a matrix in an ordered way. The potential nonadditivity of the superposed response surface increases, thereby increasing the complexity of the transformation. The goal is to create a repertoire of high-complexity basis functions for implementing input-output transforms that cannot be accommodated by programmable architectures (as discussed in section 1.2).

Three issues arise: how to migrate the tabletop prototype to a chip, how to generate a useful repertoire of transformations, and how to use these chips as molecular coprocessors for a conventional architecture or to organize them into novel architectural designs.

Current advances in lab-on-a-chip technology open up a number of possible migration pathways. Figure 1.13 visualizes one of these (Zauner and Conrad 1997). This coprocessor comprises two layers; a molecular layer that contains the macromolecules and milieu components, and an optoelectronic layer that serves as the input-output interface. The molecular layer could be a sealed fluid film, gel matrix, or Langmuir-Blodgett film (Blodgett 1935). Proteins could be embedded in the film and materials moved around using microfluidic techniques (Hadd et al. 1997; Chohen et al. 1999; Unger et al. 2000). Specific molecular components are selected to couple the molecular layer to the optoelectronic layer for input and output. A pattern of light signals introduces the pattern to be classified. The induced pattern

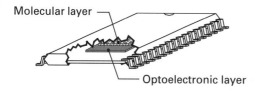

Figure 1.13
Hypothetical molecular coprocessor combining microfluidics and integrated optoelectronics. (Reproduced with permission from *Optical Memory and Neural Networks* 1997, 6: 157–173. © 1997 Allerton Press, Inc.)

of milieu features is then fused by the conformational dynamics of the embedded proteins.

The resulting conformation change produces spectroscopically identifiable signals, either directly or indirectly through catalytic change in the concentration of a light-absorbing substance. The optoelectronic layer would include integrated optics (e.g., waveguides, gratings) for coupling to the molecular layer and could incorporate integrated circuits for interfacing with a conventional electronic environment. Activities of multiple proteins in the molecular layer could be used for readout, but this depends on spectrophotometers with parallel capabilities in an appropriate wavelength range to come on-line. The choice of parameters for readout of the dynamics constitutes the interpretation.

The second issue concerns the adaptation of the physical dynamics and the interpretation. The tuning of our tabletop prototype was done by varying the substances used for coding of the inputs and essentially by ad hoc variation of the substrate concentration. A response surface was then constructed that could be used to elicit different functionalities, attention being focused in the present case on the two-variable logic functions (because only two input lines were used). The number of signal substances could be increased. The number of enzyme species included could be increased and their type varied. New macromolecular species could be evolved with specific capabilities—using, for example, protein-engineering techniques (Beaudry and Joyce 1992; Gao et al. 1997). The combinatorics clearly grows explosively, as it does in natural biological evolution. Response-surface methodology (Box and Draper 1987) can be used to prune this gigantic search space. The surfaces would be explored for features that could provide useful input-output transformations and the next steps of variation could be focused on the most interesting regions of the surface. The whole process can be automated.

The technology is available for this development program, but the evolution of suitable transforms must, of course, be a long-term, continuing process. As a first step, we envisage the development of a limited class of modules that can serve as molecular coprocessors for conventional machines. These could be used as pre-processors to transform complex input patterns into rigidly defined output patterns that can be rapidly processed by digital techniques. The conventional architecture would provide the procedural capabilities, but these would be complemented and synergized by the self-organizing dynamics of the molecular coprocessors.

As more molecular basis functions become available, it should be possible to build up an architecture with a more neuromolecular character. Artificial neural networks are essentially built up out of a set of fairly simple transforms. The situation in the brain is arguably quite different. The neuronal units exhibit a diversity of capabilities that draw on internal molecular dynamics. Complex interweavings of self-organization and procedural processes mediate what, according to our earlier considerations, are the high complexity programs that cannot be accommodated by conventional architectures.

Our group has developed a virtual system, referred to as the artificial neuro-molecular (ANM) architecture, along this line (Chen 1993). The system consists of neurons controlled by an internal signal integration mechanism modeled after the neuronal cytoskeleton. Read-in elements represent molecules of the input layer in a molecular chip; readout elements correspond to molecules that trigger output firing. Neurons fire when a locus occupied by a readout element is sufficiently activated. The input-output transform performed by the neuron is adapted by varying internal parameters (read-in locations, readout locations, structure of the signal integration network) and varying the connections to other neurons. A repertoire of special-purpose transforms is thus created. Memory manipulation mechanisms that are essentially procedural in nature are then used to orchestrate the different neuron types into assemblages capable of executing yet higher complexity transforms, again using a variation-selection evolutionary technique.

The ANM architecture has been applied to a variety of 64-bit pattern-recognition problems (the input interface being currently limited in this way). These include maze navigation (Chen and Conrad 1994), Chinese character recognition (Chen and Conrad 1997), and most recently, hepatitis diagnosis (Chen 2000). The power of the system lies in its computational adaptability properties. It is a virtual system run on top of a conventional base machine. It uses the limited resources of a low-complexity machine to achieve computational adaptability, but this must be at the expense of other desirable features that programs using the same resources differently might exhibit. The molecular processing in the neurons—particularly the readout—is, of course, nominal. The readouts are just threshold elements. It would be too computationally costly to simulate the conformational dynamics that allows context-sensitive fusion of milieu features. The reasonable supposition is that implementing the architecture with real molecules would enormously increase the complexity of the programs that it is capable of embodying, thereby affording concomitant expansion of the problem domains that it is capable of managing.

1.10   Transformal Computing

The processing capabilities of the prototype described in this chapter are, of course, extremely modest, indeed even minimal, in comparison to the architectural projections of the previous section. It is to be regarded only as an initial step designed to concretize the conformation-driven computing concept and to demonstrate its technological feasibility at the level of what might be called macroscopic fluidics. The step to lab-on-a-chip integration can readily be seen.

The important question concerns the basic claim—namely, that the conformation-driven approach should provide access to computational processes that cannot practically fit into a conventional architecture. The term *transformal computing* is apt. How would we even recognize whether a computational system performs an operation that is refractory to digital (i.e., formal) machines?

The famous thesis of Church and Turing asserts, in its strong form, that all processes in nature can be brought into the circle of formal computation (Hofstadter 1980). This is an open question. Whether the answer is affirmative or negative is not the issue with which we are concerned here. It is the practical question that is relevant. Many examples could be cited: human aesthetic judgments, legal judgments, ethical rules (like the Golden Rule), or any decision that involves an indefinitely large number of situations. Arguably, an unambiguous description of such general decision rules by formal rules (i.e., by a program in the Turing sense) is infeasible. We here enter the realm of what was referred to above as transformal computations.

Of course, we do not expect the conformation-driven technology proposed here to perform such complex human operations either. Constructing an artificial brain that comes close to the human brain, even under the reasonable assumption that conformational processing plays a key role in the human mental process, exceeds by far any expectations that we would care to project. The proper question is: Can conformational processors perform transformations that exceed the practical capabilities of formal machines; and how could such transformations be identified?

Take as a concrete example the functioning of an assembly line. Automation is limited by the speed of visual processing and by the fact that quality control problems are often ambiguous. If conformational processors were evolved and harvested that could preprocess ambiguous patterns in a manner that made them suitable for processing by vision algorithms, it would constitute what in practice might be called a transformal computation.

By choosing to look at the benchmark XOR operation, we have a fortiori precluded the possibility of finding a transformal transformation. Our objective was to demonstrate that even a single enzyme species could do more processing than is standardly attributed to the threshold elements utilized in many current neural net models. Our working hypothesis—that we can use the conformation-driven approach to escape the practical limitations of programmable machines—is based on three considerations: the complexity arguments indicating that systems with self-organizing dynamics can perform more-complex operations than systems with programmable architectures, the technological feasibility of fabricating conformation-driven modules that utilize self-organizing dynamics, and the feasibility of using an evolutionary response surface methodology for developing a repertoire of high-complexity basis transforms that can be embedded in or conjoined with higher level architectures. This is a three-point landing on theory, technology, and architecture. The pieces are present; bringing them together should yield computational capabilities complementary to and synergistic with digital capabilities.

Acknowledgments

This material is based upon work supported by the U.S. National Science Foundation under grant numbers ECS-9704190 and CCR-9610054, and by NASA under grant number NCC2-1189.

References

Ashby, W. R. 1968. Some consequences of Bremermann's limit for information-processing systems. In *Cybernetic Problems in Bionics*, ed. H. L. Oestreicher and D. R. Moore, 69–76. New York: Gordon and Breach.

Beaudry, A. A., and G. F. Joyce. 1992. Directed evolution of an RNA enzyme. *Science* 257: 635–641.

Blodgett, K. B. 1935. Films built by depositing successive monomolecular layers on a solid surface. *J. Am. Chem. Soc.* 57: 1007–1022.

Box, G. E. P., and N. R. Draper. 1987. *Empirical Model-Building and Response Surfaces*. New York: John Wiley and Sons.

Cacace, M. G., E. M. Landau, and J. J. Ramsden. 1997. The Hofmeister series: Salt and solvent effects on interfacial phenomena. *Q. Rev. Biophys.* 30: 241–278.

Chaitin, G. J. 1966. On the length of programs for computing finite binary sequences. *J. Assoc. Comput. Mach.* 13: 547–569.

Chaitin, G. J. 1974. Information-theoretic computational complexity. *IEEE Trans. Inf. Theor.* 20: 10–15.

Chen, J.-C. 1993. Computer Experiments on Evolutionary Learning in a Multilevel Neuromolecular Architecture. Ph.D. thesis, Wayne State University, Detroit.

Chen, J.-C. 2000. Data differentiation and parameter analysis of a chronic heptatitis B database with an artificial neuromolecular system. *BioSystems* 57: 23–36.

Chen, J.-C., and M. Conrad. 1994. Learning synergy in a multilevel neuronal architecture. *BioSystems* 32: 111–142.

Chen, J.-C., and M. Conrad. 1997. Evolutionary learning with a neuromolecular architecture: A biologically motivated approach to computational adaptability. *Soft Computing* 1: 19–34.

Chohen, C. B., E. Chin-Dixon, S. Jeong, and T. T. Nikiforov. 1999. A microchip-based enzyme assay for protein kinase A. *Anal. Biochem.* 273: 89–97.

Conrad, M. 1979. Mutation-absorption model of the enzyme. *Bull. Math. Biol.* 41: 387–405.

Conrad, M. 1983. *Adaptability: The Significance of Variability from Molecule to Ecosystem.* New York: Plenum Press.

Conrad, M. 1984. Microscopic-macroscopic interface in biological information processing. *BioSystems* 16: 345–363.

Conrad, M. 1990. Molecular computing. In *Advances in Computers.* Vol. 31, ed. M. C. Yovits, 235–324. San Diego: Academic Press.

Conrad, M. 1994a. Amplification of superpositional effects through electronic-conformational interactions. *Chaos, Solitons, and Fractals* 4: 423–438.

Conrad, M. 1994b. The fitness of carbon for computing. In *Molecular and Biomolecular Electronics*, ed. R. R. Birge, 43–62. Washington, D.C.: American Chemical Society.

Conrad, M. 1995. Scaling of efficiency in programmable and nonprogrammable systems. *BioSystems* 35: 161–166.

Conrad, M., and M. Volkenstein. 1981. Replaceability of amino acids and the self-facilitation of evolution. *J. Theor. Biol.* 92: 293–299.

Cornell, J. A. 1990. *Experiments with Mixtures: Designs, Models, and the Analysis of Mixture Data.* New York: John Wiley and Sons.

Davidson, A. R., and R. T. Sauer. 1994. Folded proteins occur frequently in libraries of random amino acid sequences. *Proc. Natl. Acad. Sci. USA* 91: 2146–2150.

Edsall, J. T., and J. Wyman. 1958. *Biophysical Chemistry.* New York: Academic Press.

Ellacott, S., and D. Bose. 1996. *Neural Networks: Deterministic Methods of Analysis.* London: International Thomson Computer Press.

Fischer, E. 1894. Einfluss der Configuration auf die Wirkung der Enzyme. *Berichte der Deutschen Chemischen Gesellschaft* (since 1947: *Chemische Berichte*) 27-3: 2985–2993 (in German).

Frauenfelder, H., F. Park, and R. D. Young. 1988. Conformational substates in proteins. *Annu. Rev. Biophys. Biophys. Chem.* 17: 451–479.

Freire, E. 1998. Statistical thermodynamic linkage between conformational and binding equilibria. *Adv. Prot. Chem.* 51: 255–279.

Gao, C., C.-H. Lin, C.-H. L. Lo, S. Mao, P. Wirsching, R. A. Lerner, and K. D. Janda. 1997. Making chemistry selectable by linking it to infectivity. *Proc. Natl. Acad. Sci. USA* 94: 11777–11782.

Griffith, V. V., J. A. Davis, and R. H. Kause. 1968. Learning of the exclusive-or logic function in rats. In *Cybernetic Problems in Bionics*, ed. H. L. Oestreicher and D. R. Moore, 587–595. New York: Gordon and Breach.

Hadd, A. G., D. E. Raymond, J. W. Halliwell, S. C. Jacobson, and J. M. Ramsey. 1997. Microchip device for performing enzyme assays. *Anal. Chem.* 69: 3407–3412.

Henderson, L. J. 1913. *The Fitness of the Environment.* New York: Macmillan.

Hofstadter, D. 1980. *Gödel, Escher, Bach: An Eternal Golden Braid*. New York: Vintage Books.

Kampis, G. 1991. *Self-Modifying Systems in Biology and Cognitive Science*, chap. 6, 278–343. Oxford: Pergamon Press.

Laidler, K. J., and P. S. Bunting. 1973. *The Chemical Kinetics of Enzyme Action*. 2d ed. Oxford: Clarendon Press.

Li, M., and P. Vitányi. 1997. *An Introduction to Kolmogorov Complexity and its Applications*. 2d ed. New York: Springer.

Minsky, M. L., and S. Papert. 1969. *Perceptrons: An Introduction to Computational Geometry*. Cambridge: MIT Press.

Prijambada, I. D., T. Yomo, F. Tanaka, T. Kawama, K. Yamamoto, A. Hasegawa, Y. Shima, S. Negoro, and I. Urabe. 1996. Solubility of artificial proteins with random sequences. *FEBS Lett.* 382: 21–25.

Sidgwick, N. V. 1950. *The Chemical Elements and Their Compounds*. Vol. 2. New York: Oxford University Press.

Stryer, L. 1988. *Biochemistry*. New York: W. H. Freeman.

Unger, M. A., H.-P. Chou, T. Thorsen, A. Scherer, and S. R. Quake. 2000. Monolithic microfabricated valves and pumps by multilayer soft lithography. *Science* 288: 113–116.

von Neumann, J. 1951. The general and logical theory of automata. In *Cerebral Mechanisms in Behaviour—The Hixon Symposium*. New York: John Wiley. (Reprinted in *J. von Neumann, Collected Works*, ed. A. H. Taub. Vol. 5, 288–328. New York: Pergamon Press, 1963.)

White, A., P. Handler, and E. L. Smith. 1968. *Principles of Biochemistry*. New York: McGraw-Hill.

Yamauchi, A., T. Yomo, F. Tanaka, I. D. Prijambada, S. Ohhashi, K. Yamamoto, Y. Shima, K. Ogasahara, K. Yutani, M. Kataoka, and I. Urabe. 1998. Characterization of soluble artificial proteins with random sequences. *FEBS Lett.* 421: 147–151.

Zauner, K.-P. 1996. Simulation system for studying spatially structured biochemical interactions. Master's thesis, Wayne State University.

Zauner, K.-P., and M. Conrad. 1996. Parallel computing with DNA: Toward the anti-universal machine. In *Parallel Problem Solving from Nature: PPSN IV*. Vol. 1141 of Lecture Notes in Computer Science, ed. H.-M. Voigt, W. Ebeling, I. Rechenberg, and H.-P. Schwefel, 696–705. Berlin: Springer-Verlag.

Zauner, K.-P., and M. Conrad. 1997. Conformation-driven molecular computing: The optical connection. *Opt. Mem. Neural Netw.* 6: 157–173.

Zauner, K.-P., and M. Conrad. 2000. Enzymatic pattern processing. *Naturwissenschaften* 87: 360–362.

Zauner, K.-P., and M. Conrad. 2001. Molecular approach to informal computing. *Soft Computing* 5: 39–44.

2 Molecular Recognition: Storage and Processing of Molecular Information

Tanya Sienko and Jean-Marie Lehn

Underlying every single computing system is a physical base, whether it is of semiconductor material or more complicated organic chemicals. Much of the interest expressed in molecular computing is because from one viewpoint, one is attempting to reverse the demarcation of computing into "hardware" and "software" by using the physical characteristics of the medium to carry out information processing in a desired manner. In these new systems under consideration, one cannot make a distinction between hardware and software.

"Programmability" as it is presently considered will not be taken as a given—one will have to think of "evolution," "adaptability," and "informed materials" instead. The "information" of such systems will lie in chemical and supramolecular attributes and behavior. What one gains by this is the potential ability of implementing "recognition," self-organization, and other "high-level" behaviors extremely difficult to perform according to conventional computing paradigms. Biological organisms carry out amazing feats from an information processing viewpoint. Highly specific recognition and regulation processes that occur in biology include substrate binding to a receptor protein; enzymatic reactions; assembling of multiprotein complexes; immunological antigen-antibody association; intermolecular reading, translation, and transcription of the genetic code; regulation of gene expression by NDA binding proteins; the entry of a virus into a cell; signal transduction by neurotransmitters; and cellular recognition—just to name a few.

All of this relies on what happens down at the very lowest level, the level of the molecules and of their supramolecular interactions. The basic process by which information stored in molecules is processed through their supramolecular interaction algorithms is known as *molecular recognition*. It is the topic of this chapter.

2.1 Definition of Molecular Recognition

Molecular recognition is the binding and specific selection of substrate(s) by a given receptor molecule. It is found in both organic and inorganic realms, from the lowest level to the highest. Examples (in increasingly larger systems) could be the recognition of the ammonium ion (diameter 3.4 angstroms) by a macrotricyclic cryptand, catalysis, the first step in an enzymatic reaction involving lysozyme (an ellipsoid measuring roughly 45 by 30 by 30 angstroms), and the self-replication of DNA (microns in length). Mere binding is not recognition, although it is often taken as such. Molecular recognition implies a *pattern-recognition process* through a structurally well-defined set of intermolecular interactions defining the processing algorithm. Binding of a receptor ρ (bigger part) to a substrate σ (smaller part) forms a complex, or *supermolecule*, characterized by its thermodynamic and kinetic stability and selectivity (i.e., by the amount of energy and of information brought into the operation).

The major difference between supramolecular chemistry[1] and molecular chemistry is in the type of bonds used. Whereas molecular chemistry is based on the covalent bond, supramolecular chemistry implements the intermolecular noncovalent types of binding (electrostatic interactions, hydrogen bonding, van der Waals forces, etc.). The latter are usually weaker than covalent bonding, hence supramolecular species are thermodynamically less stable, kinetically more labile, and dynamically more flexible than molecules. This "soft bonding," allowing for a more flexible exploration of the available energy surface, will turn out to have many interesting ramifications.

The effects resulting from molecular recognition are wide ranging. The physical characteristics of the supermolecule can differ radically from that of either the substrate or receptor alone, with corresponding effects on reactivity, optical behavior, charge distribution, and so forth. "Information" in a supermolecule may be stored in multiple forms: in the architecture of the receptor, in its binding sites, and in the ligand layer surrounding the bound receptor. Depending on the characteristics of the supermolecule, this information may be observed directly (as in the case of fluorescence or a chemical reaction occurring) or may contribute to such secondary effects as reactivity, kinetic effects and so on. In many cases, the receptor may strain the substrate, allowing easier cleavage (photoinduced or through the action of a third molecule). For receptors with two or more recognition sites, molecular recognition may bring components into close proximity, facilitating chemical reactions, energy transfer, or charge transfer, just to name a few possibilities.

Molecular recognition has a critical role to play in such areas as catalytic activity and membrane transport as well. Finally, there is the possibility of inducing nonlinear effects such as self-assembly and self-organization, which can lead to massive signal amplification and macroscopic changes of state. In fact, much of supramolecular chemistry can be said to concern either molecular recognition or its application, and most, if not all, biological processes involve a molecular recognition event at some stage. This chapter can only give a brief overview of this fascinating field.

---

1. The difference between supermolecular chemistry and supramolecular chemistry is that although the former is limited to the specific chemistry of the supermolecules themselves, supramolecular chemistry is broader, concerning the chemistry of all types of supramolecular entities from the well-defined supermolecular to extended, more or less organized, polymolecular associations.

2.2 Molecular Recognition: How to Do It Right the First Time

The basic tenets of molecular recognition may already be found in the "lock and key" concept, developed by Emil Fischer (1894) in his work with enzymes. The substrate—the "key"—must fit geometrically into a cleft on the receptor—the "lock." It was later recognized that such *complementarity* extends over energetic features as well as over the geometrical ones. A high level of recognition of a receptor molecule by a particular substrate σ indicates there exists a large difference between the binding free energies of σ and that of other substrates, and thus a selective binding. One may also distinguish between *positive* and *negative* recognition, depending on whether the discrimination among different substrates by a given receptor is dominated by attractive or repulsive interactions.

Factors that lead to a high degree of molecular recognition are:

1. *Steric (shape and size) complementarity.* The presence of convex and concave domains must be in the correct locations on the receptor molecule and on the substrate.

2. *Interactional complementarity.* Presence of complementary binding sites (positive/negative charges, charge/dipole, dipole/dipole, hydrogen bond donor/acceptor, etc.).

3. *Large areas of contact between receptor and substrate.* This allows for:

4. *Multiple interaction sites.* Meaning more locations on the receptor and the substrate to bind together, leading to:

5. *Strong overall binding.* Although high stability does not in principle imply high selectivity, this is usually the case. Once the molecule is bound, it does not drift away again or does so very slowly.

6. *Inclusion and Dynamics.* In addition, requiring the receptor ρ and substrate σ to be in contact over a large area will be satisfied if ρ is able to wrap around σ so as to establish numerous noncovalent binding interactions and to sense its molecular size, shape, and architecture. This is the case for receptor molecules that contain intramolecular cavities, clefts, or pockets into which the substrate may fit. In such concave receptors, termed *endoreceptors*, the cavity is lined with binding sites directed toward the bound species. In addition to maximizing contact area, *inclusion* also leads to more or less completely excluding any solvent from the receptor site, thus minimizing the number of solvent molecules that need to be displaced by the substrate on binding.

The balance between rigidity and flexibility is of particular importance for the binding and the dynamic properties of ρ and σ. Rigid, "lock and key"–type receptors are expected to present very efficient recognition with both high stability and high selectivity. More flexible receptors that bind to the substrate through an "induced fit" process may display high selectivity but have lower stability, because part of the binding energy is used up in the change of conformation of the receptor. The trade-off here is that ρ can adapt and respond to changes. Flexibility is of great importance in biological receptor-substrate interactions, where adaptation is often required. Processes of exchange, regulation, cooperativity, and allostery all require a built-in flexibility.

7. *Medium effects on molecular recognition.* It must be remembered that none of this occurs in isolation. Because effects of the surrounding medium also come into play through the interaction of solvent molecules with the receptor and with the substrate, both should present geometrically matched hydrophobic or hydrophilic domains.

Molecular recognition is markedly affected by the surrounding medium. The medium can either enhance or decrease recognition, through enthalpies and entropies of the formation of a supermolecule. Examples are the negative entropies of the formation of alkali cryptates when occurring in an aqueous solution, (Kauffmann, Lehn, and Sauvage 1976) and the increasing exothermicity of binding to cyclophane receptors as the polarity of the solvent increases (Diederich et al. 1992). The medium can also have an effect on the shape of the receptor molecules themselves—for example, hydrophobic effects may deform the receptor. Enzymes can lose all of their activity through a relatively small change in pH of the medium, which causes the enzyme to lose its tertiary protein structure—that is, it uncoils. Shape modifications can strongly influence binding properties. Such medium effects can be illustrated by the two different crystalline forms of the water-soluble salt of a macrobicyclic cyclophane, which can be crystallized in two different shapes depending on the medium: an inflated cage structure building up cylinders in a hexagonal array; and a flattened structure stacked in molecular layers separated by aqueous layers in a lamellar arrangement (Cesario et al. 1993). Such medium effects may be expected to come into play when functional molecules are incorporated into membrane phases as well as in the determination of the form and function of biomolecules.

2.3   Examples of Molecular-Recognition Processes

Most naturally occurring systems that demonstrate recognition (an enzyme recognizing its substrate molecule) involve many binding features and are too complicated to adequately model. Hence, in order to explore the basis of recognition, researchers in the field have first focused their efforts on much simpler systems for actual design,

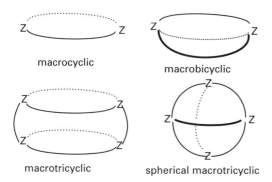

macrocyclic

macrobicyclic

macrotricyclic

spherical macrotricyclic

Figure 2.1
Some macropolycyclic structures. (From Lehn, 1973. With permission from Springer-Verlag © 1973.)

with the goal of investigating cases of increasing complexity. Much molecular recognition work has been done with macropolycyclic structures—molecules containing many branches of linked atoms—because of their suitability when designing artificial receptors. They are large (macro) and may therefore contain cavities of appropriate size and shape to contain a cation, anion, or more complex molecules.[2] Macropolycyclic structures possess numerous branches, bridges, and connections (polycyclic) that allow them to maintain the shape and to confer specific dynamic features. Figure 2.1 shows examples of macrocyclic and higher order structures.

Also, such molecules provide means for arranging geometrically the desired structural groups, binding sites, and reactive functions. When a substrate is bound into the cavity, the result is an inclusion complex, a *cryptate* designated by the mathematical inclusion sign $\subset$: (substrate $\subset$ receptor).

Exoreceptors: Outwardly Directed Molecular Recognition
Most biological examples of molecular recognition are analogous to enzymes, where the active sites are contained inside the cavity of a large protein molecule, which then binds a smaller substrate fitting into the cleft (endorecognition). Most of the work with macrocyclic/macropolycyclic architectures has been along these lines.

The opposite procedure consists of making use of an external surface with protuberances and depressions. The receptor then binds to the substrate by surface-to-surface interaction—analogous to what happens in protein-protein interactions and considered to be an outwardly directed recognition process (exorecognition). Strong

2. To give an idea on size, most cavities range from approximately 2 to approximately 15 angstroms.

and selective binding requires a large enough contact area and a sufficient number of interfaces, as well as geometrical and site complementarity, as mentioned above. Another example of exoreceptor recognition involves a molecule (ligand) containing recognition sites wrapping itself around a central metal ion. A concrete example of this will be given in the last section.

Most molecular recognition at surfaces and interfaces (monolayers, films, membranes, cell walls, organic or inorganic solids) involves outside-directed recognition sites.

Examples of Simple Molecular Recognition: Spheres, Lines, and Tetrahedra

The simplest recognition process is that of spherical substrates, because the sphere is the simplest object in three-dimensional space. These are either positive-charged metal cations (alkali, alkaline-earth, and lanthanide cations) or the negative halide anions. The receptors that recognize such species fall into three main classes: (1) natural macrocycles such as valinomycin; (2) synthetic macrocyclic polyethers, the crown ethers (and derivatives); and (3) synthetic macropolycyclic ligands, the cryptands and other types such as the cryptospherands. The major difference between the macrocycles and macropolycycles is that whereas the former have their main feature as that of a ring into which the cation is bound, macropolycycles possess by nature a three-dimensional cavity, thus allowing, in principle, a much better complementary inclusion of the substrate. Binding into a ring cavity as is found in a macrocycle does not necessarily mean binding to the "equator" of the cation only. The flexibility of the ring can allow adaptation of the ligand—as in the cubic binding of K^+ into valinomycin (figure 2.2) (Dobler 1981). As an example of spherical recognition, macrobicyclic ligands, as shown in figure 2.3, form cryptates by inclusion of a metal cation inside the molecule. This class of molecular structures shows pronounced selectivity as a function of the size complementarity between the cation and the intramolecular cavity—a feature termed *spherical recognition*. As the bridges of the surrounding molecule are lengthened, the size of the cavity increases gradually, with the most strongly bound ion becoming respectively Li^+, Na^+, and then K^+ (Lehn and Sauvage 1975; Lehn 1978). Thus these ligands present peak selectivity, being able to discriminate against cations that are either smaller or larger than their cavity. For more flexible cryptands containing longer chains, the cavities are larger and more adjustable. Thermodynamics and energetics make, of course, the question of binding more complicated than simply one of geometrical fitting. (For a review of thermodynamics data on macrocycle interactions with cations, anions, and neutral molecules, see Izatt et al. 1995.)

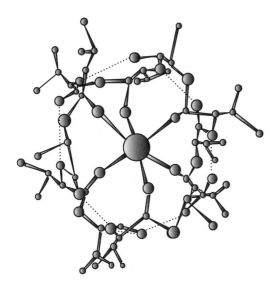

Figure 2.2
Valinomycin with K^+. (From *Ionophores and Their Structures*, M. Dobler. © 1981, John Wiley. Reprinted by permission of John Wiley & Sons, Inc.)

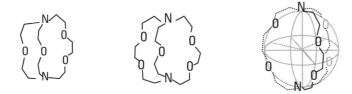

Figure 2.3
Three different examples of macrobicyclic ligands. As the size of the internal cavity gradually increases from left to right, the most strongly bound ion changes from Li^+ to Na^+ to K^+.

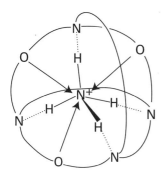

Figure 2.4
Ammonium cryptate. (Reprinted with permission from Graf et al. 1982. © 1982 American Chemical Society.)

Tetrahedral Recognition

Selective binding of tetrahedral substrates requires the construction of a receptor molecule with a tetrahedral recognition site. This may be achieved by positioning four suitable binding sites at the corners of a tetrahedron and maintaining them in the appropriate position with six bridges. Such a structure has been realized in a spherical macrotricyclic cryptand (Graf and Lehn 1975), which contains four nitrogens located at the corners of a tetrahedron and six oxygens located at the corners of an octahedron. This binds a tetrahedral NH_4^+ cation exceptionally strongly and selectively (relative to K^+, for example), forming the ammonium cryptate as shown in figure 2.4 (Graf et al. 1982; Dietrich et al. 1987). This complex presents a high degree of structural (shape and size) and interaction site complementarity between the substrate NH_4^+ and the receptor. The ammonium ion fits exactly into the cavity and is held by a tetrahedral array of $^+N-H\cdots N$ hydrogen bonds and by electrostatic interactions with the six oxygens. It should be pointed out that the molecule is firmly held inside the cavity and does not undergo internal rotation—as happens in a similar macrobicyclic molecule (figure 2.5), with which NH_4^+ can also form a cryptate (Dietrich et al. 1987).

Other Types of Molecules That Can Be Bound

The binding and recognition of *neutral molecules* make use of electrostatic, donor-acceptor, and especially hydrogen bonding interactions. Of special interest is the use of hydrogen bonding between polar sites to bind to the substrate because of the ubiquitousness of hydrogen bonding in organic systems. Here, substrate recognition results from the formation of specific hydrogen bonding patterns between complementary subunits, in a way reminiscent of base pairing in nucleic acids. Such groups

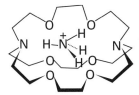

Figure 2.5
Ammonia in macrobicyclic receptor molecule. (Reprinted with permission from Dietrich et al. 1987. © 1987 American Chemical Society.)

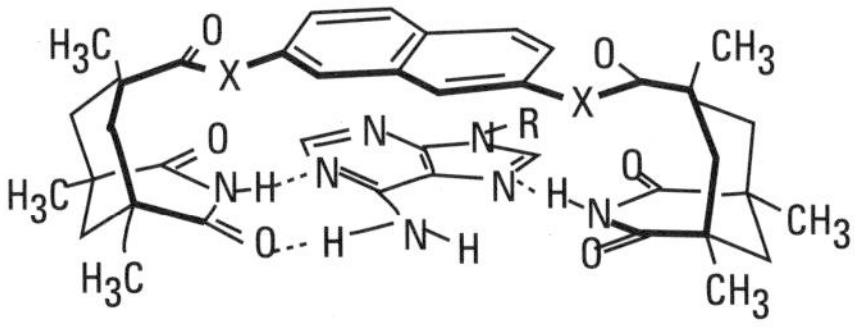

Figure 2.6
Binding of adenine in a cleft. (From Rebek, 1990. With permission from *Accounts Chem. Res.*, © 1987.)

have been positioned in acyclic or macrocyclic receptors, respectively defining clefts or cavities into which binding of substrates of complementary structures has been shown to take place. Figure 2.6 (Rebek 1988 and following references) illustrates the formation of a complex through hydrogen bonding of adenine in a cleft. Hydrogen bonding plays a major role in the recognition of nucleic acid sequences by specially designed synthetic molecules or by proteins, as well as in the recognition of oligosaccharides by proteins.

Anion Recognition

Molecular recognition investigations focused first on the complexation of metal ions and of cationic molecules. But anionic species play a very important role in chemistry and in biology. Research has become increasingly active in the area of anion complexation and recognition, involving the development of anion receptor molecules and binding subunits for anionic functional groups. Anionic substrates are large compared to cations, and possess a wide range of geometries (spherical, linear, planar, tetrahedral, and octahedral). Much work has been done on the binding of carboxylates and phosphates. The design of receptor units for these functional groups is of special interest because they serve as anchoring sites for numerous biological substrates. The strong complexation of adenosine mono-, di-, and triphosphates (AMP, ADP, and ATP) is particularly significant in view of their role in

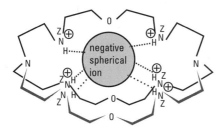

Figure 7 (a)

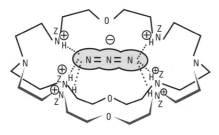

Figure 7 (b)

Figure 2.7
(*a*) Hexaprotonated form of an ellipsoidal polyammonium bis-tren macrobicycle, in this case binding a spherical halide ion. (from Dietrich et al. 1984. With permission from *Helv. Chim. Acta*, © 1984.) (*b*) Hexaprotonated form of an ellipsoidal polyammonium bis-tren macrobicycle, binding the linear triatomic anion N3⁻. (Reprinted with permission from Lehn, Sonveaux, and Willard 1978. © 1978 American Chemical Society.)

bioenergetics. Other areas of research are the development of cyclic analogues of biological polyamines (which can interact with biomolecules) and work on creating receptors containing the guanidinium group. Much attention has been paid to developing chiral receptors—that is, the molecule can come in two forms, a "left-hand" and a "right-hand" form. Such chiral receptors allow for chiral discrimination of the target molecules, analogous to what happens in biological systems.

Linear Recognition
Linear recognition can be performed with a receptor presenting two recognition sites at the opposite ends of a cavity, with the length of the cavity providing a filter as to the length of the substrate molecule that will be preferentially accepted. An example is an ellipsoidal cryptand bis-tren, as shown in figure 2.7, which strongly and selec-

tively binds N_3^- due to its size, shape, and site complementarity (Dietrich et al. 1984; Lehn, Sonveaux, and Willard 1978). This cryptand, although it also binds fluoride and chloride, does so much less well and with appreciable distortions of the ligand; it much prefers a linear molecule of a size compatible with the size of the cavity.

Another example of what could be termed linear recognition is in the hydrolysis of N-acetylglucosamine(NAG) by lysozyme. The hexamer $(NAG)_6$ is the shortest NAG oligosaccharide that is hydrolyzed rapidly. It turns out that there exist six sites on the catalyst that must be filled very specifically, each site recognizing a different part of the hexamer monomer. Anything shorter will not be sufficient (Gates 1992: 162).

2.4   Effects of Complexation

The physicochemical properties of the supramolecular species resulting from the binding of a substrate to a receptor may differ drastically from those of either of the component species, with corresponding changes in electronic, ionic, optical, and conformational properties.

An example is the formation of AC and AEC crown ether complexes and cryptates. Three major effects occur: decreased cation/anion interaction, cation protection, and anion activation. Whereas in crown ether complexes, the bound cation is still accessible for ion pairing from the open "top" and "bottom" faces, this is not (or is less) the case for the cryptates, which surround the cation more completely. Cryptate formation transforms a small metal cation into a very large, spheroidal, charge-diffuse organic cation—a sort of superheavy AC or AEC (Lehn 1980). The stability of the cryptates and the large distance imposed by the organic ligand shell separating the enclosed cation from the environment have many physical and chemical consequences. Cryptation promotes the dissociation of ion pairs, resulting in strong anion activation. It markedly affects numerous reactions, such as those involving the generation of strong bases, nucleophilic substitutions, carbanion reactions, alkylations, rearrangements, and anionic polymerizations, to name a few. Equivalently, reactions involving the cation become inhibited due to cryptation. Crown ethers and cryptands, either alone or fixed on a polymer backbone, have been used in many processes, including selective extraction of metal ions, isotope separation (Heuman 1985; Chen and Echegoyen 1992), incorporation of radioactive or toxic metals, and cation-selective analytical methods.

Another example concerns the tetrahedral binding of ammonia, as mentioned earlier. The strong binding results in an effective pK_a for bound NH_4^+ that is about six units higher than that of free NH_4^+. (Graf et al. 1982). This is an example of how large the changes may be in substrate (or in receptor) properties brought about by binding. Similar changes may take place when substrates bind to enzyme-active sites and to biological receptors.

2.5   Multiple Recognition and its Applications

Once recognition units for specific groups have been identified, one may consider combining several of them within the same structure. This leads to polytopic (many-site) coreceptor molecules containing several discrete binding subunits that may co-operate for the simultaneous binding of several substrates or of a multiple-bound substrate. Both homotopic and heterotopic receptors are possible, depending on whether the binding subunits are identical or not. Aside from the standard effects of binding on individual discrete substrates, the close proximity between bound sub-strates often allows for increased interactions. In addition, coreceptors provide a link to higher forms of molecular behavior, which includes cooperativity and allostery. *Allostery* refers to the binding at a site remote from the catalytic site. As a result of the binding, the structure of the catalytic site may change just enough so that it becomes markedly more active (or inactive). Other areas falling under this are regu-lation, as well as communication or signal transfer if a molecular/atomic species is released or taken up.

One may distinguish *cosystems,* for which the binding of several substrates is commutative, and *cascade systems,* for which the substrate binding steps must fol-low a given sequence to be effective. An example would be when a polyammonium macrocycle (an example of a homotopic substrate) first binds Cu ions, which in turn serve as interaction sites for attracting imidazole and pyrimidine into the complex (figure 2.8) (Coughlin et al. 1979).

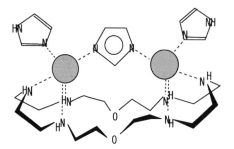

Figure 2.8
Cascade-type dinuclear copper (II) cryptate formed with a macrocyclic polyamine as the ligand. The copper ions bind first, followed by the imidazole groups. (With permission from Supramolecular Chemis-try, J.-M. Lehn. © 1995 VCH Verlagsgesellschaft.)

2.6   Molecular Recognition in Chemical Systems

Before turning to futuristic systems, it is useful to describe how molecular recognition takes place in the following areas (among others): catalysis, membrane transport, and photochemistry.

Supramolecular Reactivity and Catalysis

A catalyst is a substance that accelerates a chemical reaction but is not consumed in the reaction and does not affect its equilibrium. This occurs because a catalyst provides a new and easier pathway for reactant molecules to be converted into product molecules. The effects of molecular recognition are made manifest in systems involving enzymes and other molecules of similarly high molecular weight. Enzymes demonstrate in their high selectivity the full power of molecular recognition.

Supramolecular reactivity involves two main steps: binding, which selects the substrate, and transformation of the bound species into products within the supramolecule formed. Both steps take part in the molecular recognition of the productive substrate and require the correct molecular information in the reactive receptor. Compared to molecular reactivity, a binding step is involved that precedes the reaction itself. Catalysis additionally comprises a third step, the release of the substrate. The catalyst is then free to participate in a new cycle.

The selection of the substrate is not the only function of the binding step. In order to promote a given reaction, the binding should strain the substrate (or pair of substrates) so as to bring it toward the transition state of the reaction; thus efficient catalysis should bind the transition state more strongly than the free state of the substrate in order to lower the free energy of activation.

A major role is played by the existence of strong interactions between the substrate and the receptor site of the catalyst. They may be used to facilitate the reaction in several ways: a *thermodynamic effect* (strong binding forcing the substrate into contact with the reactive groups); a *steric effect* (i.e., fixation of the substrate being able to distort it toward its transition state geometry); and an *electrostatic (electronic, protonic, ionic) effect*, consisting of a possible activation of the functional groups of the catalyst (or substrate) by modification of their physicochemical properties as a consequence of substrate fixation (e.g., perturbation of the charge distribution in both the substrate and catalyst with respect to their free, unbound state).

Examples of catalytic behavior are processes such as ester cleavage and phosphoryl transfer in ATP hydrolysis. A case of a catalyst for the latter is as follows: a multifunctional anion receptor containing a macrocyclic polyamine as an anion binding site, an acridine group as a stacking site, and a catalytic site for hydrolysis; it

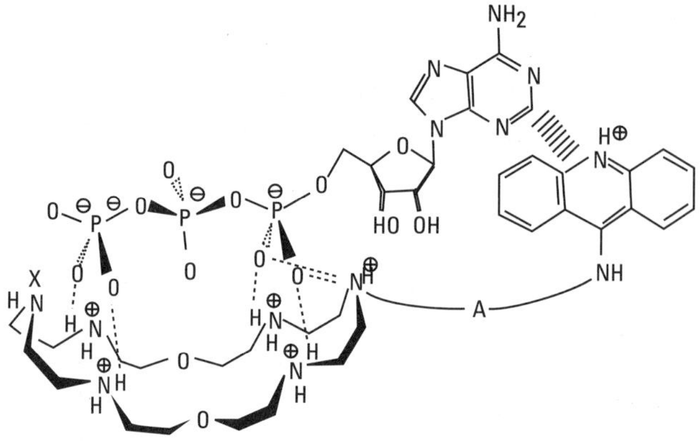

Figure 2.9
Hypothetical structure of the ATP complex in the catalysis of ATP hydrolysis. (Reprinted with permission from Hosseini, Blacker, and Lehn, 1990. © 1990 American Chemical Society.)

acts as a catalyst in ATP hydrolysis with increased ATP/ADP selectivity. One possible pathway is shown in figure 2.9 (Hosseini, Blacker, and Lehn 1990). Another area of major interest, as mentioned above, is molecular recognition of the structural and base sequence features in DNA together with the selective cleavage of nucleic acids. Being able to design selective DNA and RNA cleavage reagents is a very active area of research at present, particularly in light of their potential uses in biotechnology.

A further step beyond bond cleavage is the design of systems capable of inducing bond formation. To this end, the presence of several binding and reactive groups is essential. Such is the case for coreceptor molecules in which subunits may cooperate for substrate binding and transformation (figure 2.10) (Lehn 1995).

This ability of bringing together substrates and cofactors, mediating reactions between them within the supramolecular architecture, is called cocatalysis. As an example, the same macrocycle as was used in the studies of ATP hydrolysis was also found to mediate the synthesis of pyrophosphate from acetylphosphate (Lehn 1979, 1986).

Another example of interest is the enhanced ligation of DNA, effected by an imidazole-functionalized spermine binding in the minor groove of the double helix (figure 2.11) (Zuber, Sirlin, and Behr 1993).

Carrier-Mediated Transport

The assisted transport of molecules across membranes is extremely important for processes in biology. This is of particular significance when the flow of molecules

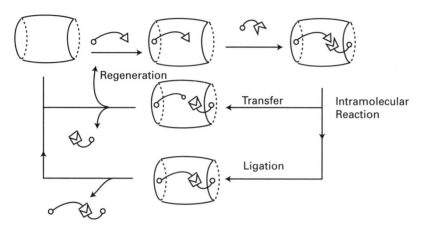

Figure 2.10
Cocatalysis cycle, with final products either being the transfer of a subunit or the ligation of two subunits. (With permission from *Supramolecular Chemistry*, J.-M. Lehn. © 1995 VCH Verlagsgesellschaft.)

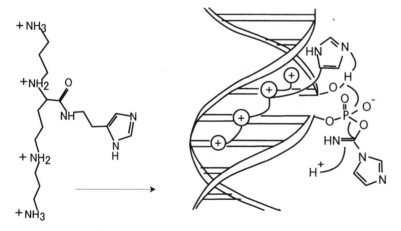

Figure 2.11
Enhancement of ligation of DNA as effected by an imidazole-functionalized spermine binding in the minor groove of the double helix. (Reprinted with permission from Zuber, Sirlin, and Behr. © 1993 American Chemical Society.)

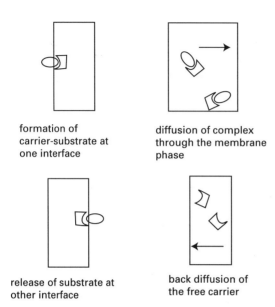

formation of
carrier-substrate at
one interface

diffusion of complex
through the membrane
phase

release of substrate at
other interface

back diffusion of
the free carrier

Figure 2.12
Schematic showing the four steps of a transport cycle.

occurs against a gradient or occurs faster than free diffusion would allow. Biological systems accomplish this feat through the judicious use of molecular recognition and transport processes. Carrier-mediated transport consists of the transfer of a substrate across a membrane, facilitated by a carrier molecular located in the membrane. It is a cyclic process comprising four steps, as shown in figure 2.12: (1) formation of the carrier-substrate complex at one interface; (2) diffusion of the complex through the membrane phase; (3) release of the substrate at the other interface; and (4) back diffusion of the free carrier.

Because of its cyclic nature, this process presents analogies with molecular catalysis; it may be considered as physical catalysis producing a change in location. In transport, the substrate is translocated, just as chemical catalysis produces a transformation into products. The carrier is the transport catalyst that strongly increases the rate of passage of the substrate with respect to free diffusion and shows enzyme-like features.

Carrier design requires taking into account factors specific for transport processes. Whereas a molecular receptor should display high stability, high selectivity, and a slow exchange rate with respect to its substrate, a carrier molecule should be highly selective but should not bind its substrate too tightly. It must be flexible enough to allow sufficiently fast exchange rates for loading and unloading and to avoid carrier saturation. In addition, the carrier must have a suitable lipophilic-hydrophilic balance so as to be readily soluble in the membrane phase, while retaining the ability to reach the interface and enter into contact with the aqueous phase. Finally, it should not be too bulky to diffuse rapidly.

A major goal in transport chemistry is to design carriers and processes that involve the coupled flow of two (or more) species in either the same (symport) or in opposite (antiport) directions. Such parallel or antiparallel vectorial processes make it possible to set up a pumped system in which a species is carried in the potential created by physicochemical gradients of electrons (redox gradient), protons (pH gradient), or other species (concentration gradient). Gradients may be generated by chemical reactions, as occurs in vectorial bioenergetics. For transport, either two or more individual carriers for different substrates may be used simultaneously or the appropriate subunits may be introduced into a single species, a so-called cocarrier. In such coupled systems, carrier design allows transport processes to be endowed with regulation of rates and selectivity, as well as with coupling to energy sources for the transport of a species against its own concentration gradient.

Photonic Molecular Devices
One reason for the emphasis on photochemistry is due to its potential for devising (a) parallel input, (b) processing, and (c) output functions. How to read information in and out of molecular systems should be considered as one of the defining problems of the field. This is particularly true in light of the fact that much of the information stored may not even be localizable. Even if it is, the value may make no sense unless it is compared to the measured values of all other incident values in the same system. An example is the location of the "information" encoded in a neural network. Many of the systems under discussion will require some form of parallel output or value definition arising from collective behavior.

The formation of supramolecular entities from photoactive components may be expected to perturb the ground-state and excited-state properties of the individual species, giving rise to novel properties that define a supramolecular photochemistry. This could include such features as excitation energy migration, photoinduced charge separation by electron or proton transfer, perturbation of optical transitions and polarizabilities, modification of redox potential or excited states, photoregulation of binding properties, and selective photochemical reactions, among other possibilities.

Supramolecular photochemistry, like catalysis, may involve three steps: binding of substrate and receptor, mediating a photochemical process (such as energy, electron, or proton transfer), followed by either restoration of the initial state for a new cycle or a chemical reaction.

In principle, supramolecular photonic devices require a complex organization and adaptation of the components in space, energy, and time, leading to the generation of photosignals by energy transfer (ET) or electron transfer (eT), substrate binding, chemical reactions, and so on. Numerous types of devices may thus be imagined, involving oriented energy migration, antenna effects, vectorial transfer of charge, conversion of light into chemical energy, optical signal generation, and photo-switching, to name a few. Being able to carry out separately the various steps of an overall photochemical process (such as in conversion of absorbed light into emitted light of another wavelength, for example) would allow the customization and opti-mization of each part. Light conversion requires a device involving three basic oper-ations and consisting of two discrete components: (a) a light collector (antenna) using strongly absorbing units and (b) an emitter, thus allowing the separate optimization of absorption and emission. For maximum effectiveness, intercomponent energy transfer between the antenna and emitter must occur as efficiently as possible. Hence the three-step mode of absorption, energy transfer, and emission.

As an example of such a process, luminescent cryptates of europium(III) and ter-bium(II) have been formed with macrobicyclic structures including various groups that can serve as light-collecting antenna components. These complexes present a unique combination of features arising from both their cryptate structure and the nature of the emitting species: protection of the included ion from deactivation due to interaction with water molecules; very high thermodynamic stability and kinetic inertness; multiple photosensitizing groups suitable for energy transfer and displaying strong UV light absorption; and characteristic long wavelength and long lifetime of the emission. They display a bright luminescence in an aqueous solution, whereas the free ions do not emit under the same conditions. Absorption of UV light by the organic antenna groups is followed by energy transfer to the included lanthanoid cation, which then emits its characteristic visible radiation (figure 2.13).

Such photoactive cryptates are of interest as novel luminescent materials and as labels for biological applications such as labeling of monoclonal antibodies, oligo-nucleotides, and membrane components (Prat, Lopez, and Mathis 1991; Lopez et al. 1993). Linked, cascade systems performing very long range energy transfer (VLRET) may be imagined as well. Such systems could be considered as examples of supra-molecular wires in the field of molecular and supramolecular electronics.

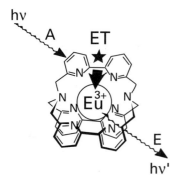

Figure 2.13
Eu(III) cryptate showing the three steps (absorption, energy transfer, and emission) in light conversion. (Reprinted with permission from *Supramolecular Chemistry*, J.-M. Lehn. © 1995 VCH Verlagsgesellschaft.)

Another area of interest is the use of receptor molecules bearing photosensitive groups. Such molecules may display marked modifications in their photophysical properties on the binding of substrate species, leading to changes in their light absorption (color generation) or emission features, allowing their detection by spectroscopic measurements.

Chromo- or lumino-ionophores of macrocyclic or macropolycyclic type respond to the binding of metal ions and may be of much interest as analytical tools for environmental applications or for the study of ionic changes in biological processes such as cell signaling. These types of receptors combine the strong and selective complexing ability of cryptands with the intense absorption or emission properties of photosensitive groups (azophenol, spirobenzopyran, anthracene, or coumarin). They display marked changes in absorption on complexation of alkali-metal cations or protonation, thus acting as fluorescent signaling systems.

Yet another example is the strong enhancement of the acridine fluorescence observed when ATP binds to a receptor molecule formed by a (24)-N_6O_2 macrocycle bearing a lateral acridine group (Hosseini, Blacker, and Lehn 1990). This receptor is a sensitive and selective ATP probe that generates a fluorescence signal on ATP binding.

One present, very active area of research is the search for substances effecting single- or double-strand nucleic acid recognition and fitted with a photoreacting group to perform sequence-specific photocleavage on DNA or RNA.

The field of supramolecular photochemistry is a rapidly expanding field and promises much activity in the years to come.

2.7   Self-Assembly, Self-Recognition, and Self-Organization

The potentially most far-reaching aspect of molecular recognition lies in its application in self-assembly and/or self-organization. Self-assembly refers to the more or less automatic putting together of parts, based almost purely on molecular recognition. Self-organization refers to self-assembly with the generation of organized entities and may result in networks and feedback systems on different levels.

Self-organization may display positive cooperativity, implying that a given step in the assembly sets the stage for and facilitates the following one. It is self-assembly driven to completion. Positive cooperativity is a basic characteristic of molecular amplification devices, because once initiated, the subsequent steps of the assembly are facilitated. It represents a nonlinear process and confers features of an *error filter*; only the correct input will, in principle, lead to creating the cooperative structure. In addition, the dynamic features of supramolecular binding make these systems able to undergo annealing and self-repair defects. The ability to "explore" the available energy surface more freely than is possible with covalent bonding allows such systems to exchange incorrect components for correct ones, thus allowing a form of self-maintenance and error correction. They can also display adaptation by being able to react to environmental changes and to adjust to novel conditions.

Self-Assembled Entities—Micelles and LB Films

Micelles, which are either globular or cylindrical constructions, are formed when a soluble surfactant dissolved in a solvent (usually aqueous) reaches a certain concentration (critical micelle concentration). Such surfactants are usually in the form of hydrocarbon chains with a hydrophilic "head" and a hydrophobic "tail." At the critical concentration, the molecules begin to associate, with the chains packing together (like a sea urchin) and the hydrophilic heads facing the water. Reactant molecules with nonpolar groups may have a much greater affinity for the interior of the micelle than for the polar aqueous phase or the interfacial regions. Consequently, some reactants are concentrated in the micelles, where the high local concentration may favor reactions between them.

In polymerization processes, the micelles can stabilize free-radical initiators by isolating single radicals and preventing the chain termination that results from the reaction of two radicals—at least until another radical enters or is formed within the micelle. This results in higher molecular weight products—so-called emulsion polymerization. In solution, the termination reactions are faster and the average molecular weight is much lower.

Spherical micelles are predominantly formed by surfactants with bulky or charged head groups slightly above the critical micelle concentration. With increasing concentration, there is competition among the micelles for water molecules forming their solvation shell, resulting in cylindrical structures (Gates 1992: 129).

Langmuir-Blodgett Films
In the formation of self-assembled layers of Langmuir-Blodgett (L-B) films, a surfactant that is insoluble in water (a fatty acid molecule with a hydrophilic part [carboxyl group] and a hydrophobic part [a long hydrocarbon chain]) is spread in an organic solvent on the water surface. After evaporation of the solvent, the molecules can be pushed together with a movable barrier until they are densely packed, forming a compact monolayer one molecule thick. This monolayer can then be transferred to the surface of a solid support—for instance, a glass slide. The carboxyl groups of the fatty acid molecules bind to the surface of the glass slide and the ends of the hydrocarbon chains are now facing the air. When dipping in the slide again, it is covered by a second layer of fatty acid in reverse orientation, the molecular "tails" of the two layers facing each other. This can be repeated many times. This technique (the Langmuir-Blodgett technique) has been used as a way to produce supramolecular arrangements with increasing complexity (Kuhn and Forsterling 2000).

Examples of Self-Organization Processes
Molecular organization and self-assembly into layers, membranes, vesicles, construction of multilayer films, and so on make it possible to build up specific supramolecular architectures. Performing the polymerization of the molecular components is a major step in increasing control over the structural properties of such assemblies. Outfitting these polymolecular entities with recognition units and reactive functional groups may lead to systems performing molecular recognition or supramolecular catalysis on external or internal surfaces of organic materials (molecular layers, membranes, vesicles, polymers, etc.) or on inorganic materials (zeolites, clays, sol-gel preparations, etc.). Control of the distance between different reaction sites is already possible in a crude way by incorporating the wished-for reaction site in an L-B film (either at the head or the tail of a fatty acid) and then building up, layer by layer. Undoubtedly, as research progresses in this area, finer and finer control will be obtained over both the ability to incorporate different reaction sites in a "network" molecule, and the ability to judiciously control their level of polymerization.

The further interest in self-organization, aside from the possibility of creating devices out of self-assembling components, is the possibility of being able to trigger supramolecular assemblies by optical, electrical, or chemical stimuli that result in a large-scale change of the organization, thus amounting to signal amplification and expression on the macroscopic level. Such a case of signal amplification is given below.

If two (or more) complementary units A or A′ are grafted onto a backbone (also called a template), mixing the two can lead to the self-assembly of a linear or cross-linked, main-chain supramolecular "copolymer" species.

As an example of this, condensation of the complementary groups 2,6 diamino-pyridine P and uracil U with long chain derivatives of L-, D-, or meso (M) tartaric acid yields substances LP_2, LU_2, MP_2, MU_2, and so on; each contains two identical units capable of undergoing association via triple hydrogen bonding (Fouquey, Lehn, and Levelut 1990). Whereas the individual (pure) species are solids, the mixtures $(LP_2 + LU_2)$, $(DP_2 + LU_2)$ and $(MP_2 + MU_2)$ display liquid crystalline behavior. The overall process thus may be described as the self-assembly of a supra-molecular liquid-crystalline polymer based on molecular recognition. Varying the concentration allowed one to track, via electron microscopy, the progressive assembly of supramolecular-polymolecular entities from small up to very large ones: small nuclei → filaments → treelike structures → fibers. The species formed presented helicity induced by the chirality of the original components and successively transferred to the larger scale entities. A mixture of all four of the components yielded long superhelices of opposite handedness that coexisted in the same sample—in other words, spontaneous resolution through chiral selection in a molecular recognition-directed self-assembly. Here, molecular chirality is transduced into supramolecular helicity, which is then repeated in the structure of the material at nanometric and micrometric scales, amounting to a *size amplification of chirality*.

It should be pointed out that the separation of material into mesoscopic entities of one or the other chirality implies a sorting out of molecular components. Due to the supermolecular nature of the bonds, this signal can be reversed and the system dissolved back into its components simply by heating.

Another example of complex self-assembly is the formation of double-stranded helices—termed *helicates*—around metallic ions of specific coordination geometries. Certain molecular strands containing two to five $2, 2'$ bipyridine groups will spontaneously assemble in the presence of Cu(I) ions. This double helix structure results from the tetrahedral-like coordination imposed by each Cu(bipy)$_2^{2+}$ site and from the design of the ligands, which disfavors binding to only a single strand. Using a slightly different molecular chain and metal ions, which favor an octahedral symmetry (nickel [II]), one can produce similar triple helical complexes, as shown in figure 2.14 (Kraemer, Lehn, and Marquis-Rigault 1993).

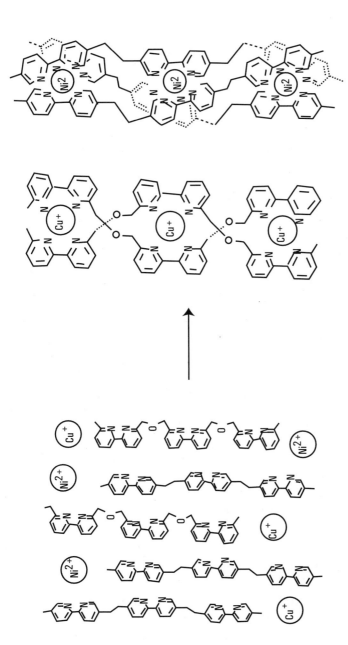

Figure 2.14
Self-recognition in the self-assembly of double and triple helices from a mixture of two different oligobipyridine strands and of Cu(I) and Ni(II)ions (ClO$_4^-$ counter-ions not shown) (Krämer, Lehn, and Marquis-Rigault. © 1993 *Proc. Natl. Acad. Sci. USA.*)

This can been seen as a sort of molecular program being carried out, with the information carried both in the strands and in the ions. Molecular programming involves the incorporation of instructions into molecular components for the generation of the desired supramolecular architecture. Depending on the design of the interaction patterns between the components, more or less strict programming of the output entity will be achieved. The program is molecular, the information being carried in the covalent framework—while its operation through noncovalent recognition "algorithms"—is supramolecular. The processing of molecular information via molecular recognition events implies the passage from the molecular to the supramolecular level. In the example outlined above, in addition to the nature and the coordination geometry of the metal ions involved, three main features that bear structural information determining the nature and shape of the helical species formed may be distinguished: (1) the precise structure of the binding site—it specifies the ability to coordinate metal ions with a given geometry as well as the number of strands bound; (2) the spacer separating the binding sites—it must favor inter- over intrastrand binding, and it influences the tightness of the helix (the pitch) through the rotation of one metal center with respect to the next; and (3) most important, the configuration of the coordination centers determines whether the structure is indeed of a helical nature; helicity implies that all metal centers have the same screw sense. The program containing all these information features is molecular and linear. Its operation is supramolecular and takes place through the reading of the information according to the coordination algorithm of the metal ion.

The full power of such applied molecular recognition comes to fruition in such systems. When all of the components (both types of bipy [bipyridine] strands and both types of metal ions) are mixed together, only the "pure" double helices containing Cu(I) and the triple helicate with Ni(II) were formed, with no crossover (Krämer 1993). This is an example of a parallel operation of two "programmed" molecular systems leading to the clean self-assembly of two well-defined helical complexes from a mixture of their four components.

2.9   Thermodynamics, Information, and Entropy

Whereas questions about the interplay of limitations on information and entropy for most present computer system technologies remains more theoretical than actual, in systems using molecular recognition, this is a factor that must be considered from the outset. It has already been mentioned that one reason for the present emphasis on photochemistry is due to its possibilities for (a) parallel input, (b) processing, and (c) output. How to read information in and out of molecular systems should be considered as one of the defining problems of the field. Many of the systems under discussion will require some form of parallel output or defining value arising from collective behavior. Although single-atom observing devices such as STMs and AFMs have been developed, it will be hard to build a device that would allow interaction with all possible molecular units in the system in a reasonable amount of time. It would be much better to use the self-organizing behavior of the system to provide a signal at the macroscopic level. We have already seen this as a possibility with the example given above of size amplification of chirality.

By allowing the spontaneous but controlled buildup of complex systems from their components, self-organization also provides means of bypassing tedious nanofabrication and nanomanipulation procedures, a feature of great interest for nanotechnology.

In molecular systems, unlike present-day computers, there is no real split between hardware and software. It is theoretically possible to develop a molecular version of the 0s and 1s of present-day magnetic or optical memory using supermolecules with bipolar or multipolar states. It should be kept in mind, however, that it may be impossible to easily access the information without erasing it or perturbing it to the point where it loses its value. Although in many cases it may be possible to conceive of ways around this problem (e.g., regeneration of the data), it should be noted that putting such a scheme into effect may negate many of the putative advantages of molecular systems (quick reaction time, fuzzy logic, etc.). Add to this the inherent "floppiness" of molecular systems (because one is invariably working at nonzero temperatures) and the possibility of parallel/competing processes occurring. The result is that one starts to address problems that sound very much like that found in quantum mechanics—the inability of "knowing" what a particular state is without perturbing it, the spreading out of probability waves (here in chemical systems, it is information waves), and the overlapping and mixing of different states. The major stumbling block with using molecular systems may not be technical; the challenge is being able to conceive how to adequately make use of their properties!

Chemical systems may store information either in an analog fashion, in the structural features (size, shape, nature, and disposition of interactions sites) of a molecule or a supermolecule; or in a digital fashion, in the various states or connections of a chemical entity. The evaluation of the information content of a recognition process based on structural sensing in receptor-substrate pairs requires an assessment of the relevant molecular characteristics. Recognition is not an absolute but a relative notion. It results from the structural (and eventually dynamical) information stored in the partners and is defined by the fidelity of its reading, which rests on the difference in free energy of interaction between states, represented by different receptor-substrate combinations. It is thus not a yes/no process but is relative to a threshold level separating states and making them distinct. It depends on free energy and, consequently, on temperature. The parameter kT could be a possible reference quantity against which to evaluate threshold values, differences between states, and reading accuracy. Both analog and digital processing of chemical information depend on such factors.

As an example of how both thermodynamics and structural factors come into play in self-recognition, let us examine the example given above, of the multicomponent self-assembly of the oligobipyridine strands around different ions. Here, we have three structural factors: (1) the structural features of the ligands (nature, number, and arrangement of the binding subunits; nature and position of the spacers), (2) the coordination geometries of the metal ions, and (3) the steric and conformational effects within the different assembled species resulting from the various possible combinations of ligands and metal ions in a given mixture. We also have two thermodynamic factors: (1) the energy-related principle of "maximal site occupancy," which implies that the system evolves toward the species or the mixture of species that presents the highest occupancy of the binding sites available on both the ligand and the ions (i.e., site saturation) and (2) the entropy factor, which favors the state of the system with the largest number of product species. Of course, other factors may contribute, such as the binding of other species present in the medium and environmental effects.

We have already mentioned before that these are all chemical systems following a natural process (i.e., entropy always increases). The decrease in entropy implied in information storage in a covalent structure is (over)compensated by the entropy increase occurring in the course of the stepwise synthesis of the "informed" molecule in question.

Another aspect of "information transfer" is what happens in self-replication. Here, a molecule catalyzes its own formation by acting as template for the constituents, which react to generate a copy of the template. Such systems display autocatalysis and may be termed *informational* or *noninformational*, depending on whether or not replication involves the conservation of a sequence of information (Orgel 1992). In self-replicating systems employing three starting constituents, competition between them can occur. Such processes are on the way to systems displaying information transfer, whereas the two-component ones are noninformational.

Entities resulting from self-assembly and self-organization of a number of components may undergo self-correction and adaptation. Such features might also explain why large multisite protein architectures are formed by the association of several smaller protein subunits rather than from a single long polypeptide.

In a broader perspective, these results point to the emergence of a new outlook involving a change in paradigm, from "pure compounds" to "instructed mixtures," from "unicity" (pure substance) to "multiplicity + information" (mixture of instructed components and program). Rather than pursuing mere chemical purity of a compound or a material, one would seek the design of instructed components that, as mixtures, would lead through self-processes to the spontaneous and selective formation of the desired (functional) superstructures.

Beyond programmed systems, the next step in complexity consists in the design of chemical "learning" systems, systems that are not just instructed but can be trained, that possess self-modification ability and adaptability in response to external stimuli. This opens perspectives toward systems that would undergo evolution (i.e, progressive change of internal structure under the pressure of environmental factors). It implies also the passage from closed systems to open systems that are connected spatially and temporally to their surroundings.

The progression from elementary particles to the nucleus, the atom, the molecule, the supermolecule, and the supramolecular assembly represents steps up the ladder of complexity. Particles interact to form atoms, atoms to form molecules, molecules to form supermolecules and supramolecular assemblies, and so on. At each level, novel features appear that did not exist at a lower one. Thus a major line of development of chemistry is toward complex systems and the emergence of complexity. Complexity implies and results from multiple components and interactions between them with integration (i.e., long-range correlation, coupling, and feedback). It is interaction between components that makes the whole more than the sum of the parts and leads to collective properties. The species and properties defining a given level of complexity result from, and may be explained on the basis of the species belonging to the level below and of their multibody interactions.

Because the higher depends on the lower, we work our way backward from organism to interacting assemblies down to supramolecular entities and to the recognition process. Molecular recognition is the level at which information processes and programming procedures are implemented in chemical systems, based on the storage of information in the molecular components and its supramolecular processing through specific interactional algorithms. It brings to light the third basic feature of chemical systems, in addition to matter and energy: information.

References

Blasse, G., G. J. Dirksen, D. Van der Voort, N. Sabbatini, S. Perathoner, and J.-M. Lehn. 1988. [Eu bpy·bpy·bpy]$^{3+}$ Cryptate: Luminescence and conformation. *Chem. Phys. Lett.* 146: 347–351.

Cesario, M., J. Guilhem, J.-M. Lehn, R. Meric, C. Pascard, and J.-P. Vigneron. 1993. Medium effects in action, visualized by the crystal structures of open and closed forms of a molecular receptor. *J. Chem. Soc., Chem. Commun.* 6: 540–543.

Chen, Z. and L. Echegoyen. 1992. Redox-active polyether ligands: Toward metal ion isotopic separation. In *Crown Compounds: Toward Future Applications*, ed. S. R. Cooper, 27. Weinheim: VCH.

Coughlin, P. K., J. C. Dewan, S. J. Lippard, E. K. Watanabe, and J.-M. Lehn. 1979. Synthesis and structure of the imidazolate bridged dicopper (II) ion incorporated into a circular cryptate macrocycle. *J. Am. Chem. Soc.* 101: 265–266.

Diederich, F., D. B. Smithrud, E. M. Sanford, T. B. Wyman, S. B. Ferguson, D. R. Carcanque, I. Chao, and K. N. Houk. 1992. Solvent effects in molecular recognition. *Acta Chem. Scand.* 46: 205–215.

Dietrich, B., J. Guilhem, J.-M. Lehn, C. Pascard, and E. Sonveaux. 1984. Molecular recognition in anion coordination chemistry. Structure, binding constants and receptor-substrate complementarity of a series of anion cryptates of a macrobicyclic receptor molecule. *Helv. Chim. Acta* 67: 91–104.

Dietrich, B., J.-P. Kintzinger, J.-M. Lehn, B. Metz, and A. Zahidi. 1987. Stability, molecular dynamics in solution, and x-ray structure of the ammonium cryptate [NH$^+$.cn$^+$nd.2.2.2] hexafluorophosphate. *J. Phys. Chem.* 91: 6600–6606.

Dobler, M. 1981. *Ionophores and their Structures*. New York: John Wiley.

Fischer, E. 1894. Einfluss der Configuration auf die Wirkung der Enzyme. *Ber. Deutsch. Chem. Ges.* 27: 2985–2993.

Fouquey, C., J.-M. Lehn, and A.-M. Levelut. 1990. Molecular recognition directed self-assembly of supramolecular ligand crystalline polymers from complementary chiral components. *Adv. Mater.* 2: 254.

Gates, B. 1992. *Catalytic Chemistry*. New York: John Wiley and Sons.

Graf, E., and J.-M. Lehn. 1975. Cryptates. XVII. Synthesis and cryptate complexes of a spheroidal macrotricyclic ligand with octohedrotetrahedral symmetry. *J. Am. Chem. Soc.* 97: 5022–5024.

Graf, E., J.-P. Kintzinger, J.-M. Lehn, and J. LeMoigne. 1982. Molecular recognition. Selective ammonium cryptates of synthetic receptor molecules possessing a tetrahedral recognition site. *J. Am. Chem. Soc.* 104: 1672–1678.

Heuman, K. G. 1985. Isotopic separation in systems with crown ethers and cryptands. *Topics Curr. Chem.* 127: 77–132.

Hosseini, M. W., A. J. Blacker, and J.-M. Lehn. 1990. Multiple molecular recognition and catalysis. A multifunctional anion receptor bearing an anion binding site, an intercalating group, and a catalytic site for nucleotide binding and hydrolysis. *J. Am. Chem. Soc.* 112: 3896–3904.

Izatt, R., K. Pawlak, J. S. Bradshaw, and R. L. Bruening. 1995. Thermodynamic and kinetic data for macrocycle interaction with cations, anions, and neutral molecules. *Chem. Rev.* 95: 2529–2586.

Kauffmann, E., J.-M. Lehn, and J. P. Sauvage. 1976. *Helv. Chim. Acta* 59: 1099–1111.

Krämer, R., J.-M. Lehn, and A. Marquis-Rigault. 1993. Self-recognition in helicate self-assembly: Spontaneous formation of helical metal complexes from mixtures of ligands and metal ions. *Proc. Natl. Acad. Sci. USA* 90: 5394–5398.

Kuhn, H., and H.-D. Forsterling. 2000. *Principles of Physical Chemistry*. New York: John Wiley and Sons.

Lehn, J.-M. 1973. Design of organic complexing agents. Strategies towards properties. *Struct. Bond.* 16: 1–69.

Lehn, J.-M. 1978. Cryptates: The chemistry of macropolycyclic inclusion complexes. *Acc. Chem. Res.* 11: 49–57.

Lehn, J.-M. 1979. Macrocyclic receptor molecules: Aspects of chemical reactivity. Investigations into molecular catalysis and transport processes. *Pure Appl. Chem.* 51: 979–987.

Lehn, J.-M. 1980. Cryptate inclusion complexes. Effects on solute-solute and solute-solvent interactions and an ionic reactivity. *Pure Appl. Chem.* 52: 2303–2319.

Lehn, J.-M. 1986. Ann. N.Y. Acad. Sci. 471: 41–50.

Lehn, J.-M. 1995. *Supramolecular Chemistry*. Weinheim: VCH.

Lehn, J.-M., and J.-P. Sauvage. 1975. Cryptates. XVI. [2]-cryptates. Stability and selectivity of alkali and alkali-earth macrobicyclic complexes. *J. Am. Chem. Soc.* 97: 6700–6707.

Lehn, J.-M., E. Sonveaux, and A. K. Willard. 1978. Molecular recognition. Anion cryptates of a macrobicyclic receptor molecule for linear triatomic species. *J. Am. Chem. Soc.* 100: 4914–4916.

Lopez, E., C. Chypre, B. Alpha, and G. Mathis. 1993. Europium (III) trisbipyridine cryptate label for line-resolved fluorescence detection of PCR products fixed on a solid support. *Clin. Chem.* 39: 196–201.

Orgel, L. E. 1992. Molecular recognition. *Nature* 358: 203–209.

Prat, O., E. Lopez, and G. Mathis. 1991. Europium (III) cryptate: A fluorescent label for the detection of DNA hybrids on solid support. *Anal. Biochem.* 195: 283–289.

Rebek, J. 1990. Molecular recognition and biophysical organic chemistry. *Acc. Chem. Res.* 23: 399–401.

Zuber, G., C. Sirlin, and J.-P. Behr. 1993. Gene transfer with a series of lipophilic DNA-binding molecules. *J. Am. Chem. Soc.* 115: 4939–4940.

3 Computing in Reaction-Diffusion and Excitable Media: Case Studies of Unconventional Processors

Andrew Adamatzky

Recently, we have seen an explosive growth of interest in nonstandard computing architectures, materials, and algorithms: molecular electronics, quantum computation, genetic algorithms, membrane computing, DNA computing, and many others. Computation based on wave dynamics and reaction-diffusion processes in physical, chemical, and biological systems (generally classified as nonlinear media) is one of the new approaches being followed (Adamatzky 2001). In this chapter, we will provide a brief account of the subject.

Target waves, spiral waves, and self-localized mobile excitations, to mention a few, are typical space-time patterns in active nonlinear media. Is it possible to employ these phenomena to carry out something useful, to process images, to compute logical functions, to control robots? The answer is yes; we shall prove it in this chapter. Consider, for example, an active chemical medium and a change in the concentration of reagents at a few sites: Diffusive or phase waves are generated and spread, they interact with each other and form dynamic or stationary patterns as a result of their interactions. The medium's microvolumes update their states simultaneously. Aside from a small degree of asynchronous acting that can be neglected, molecules also diffuse and react in parallel. Thus the medium can be thought of as a massive parallel processor. In this wet processor, data and the results of a computation are encoded as concentration profiles of reagents, while the computation is achieved by the spreading and interaction of the waves. In this chapter, we show how these wet processors work and how they employ space-time dynamics in the form of activity patterns to perform useful computations. We demonstrate how various problems are solved in active nonlinear media, where data and results are given by spatial defects, and information processing is implemented by the spreading and interaction of phase or diffusive waves.

The field of reaction-diffusion and excitable computing is rapidly expanding. It has already affected domains as diverse as smart materials, computational complexity, theory of computation, robotics, logic, and mathematical physics. Lack of space prevents us from exposing the full spectrum of results obtained in the field; we would rather refer the reader to present textbooks (Adamatzky 2001, 2002), where every element of this unconventional computing has been scrutinized. This chapter is restricted to discussing classical examples of wet processors, exemplifying critical issues of the research, and outlining our perspective for further studies.

3.1   Reaction-Diffusion and Excitation

A great variety of natural processes can be described in terms of propagating fronts. Well-known phenomena include: the dynamics of excitation in heart and neural tissue, calcium waves in cell cytoplasm, the spreading of genes in population dynamics, and forest fires. All these systems, and many more, are capable of implementing some basic computational operations. In this chapter, we consider mostly those based on wave dynamics in nonlinear chemical systems.

A nonlinear chemical medium is bistable: Each microvolume of the medium has at least two steady stable states, and the microvolume switches between these states. In the chemical medium, fronts of diffusing reactants propagate with constant velocity and wave form; the reagents of the wave front convert reagents ahead of the front into products left behind (Epstein and Showalter 1996). In an excitable chemical medium, the wave propagation occurs because of coupling between diffusion and autocatalytic reactions. When autocatalytic species are produced in one microvolume of the medium, they diffuse to the neighboring microvolumes and thus trigger an autocatalytic reaction there. That is why an excitable medium responds to perturbations that exceed a excitation threshold by generating excitation waves (Epstein and Showalter 1996; Adamatzky 2001).

Why are excitation waves so good for computing? Unlike mechanical waves, excitation waves do not conserve energy but conserve waveform and amplitude; they do not interfere, and generally do not reflect (Krinsky 1984). Because of these properties, excitation waves can play an essential role of information transmission in active nonlinear media processors.

3.2   What Is a Reaction-Diffusion Processor?

A reaction-diffusion processor is merely a container, or a reactor, filled with chemicals, or reagents. The reactor transforms input data to output data in a sensible and controllable way via spatial spreading and interaction of the reactants. A medium of the reactor is at rest at the beginning of a computation. Data are transformed into the configuration of a geometrical object; this configuration is cast onto the medium. After projection, the elements of the data configuration form a pattern of local disturbances in the medium's characteristics—drops of a reagent or an excitation pattern. These local disturbances generate waves. The waves spread in the medium. Eventually, the waves, originating from different data sources, meet. They somehow interact and produce either a concentration profile of a precipitate or a stationary pattern of activity. This emerging pattern represents the result of the computation.

We would rather transform our problems to make them solvable in a nonlinear media instead of trying to modify the media to solve the problems.[1] Most problems with natural spatial parallelism, it is hoped, can be solved in a computation-efficient manner in nonlinear active media (Adamatzky 2001).

A computation in a chemical medium can be accomplished in two ways: structured or architecture-free. The structured computation is implemented in a chemical reactor subdivided into domains with different reagents. Usually the structure of the reactor imitates conventional logical circuits, where wires are simulated by tubes with flowing reagents and logical gates are realized by physical junctions of two or more tubes; alternatively, logical circuits can be drawn as channels in an excitable medium. Such implementation of reaction-diffusion information processing demonstrates the viability of chemical computing in principle but gives nothing new from the computer architecture point of view.

Architecture-free chemical processors are of much more interest. They can be classified into two subtypes: integral computers and spatial computers. In the processors of the first subtype, all spatial differentiation has been eliminated by stirring. The essence of the computation lies in the appearance and development of linked reactions and compounds in which certain characteristics of identity and concentration can be identified as outcomes of useful computation for some problem defined by the initial state and external inputs. Three remarkable examples of stirred processors include a chemical kinetic representation of a Turing machine (Hjelmfelt, Weinberger, and Ross 1991; Hjelmfelt and Ross 1993; Laplante, Pemberton, and Ross, 1995); abstract chemical reactors for parity checking and sorting (Banzhaf, Dittrich, and Rauhe 1996); and metabolic computations (Ziegler, Dittrich, and Banzhaf 1997).

The architecture-free processors of the second subtype exploit local changes and spatial differentiation in nonstirred reactors with typically simpler chemical reactions. Many basic forms of image processing are executed in parallel in such chemical computing devices (Rambidi and Chernavskii 1991; Rambidi 1992; Rambidi, Maximychev, and Usatov 1994, 1994a; Rambidi and Yakovenchuk 1999). The nonstirred active chemical media exhibit also a wide spectrum of dynamic behaviors, which could be extremely useful from a practical point of view (see Adamatzky 2001 for a detailed treatment).

---

1. As Lord Kelvin wrote in 1876: "It may be possible to conceive that nature generates a computable function ... directly and not necessarily by approximation as in the traditional approach."

Consider a Belousov-Zhabotinsky medium—the most widely known example of an active chemical medium. In the family of chemical oscillators, the Belousov-Zhabotinsky thin-layer reaction has been the most investigated, and thus the most appropriate for laboratory experiments. The nonstirred layer of an oscillating reaction can be seen as a massively parallel processor, where every elementary processor is represented by a microvolume reactor. The state of the microvolume can be identified with the reduced/oxidized state of the bromate component. Information processing media of the Belousov-Zhabotinsky type are specialized processors where the statement of the problem, the computational processes, and the results of the computations are all represented in the states (e.g., reagent local concentrations) of the microvolumes. The evolution over time of such reaction-diffusion processors leads to a spatiotemporal dissipative structure that can be interpreted as the solution of the problem. The computation in a Belousov-Zhabotinsky processor takes place when waves are generated, spread, and interact with each other, and perhaps result in external representations of information (e.g., light patterns). The abilities of excitable media for more complex image analysis (Rambidi, Maximychev, and Usatov 1994; Rambidi et al. 2002) and for the solution of spatially based problems (e.g., the shortest path problem; Steinbock, Toth, and Showalter 1995; Rambidi and Yakovenchuk 1998; Rambidi et al. 2002) have been well demonstrated recently.

3.3   How Do We Simulate Reaction-Diffusion Processors?

Cellular automata models of reaction-diffusion and excitable media capture essential aspects of natural media in a computationally tractable form. A cellular automaton is a lattice of uniform finite automata. The automata evolve in a discrete time and take their states from a finite set. All automata of the lattice update their states simultaneously. Every automaton calculates its next state depending on the states of its closest neighbors.[2]

3.4   Specialized Processors

The spatial representation of a problem is a key feature of reaction-diffusion processors. Data and results are represented through concentration profiles of the reagents or spatial configurations of activity patterns. A computation is defined in

---

2. We refer a reader to an excellent book by Chopard and Droz (1999) to gain background knowledge on cellular automata simulations of physical phenomena; see also Adamatzky (2001) for specific cellular-automaton models of reaction-diffusion computing.

a physical space as well. The computation is realized by spreading and interacting waves of the reagents or excitation patterns. A computational code, or a program, is interpreted in a list of possible reactions between the diffusing components and in a form of diffusive or excitation coupling between microvolumes of the computing medium. Usually, such properties could not be changed online. But they can be determined and adjusted to work toward the solution of a particular problem. Therefore most reaction-diffusion processors are intentionally designed to solve a few particular problems—they are specialized. To give the reader a sense of these specialized processors in both automata and laboratory forms, the following sections will show designs of reaction-diffusion processors that subdivide a space and approximate a skeleton of a planar shape.

3.5 Plane Subdivision

Let P be a nonempty finite set of planar points—a Voronoi diagram of the set P is a partition of the plane into such regions, each for any element of P, that a region corresponding to a unique point p contains all those points of the plane that are closer to p than to any other node of P. A unique region assigned to point p is called a *Voronoi cell* of the point p; a union of all the edges of the Voronoi cells determines the Voronoi diagram.

Assuming the computing space is homogeneous and locally connected (à la cellular automata, where every node is coupled to its closest neighbors by the same diffusive links), we can easily draw a parallel between the distance and the time. There is a very simple intuitive technique for detecting the bisector points separating two given points of the set P. If we drop reagents at these two nodes, the diffusive waves (or phase waves if an active substrate) spread outward from the originating points with the same speed; they travel the same distance from the sites of origination before they meet with one another. The points where the waves meet are the bisector points.

In a naive version of reaction-diffusion computing of a Voronoi diagram, one needs two reagents and a precipitate to mark a bisector separating two points—that is, n reagents are required to approximate a Voronoi diagram of n points. We place n unique reagents on n points of the given set; waves of these reagents spread around the space and interact with each other when they meet. When at least two different reagents meet at the same or adjacent sites of the space, they react and form a precipitate, resulting in: the reaction-sites that contain the precipitate represent edges of the Voronoi cell and therefore constitute the Voronoi diagram. Actually, the number of reagents can be sufficiently reduced (literally to just two states) in cellular-automaton models: when the topology of the spreading waves of the excitation is taken into account (Adamatzky 2001), and in real experimental wet processors (Tolmachev and Adamatzky 1996; Adamatzky and De Lacy Costello 2002a).

In cellular-automaton models (Adamatzky 2001), a colored precipitate is formed when chemical waves collide with each other: colored sites are sites of Voronoi diagram edges, uncolored sites are simply "planar points." If we try to implement this idea in a real chemical medium, we find an even simpler solution: when two or more wave fronts collide, no colored precipitate will form at sites of their collision, while all other parts of the medium are colored with the precipitate. Thus the Voronoi diagram is represented by light (or uncolored) loci of the chemical medium.

A palladium processor (Tolmachev and Adamatzky 1996; Adamatzky and De Lacy Costello 2002a, 2002b) is a first-ever specialized chemical computer after Belousov-Zhabotinsky processors (see, e.g., Kuhnert, Agladze, and Krinsky 1986; Rambidi and Chernavskii 1991; Rambidi, Maximychev, and Usatov 1994; Rambidi et al. 2002) to be used for image processing and computational geometry. An active planar substrate is prepared by mixing agar gel with a solution of palladium chloride. This thin film of agar is placed on an acetate film. Sites corresponding to the planar points, which must be subdivided by Voronoi bisectors, are marked by drops of potassium iodide solution. The potassium iodide diffuses from the given points and fills almost the entire reaction space with a dark color, because a precipitate of palladium iodide is produced as the result of the reaction. When two diffusive wave fronts meet with one another, no precipitate is formed (this may happen due to exhaustion of potassium iodide, or concentration inhibition of the reaction, or even physical interaction—e.g., repulsion—of the diffusive fronts). Thus the bisectors of the Voronoi diagram are represented by colorless zones of the reaction space, as shown in figure 3.1.

3.6 Skeletonization

A skeleton of a planar contour is a set of centers of bitangent circles that lie entirely inside the contour. One can construct a skeleton in a chemical medium using one of two following approaches: The first is based on excitation wave dynamics in Belousov-Zhabotinsky reactions, the second employs precipitation. Both approaches are based on Blum's ideas of grass fire transformation (Blum 1967, 1973).

The Belousov-Zhabotinsky computing medium stays in a trigger mode, wherein every elementary microvolume switches from one stable state to another. This co-

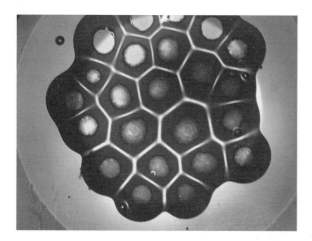

Figure 3.1
Voronoi diagram, constructed in experimental reaction-diffusion processor. Bisectors are seen as light (uncolored) segments. Original data points are represented by light discs. (With permission of Benjamin de Lacy Costello, Bristol, UK.)

herent switching results in the spreading of wave front of the switching states. A laboratory prototype of a Belousov-Zhabotinsky processor is a thin, 0.5–1.5 mm, nonstirred reagent layer, placed in a siliconized reaction vessel. Two states of a microvolume can be classified by their colors: red and blue. Initially, a contour of a planar shape is projected onto the reaction space. The circular waves are generated. The waves run away from every point of the contour. Two wave fronts are formed— one wave front spreads inward the contour, another runs outward. Sites of meeting of inward-running waves are registered optically. They represent segments of a skeleton of the planar shape (Rambidi, Maximychev, and Usatov 1994a). The only disadvantage of the technique is that no stationary structure is formed.

We can avoid the unpleasant experience of having to chase an ever-changing wave front if we use a set of reactions wherein a colored precipitate is produced. Essentially the same palladium processor discussed with regard to the Voronoi diagram can easily handle this skeleton problem. We do not apply drops of potassium iodide but prepare a contour cut of a filter paper saturated with this reagent; the filter-paper contour is applied onto the gel with the palladium chloride. Diffusive wave fronts of potassium iodide spread inward (actually, they spread outward also but we do not care about this) from the contour. When and where wave fronts meet, no precipitate is formed, and thus a skeleton is seen as uncolored sites of the chemical processor (figure 3.2).

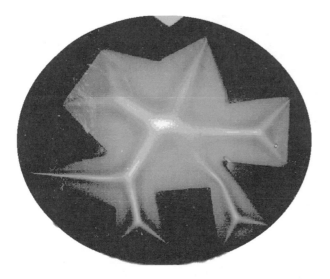

Figure 3.2
Skeleton of a planar shape constructed in experimental reaction-diffusion processor. Data shape is shown in black color, segments of the skeleton are uncolored. Photo of the original chemical processor designed by D. Tolmachev in 1996.

Unfortunately, the palladium processor (and its analogues, see Adamatzky 2001) is not simply a specialized processor, it has to be considered a disposable processor (the palladium processor is analogous to a photographic paper or a recordable compact disc, while the Belousov-Zhabotinsky processor is like an hourglass or a rewritable compact disc).

3.7   Reaction-Diffusion Robots

Unconventional robotics closely follows unconventional computing. Evolutionary computing excited a wave of research in evolving novel robotic architectures, while smart materials opened previously unexplored routes in the design of artificial muscles and polymer-based actuators. Studies in collective intelligence pushed forward research in emergent phenomena in collectives of minimalist robots. Reaction-diffusion robots may therefore appear to naturally follow from reaction-diffusion computing.

If one were to apply theoretical advances or experimental achievements of active nonlinear medium computing to robotics, one would probably start with designing unconventional controllers for mobile robots. An unconventional controller could employ some implicit forms of computation (e.g., wave computation, in which local microprocesses of wave generation and spreading may result in certain macroscopic phenomena), which can be used as a guidance of the robot motion.

The first-ever approach to control a mobile robot by a chemical medium was presented by Ziegler, Dittrich, and Banzahf (1997), where, in this design, chemical reaction chains were employed. A light-seeking robot is under consideration (Ziegler, Dittrich, and Banzahf 1997): In this case, a controller is a chemical reactor with several reagents. There are some connections between the light sensors and the reactor, and between the reactor and the motors. Changes in the values of light sensors lead to changes in the concentration of reagents in the reactor. The chemical reactions between the metabolites result in the corresponding changes in robot behavior (some results of the simulation experiments, plus graphs of the appropriate metabolic networks can be found in Ziegler, Dittrich, and Banzahf 1997).

Another approach, developed by Adamatzky and Colleagues (Adamatzky et al. 1999; Adamatzky and Melhuish 2000, 2002; Adamatzky 2001), is to exploit space-time excitation dynamics in nonlinear media. Obviously, if we talk about a light-seeking robot, we keep the light-sensitive Belousov-Zhabotinsky reaction in mind. Assume that the chemical medium, constituting the controller, is light sensitive. Every microvolume excites with a probability, or intensity, proportional to its relative distance from a source of light. Therefore microvolumes at those edges of a reactor that are closer to the light target are excited and generate spreading waves of excitation that travel inward in the reactor space. Velocity vectors of the wave fronts, being inverted, indicate a direction toward the source of light. The vector, indicating the position of the light target, is used as a base to rotate the robot hosting the reactor. The waves are generated continuously during the robot movement. Therefore the direction vector may be recalculated at every step of the robot movement. Thus the robot can even chase a mobile target. This idea is illustrated in figure 3.3, where a light target, contours of wave fronts, wave velocities, and the direction vector to target are indicated. Preliminary tests with an experimental Belousov-Zhabotinsky reaction coupled to a vector-to-target extracting optical system (Adamatzky et al. 2002c) have already proved the feasibility of this approach.

An unconventional, wet-ware controller would greatly benefit from the coupling with wet actuators—for example, electroactive polymers (Kennedy, Melhuish, and Adamatzky 2001) or oscillating pH-sensitive gels (Yoshida, Yamaguchi, and Ichijo 1996; Tabata et al. 2002).

Looking again at Adamatzky and Colleagues' ideas (Adamatzky et al. 1999) on wave control of robots' phototactic behavior using a Belousov-Zhabotinsky medium, one realizes there is a huge disadvantage in this approach: Local vectors, and then a

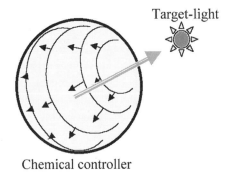

Chemical controller

Figure 3.3
A sketch of a light-sensitive chemical controller. Target-light stimulates wave generation in a reactor. Wave dynamic determines local repulsive vector field, inverted global vector guides a robot to the target.

global vector, are calculated "externally"—patterns of excitation in a Belousov-Zhabotinsky thin layer are processed by a camera coupled with not-too-complicated software, then information on the global vector is passed to the motor controllers of the robot. It would be incomparably better to couple an array of "autonomous" propulsive actuators made of chemo- or magnetosensitive polymers, and thus implement a membrane of artificial paramecium cilia, which would bend coherently when waves of excitation travel along it.

A breakthrough experiment—implementation of ciliary motion in an array of gel actuators controlled by a Belousov-Zhabotinsky reaction—has been reported by Tabata and Colleagues (Tabata et al. 2002). Combining X-ray lithography with a micromolding technique, Tabata and Colleagues produced an array of conical "cilia" made of isopropylacrylamide gel (figure 3.4). This gel contains a catalyst used in the Belousov-Zhabotinsky reaction (ruthenium bypyridine). The gel array of actuators was immersed in the solution, which included all other necessary components to carry out the Belousov-Zhabotinsky reaction. The reaction was initiated in the gel and waves of oxidation spread along the gel sheet, where passing wave fronts changed hydrophilic-hydrophobic properties of polymer chains and thus caused swelling/deswelling of the gel actuators. Mechanical oscillations induced by chemical waves could therefore be observed (Tabata et al. 2002).

3.8 Computation Universal Processors

The preceding sections dealt with specialized processors—the processors designed exclusively to solve some particular problems. One could not use an unmodified re-

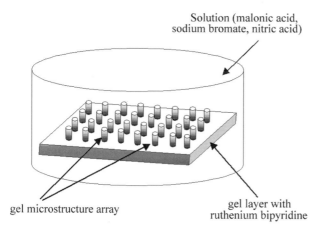

Solution (malonic acid,
sodium bromate, nitric acid)

gel microstructure array

gel layer with
ruthenium bipyridine

Figure 3.4
A ciliate sheet: a micro-array of oscillating gel actuators is coupled with Belousov-Zhabotinsky reaction.
(After Tabata et al. 2002.)

action-diffusion processor specialized to construct a skeleton to do arithmetical calculations or logical reasoning. Specialization offers relative simplicity in architectural
design and efficiency in its functioning, but lacks applicability to all cases. A device is
called *computation universal* if it calculates—at least *in posse*—any computable logical function. Formally, to prove a physical system's universality, we should demonstrate that a functionally complete logical set (e.g., {NOT, OR}, {NOT, AND}, or Sheffer
stroke) can be implemented in the space-time dynamics of the system. Namely, we
have to represent quanta of information, usually TRUE and FALSE values of a Boolean
variable, routes of information transmission, and logic gates—where information
quanta are processed—in states of the given system. That is, a primitive logical circuit should be constructed. This can be done in two ways.

First, a Boolean circuit could be embedded into a system in such a manner that all
elements of the circuit are represented by the system's stationary states; the architecture is static and its topology is essential for a computation. We would call this an
architecture-based universality.

Second, we could adopt techniques of a dynamic or collision-based computing that
employs finite patterns—mobile self-localized excitations—which travel in space and
execute computation when they collide with each other. Truth values of logical variables are represented by the absence of traveling information quanta or by various
states of the quanta. There are no predetermined wires: patterns can travel anywhere
in the medium; a trajectory of a pattern motion is analogous to a instantaneous wire.
A typical interaction gate has two input "wires" (trajectories of the colliding mobile

localizations) and, typically, three output "wires" (two "wires" represent the localizations' trajectories when they continue their motion undisturbed, the third output gives a trajectory of a new localization, formed in the result of the collision of two incoming localizations).

3.9 Stationary Circuits

A stationary, or architecture-based, universality is usually achieved by "conventional" techniques: One simply fabricates varieties of traditional computers made of nonstandard materials (tubulin microtubles, glass tubes filled with chemicals, artificially grown silicon-neuron interfaces). Here, we consider three illustrative examples of reaction-diffusion logical gates.

The first example is a mass-transfer or kinetic-based logical gate (Hjelmfelt, Weinberger, and Ross 1991; Hjelmfelt and Ross 1993; Blittersdorf, Müller, and Schneider 1995). Typically, several reactors are connected through peristaltic pumps (figure 3.5a). Concentrations of reagents in a few reactors represent values of input logical variables and other (usually sinks of the reactor network) values of outputs. To construct a particular logical gate, one directly adjusts flow rates between the reactors.

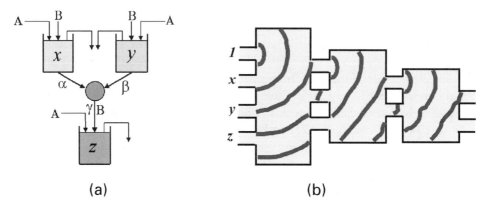

(a)   (b)

Figure 3.5
Architecture-based chemical gates. (a) A mass-transfer chemical device for computation of basic logical functions: x, y and z are acidity levels in the reactors; A and B are feeding tubes for supply of reagent A and B solutions with an indicator; α and β are coupling coefficients, and γ is a flow rate. Modified after (Blittersdorf et al 1995) (b) A wave realization of x OR y OR z gate. Waves in output chambers are asynchronous when all three input variables take the value FALSE. If one of the inputs is TRUE, represented by an excitation wave, the output chambers exhibit synchronous waves, that is represent TRUE. (Modified after Steinbock, Kettunen, and Showalter 1996.)

The second example exploits the fine characteristics of wave dynamics in excitable media. There are two types of wave gate (Toth and Showalter 1995; Steinbock, Kettunen, and Showalter 1996). In the gates, Boolean states of inputs and outputs are represented by the presence or absence of a phase wave at a specified location of the tube-based circuit. The first wave gate (Toth and Showalter 1995) employs particulars—namely, a wave-nucleation size critical for successful generation of a wave—of wave interactions in the Belousov-Zhabotinsky reaction. The Belousov-Zhabotinsky logic circuit comprises several very narrow tubes filled with a Belousov-Zhabotinsky medium; the tubes are connected via expansion chambers or junctions where logical functions are implemented. In experimental realizations of AND wave gates, the size of wire tubes is selected such that if a single excitation wave reaches an expansion chamber along one tube, it will not generate any excitation in the chamber. Two waves satisfy a critical nucleation radius constraint and thus will generate excitation in the chamber. The second wave gate (shown in figure 3.5b) is based on ideas of geometrically constrained excitable media. Logic operations are determined by the geometry of tubes and chamber connections. The operations are expressed in (a) synchronous occurrences of excitation waves in the output tubes of the Belousov-Zhabotinsky circuit (figure 3.5b).

The third example undermines our "perfect" division of all reaction-diffusion processors into either specialized or universal. We show that an XOR gate ($z = x$ XOR $y =$ TRUE if $x \neq y$) can be implemented in a very simple modification (De Lacy Costello 2002) of the palladium processor discussed in relation to image processing in previous sections. The gate looks like a letter T made of gel (the gel is mixed with palladium chloride). Shoulders of the T are the gate's inputs, and the vertical segment is an output (figure 3.6): presence\absence of the palladium-iodide species indicate TRUE\FALSE values for the input variables. To specify TRUE value for an input, we put a drop of potassium iodide to an appropriate shoulder (figure 3.6b). The potassium iodide diffuses along the gel strip; palladium-iodide species are formed and color the gel. When both shoulders initially contain drops of potassium iodide, a middle part of the vertical segment will remain uncoloured due to the mechanics of diffusive waves interaction (figure 3.6c; see details in Adamatzky and De Lacy Costello 2002a, 2002b). When only one of the shoulders contains potassium iodide, all gel strips become colored (figure 3.6b). When "nothing happens" (or when both shoulders of the gate contain potassium iodide), at least the central part of the vertical strip will be uncolored (figure 3.6c). Thus, assuming colored sites of the gel represent the value TRUE and uncolored the value FALSE, we demonstrate that the T-shaped gel implements the gate XOR.

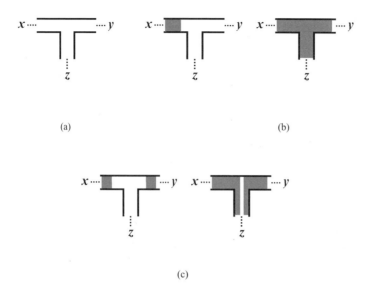

Figure 3.6
A palladium-based XOR gate (colored zones represent precipitating palladium-iodine species). (*a*) The gate architecture, this also reflects the situation $x = $ FALSE and $y = $ FALSE. (*b*) Reaction development in the gate for $x = $ TRUE and $y = $ FALSE. (*c*) Formation of a bisector (uncolored strip) when two diffusive fronts "collide": this happens when $x = $ TRUE and $x = $ TRUE.

3.10 Dynamical Circuits: Collision-Based Computing

In dynamical circuits, autonomous signals travel in a uniform space. Truth values are represented by either the presence or absence of information quanta or by various states of the traveling pattern, and perform computation by colliding with other traveling signals. The traveling is analogous to information transfer, while collision is an act of computation—thus we call the setup *collision-based computing*. There are three sources of collision-based computing: a proof of universality of Conway's Game of Life via collisions of glider streams (Berlekamp, Conway, and Guy 1982); a conservative logic and its implementation in a billiard ball model (Fredkin and Toffoli 1982); and a concept of computation in cellular automata with soliton-like patterns—the particle machines (Steiglitz, Kamal, and Watson 1988; classical papers and recent advances can be found in Adamatzky 2002).

In a series of papers (see, e.g., Adamatzky 1998, 2000, 2001), it was proved that two- and three-dimensional cellular automata models of excitable media are minimal computationally universal machines. The model and accompanying results are too technical to talk about in the present chapter. Suffice it to say that logical gates in discrete excitable lattices can be implemented via the collision of two or more particle-like waves—compact mobile patterns of excitation with particle-like behavior. These waves are similar to nonlinear self-localized excitations found in physical systems (e.g., breathers and solitons). Because this book is preferentially about wet-ware rather than abstract constructs, we will provide mainly computational examples of "natural" systems that can do collision-based computing. We will discuss breathers in DNA molecules, mobile excitations in molecular arrays, and quasiparticles in gas-discharge systems.

Forinash and others (Forinash, Peyrard, and Malomed 1994; Forinash, Cretegny, and Peyrard 1997) studied a Hamiltonian with two variables, which describes the transverse displacement of a DNA molecule under different values of the coupling between nucleotides along the same strand. They observed the spontaneous formation of intrinsic local modes, which, as the authors predicted, emerge because of localization of thermal fluctuations and grow due to the exchange of energy. In computational experiments, using a numerical solution of the equation of motion, Forinash and Colleagues demonstrated that a typical self-localization—a breather—is mobile: Being excited, the breather travels along DNA strands. The breathers interact with each other and with defects, natural or artificial, in the DNA molecule (Forinash, Cretegny, and Peyrard 1997).

What types of breather-collision-based gates can be implemented in a DNA molecule? We display a modest catalog of DNA breather gates in figure 3.7. The gate 1G-A is quite a common gate in the family of collision-based gates: When two breathers collide, they undergo phase shifts and thus arrive to checkpoints earlier or later than noncolliding breathers. In some cases, a third localization is formed in the collision of two breathers. Usually it remains immobile; this stationary localization depicts a logical conjunction of two variables represented by the colliding breathers (figure 3.7, 1G-B). The gate 1G-C is an amalgam of the two previous gates: Colliding breathers are delayed or sped up and the third stationary localization is formed.

The next four gates (1G-D, 1G-E, 1G-F, and 1G-G) are derived from the interaction of a breather with an impurity (Forinash, Peyrard, and Malomed 1994) in a model of a chain of harmonically coupled particles influenced by asymmetric on-site potentials. Both resting and excited impurities are considered. When a breather collides with a resting impurity, four possible outcomes of the collision are expected, depending on the breather's amplitude and the mass of the impurity: (1) the breather passes through the impurity without any sufficient changes in the breather's form and energy, (2) the breather is trapped by the impurity and it stays at the impurity site

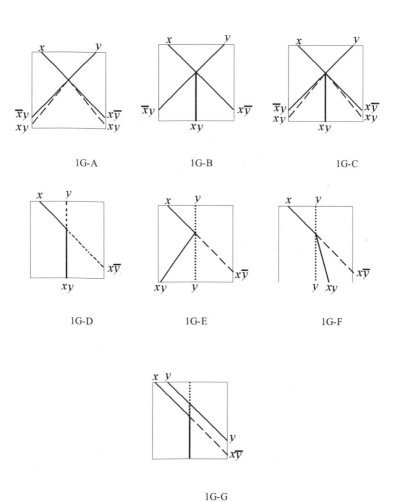

Figure 3.7
Catalog of spatio-temporal gates implemented in a model of a DNA molecule in the collisions between two breathers (1G-A, 1G-B, 1G-C) or between one (1G-D, 1G-E, 1G-F, 1G-G) or two (1G-G) breathers and an impurity. Time goes downward. Positions of nucleotides are indexed rightward.

(1G-D), (3) one part of the breather excitation becomes trapped by the impurity mode, the other part is reflected (splitting or partial reflection of the breather by impurity: 1G-E), and (4) the breather is reflected by the impurity.

The second scenario above—the "breather-impurity" collision—gives us the construction of the gate 1G-D. Assume a resting impurity is not detected, thus when a breather collides with the impurity and becomes trapped, a conjunction of two Boolean variables represented by the breather and the impurity is calculated. The gate 1G-E is devised from the third and the fourth scenarios of the collision. In some cases, it is also possible to slow down a breather by an impurity: The breather may be trapped at the impurity site for a long time until it escapes later with a reduced velocity (Forinash, Peyrard, and Malomed 1994; figure 3.7, 1G-F).

What happens when a breather collides with an excited impurity? Results of the collision depend on the relative phases of the breather and the impurity (Forinash, Peyrard, and Malomed 1994): The breather is trapped by the impurity if the distance between the initial position of the breather and impurity sites is odd; the breather passes through the impurity otherwise. Let two breathers head for a resting impurity. We can adjust their distances such that the following scenario occurs: The first breather passes through the impurity and leaves the impurity in an excited state. The second breather therefore collides not with the resting impurity but with the excited one. Depending on the distance between these two breathers, the second breather may be captured by the impurity or pass along it (Forinash, Peyrard, and Malomed 1994). Thus we obtain the structure of the gate 1G-G.

For a certain set of parameters, it is possible to implement a fusion of two breathers via collisions with a resting impurity: The breathers are fused in a single (im)mobile breather (Forinash, Peyrard, and Malomed 1994). When two breathers pass through a resting impurity, the first breather may be trapped. When a second breather arrives at the impurity site, it is also trapped. The trapping is reversible because both captured breathers give rise to a larger breather that can start its own motion. This means a resting impurity can play the role of a summator—we set up the parameters in such a fashion that only the energy of n breathers, trapped by the impurity, is enough to start a large mobile breather. The impurity may be considered an elementary threshold summator, which takes the value 1 if it accumulates at least n breathers, and the value 0 otherwise.

Our speculations about possible designs of one-dimensional breather machines fit well in a framework of computation in one-dimensional cellular automata, where interaction of traveling signals is the main issue (see, e.g., Mazoyer 1999; Delorme and Mazoyer 2002). We also briefly mention that the automaton representation of localized excitations and its application to computing in regular structures and bulk media received much attention in the academic community after the advent of the Park-Steiglitz-Thurston model of soliton-like mobile patterns in one-dimensional cellular automata (Park, Steiglitz, and Thurston 1986; Steiglitz, Kamal, and Watson 1988; Jakubowski, Steiglitz, and Squier 2002).

Two-dimensional computers exploiting the principles of collision-based computing can be fabricated from molecular aggregates capable of directed transfer of energy. What happens when we optically excite an electronic system in light-sensitive molecular aggregates? Two competitive mechanisms are activated: localization and delocalization (Toyozawa 1983). The first mechanism is based in the imbalance of forces activated by electronic charge redistribution and acts on relevant atoms to find new equilibria of molecular configuration coordinates; this destroys resonance of electronic excitation to the neighboring sites. The second mechanism relies on molecular resonance; it is responsible for the transfer of excitation from one site of the molecular aggregate to another site. The localization of excitation emerges due to interplay between the localization and delocalization. Scheibe aggregates are the most suitable candidates for the role of a molecular-array computer.

To make a Scheibe aggregate, we mix oxacyanine dye molecules with inert molecules to form a monomolecular array. Then we add thiacyanine dye molecules: Donor molecules of the oxacyanine group are replaced by acceptor molecules of the thiacyanine group (Bücher and Kuhn 1970; Moebius and Kuhn 1979; Bartnik and Tuszynski 1993); the fabricated array can then be transferred to a solid substrate. If the array contains at least one acceptor molecule to 10^4 donor molecules, it absorbs energy of photons and transfers this energy over long distances without losses sufficient for degradation (Moebius and Kuhn 1979; Bartnik and Tuszynski 1993). When a photon is absorbed into the aggregate, a domain of excitation is generated: The domain occupies eight molecules nearest to the acceptor molecule, which oscillate in phase at the frequency of fluorescence. The domain moves across the monomolecular array (Bartnik, Blinowska, and Tuszynski 1991, 1992) with supersonic speed; the domain's size (about 27×27 Å) is conserved. This domain is called an *exciton* (Nolte 1975; Moebius and Kuhn 1979).

The moving excitons may undergo mutual annihilation when within each other's influence (Kenkre 1983), thus a gate NOT(y) AND x can be implemented in exciton collisions (figure 3.8a). Actually, we can find two-dimensional analogies of almost all DNA breather gates; the time-space separation of input and output trajectories in DNA breather gates is substituted here by space-space separation of exciton trajectories in molecular arrays. Let us mention a few exemplar collisions:

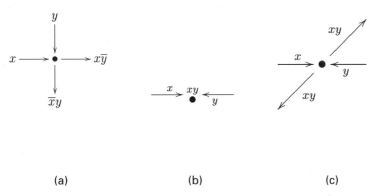

(a)   (b)   (c)

Figure 3.8
Exemplar gates realized in collision of two-dimensional self-localized excitations.

The colliding of two localizations can produce the third stationary localization: This stationary localization represents a conjunction of the signals represented by two colliding localizations (figure 3.8b). The stationary localization can be detected via a collision with another mobile localization. For a particular set of parameters, two colliding localizations form an unstable bound state and split again, hence angles of their velocity vectors are changed. This gives us quite a peculiar topology of the AND gate (figure 3.8c).

Conditions may also be satisfied when a third mobile (daughter) localization is formed in the binary collision of localizations. This new localization may be diverted to other routes and thus multiplication of a signal is implemented.

To realize the logical truth constant, we need a continuous stream of mobile localizations. Such a stream could be generated by some kind of a particle-gun, which periodically produces the coherent mobile patterns. Several types of guns of self-localized excitations in two and three dimensions are studied in Adamatzky (1998, 2001). Despite their sound theoretical background and great variety of forms, the experimental verification of such guns only recently was confirmed. Namely, in numerical experiments based on solutions to the discrete nonintegrable thermalized Schrödinger equation, Rasmussen and Colleagues (1999) demonstrate that discrete breathers cause large phonon fluctuations in their neighborhood. The fluctuations increase a probability of new breather generation in the vicinity of the old one. This newly born breather may be ejected as a propagating breather; meantime, the stationary "old" breather recovers after the generation of the mobile "daughter" breather and repeats the "labor."

Recently, we were studying universal computation in simulated and laboratory prototypes of active chemical media or in their discrete analogues (i.e., excitable lattices; Adamatzky 1998, 2000, 2002). As a result, our collision-based computing model of universal reaction-diffusion computers lacked an experimental proof. Luckily, the situation changed because of experimental findings obtained in Professor Purwins's laboratory (University of Münster), using an experimental setup based on a gas discharge system (a mixture of argon with air between two planar electrodes, a highly resistive semiconductor anode, and a metallic cathode). It was shown that with increasing voltage supply, a number of current density filaments or quasi-particles are formed (Bode and Purwins 1995). The filaments may travel in the system and collide with each other. Experimentally observed collisions include quasi-elastic collision, annihilation, formation of bound state of two quasiparticles, and generations of the third quasiparticle (due to interaction of the quasiparticles' oscillating tails) (Astrov and Purwins 2001)—that is, the full spectrum of collisions sufficient to implement a functionally complete system of logical functions. In terms of a two-component reaction-diffusion system, a current density distribution or a concentration of charge carriers in the gap between electrodes is analogous to an activator, and an increase in voltage drop, diffusing from domains with over-threshold current, is an inhibitor.

The findings were confirmed in numerical simulations of the three-dimensional system, where for certain combinations of reaction rates and diffusion speeds of inhibitor and activator, one can produce the development of quasiparticles (Schenk et al. 1999; Liehr, Bode, and Purwins 2001). The structure of the quasiparticle—with an activator-head and an inhibitor-tail—gives an excellent continuous-space analogue of our early discrete models of particle-like waves in three-dimensional lattices (Adamatzky 1998, 2001).

3.11   Discovering Computing Abilities

How do we find reaction-diffusion or excitable media to fulfill our "computational dreams" in very real wet-ware? There is not much choice at the moment. Regarding oscillating chemical reactions, there are dozens of them and most reactions look quite similar, hence almost everybody mainly experiments with Belousov-Zhabotinsky media. The advantage of such ubiquity is the chance to verify each other's experiments. At the molecular level, the situation is not as good: We can fabricate molecular arrays, but there exist almost no reports on any feasible computing experiments, either with "classical" waves or with mobile self-localizations.

Which problems can be solved in what types of nonlinear media? Should we fabricate these media from scratch or could we instead search for already existing species in nature? In one of the author's papers (Adamatzky 2001), the reader can find a study of which behavioral parameters of a medium's local elements are essential when classifying morphological, dynamic, and computational aspects of excitable lattices. In this chapter, we would rather provide an example demonstrating an impressive potential arising from very simple parameterization.

A threshold of excitation seems to be the most suitable parameter in the case of excitable media. Unfortunately, knowing the excitation threshold does not give us a complete description of space-time excitation dynamics. To discover richer regimes of the dynamics and thereby find new computing abilities, we can "upgrade" the excitation threshold to an excitation interval. In a lattice with local transition rules and an eight-cell neighborhood, a cell is excited if the number of excited neighbors belongs to a certain interval $[\phi_1, \phi_2]$, $1 \leq \phi_1 \leq \phi_2 \leq 8$. Using excitation intervals, we classify the lattice excitation regimes and select those suitable ("suitability" being decided based on our previous experience and intuition) for wave-based computing. As we see in figure 3.9, the evolution of excitable lattice from senseless quasi-chaotic activity patterns to the formation of protowaves and then proper labyrinthine-like structures is guided mainly by the upper boundary of the excitation interval $[\phi_1, \phi_2]$. When the boundary ϕ_2 is increased, the computation capabilities of the medium are changed from chaos to a wave dynamic that implements image processing (contouring, segmentation, filtration) then to a quasiparticle dynamic that supports universal computation (via colliding localizations; see previous sections on universal computing) then to the solution of computational geometry problems (shortest path, spanning tree) (Adamatzky 2001).

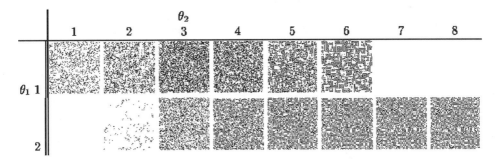

Figure 3.9
Morphology of interval classification.

We would like to stress that the excitation interval discussed in the previous section may be analogous to (1) Langton's λ parameter (Langton 1990), which opened a new field of research in complex systems and emergence of computation; (2) temperature in the lattice swarm models of hot sand (Adamatzky 2000a; an abstract temperature determines transitions between various types of two-dimensional patterns); and (3) laboratory experiments with a nonstirred Belousov-Zhabotinsky reaction (Masia et al. 2001); where the increasing temperature evokes mode transitions from periodic oscillations to quasi-periodic oscillations to chaos.

3.12 Discussion

We have not aimed to provide an overly general explanation nor to offer a complete theory of reaction-diffusion and excitable computing. Rather, we have tried to inspire the reader to move toward still-virgin sites of the field of nonlinear media-based unconventional computing. Thus we have studied several cases of reaction-diffusion processors from computational geometry to robotics to universal machines. Because a more detailed treatment of computing in nonlinear media is already offered (Adamatzky 2001; Rambidi et al. 2002; Adamatzky 2002), in this chapter we simply presented an outline and discussed some recent discoveries in the field.

All considered algorithms of reaction-diffusion computing were tested in cellular-automata models. In automata models, we demonstrated that a dynamic of reaction and diffusion can be successfully employed in the designing of massively parallel processors for image computational geometry and optimization. Analysis of space-time dynamics of cellular automata models helped us draw a picture of intuitive design of real-life processors. Several real-life processors were fabricated thereby.

In conclusion, we would like to mention two very prospective fields where the reaction-diffusion paradigm can be efficiently applied: evolvable hardware (Miller et al. 2000; Miller and Hartmann 2001) and collective behavior and consciousness.

Considering the pros and contras of field-programmable gate arrays, Miller stresses that hence designed for conventional electronics, the programmable gate arrays are not "rigid" structures and therefore allow the exploitation of physics- and chemistry-based computing (Miller 2000). He thus invites us to take advantage of possibly coupling "conventional" silicon gate arrays with molecular and chemical nonlinear media, and to fabricate field-programmable *matter* arrays. One of the possible designs of the field-programmable matter arrays is shown in figure 3.10. A configuration of this new smart material is thought to be achievable via variations of voltages on the array's input wires. The idea fits well into a "programmable matter" concept (Toffoli and Margolus 1991) and it already has been supported by some

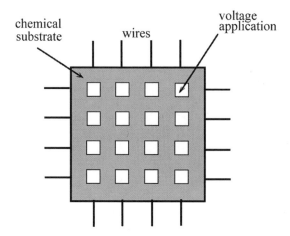

Figure 3.10
Julian Miller's field programmable matter array. (After Miller 2000.)

experiments on field-based control of excitation dynamics in a Belousov-Zhabotinsky medium (Marek and Ševčíková 1984; Ševčíková and Marek 1986).

Can we apply a reaction-diffusion paradigm to study collective behavior of intelligent entities or even to give yet another nonstandard interpretation of cognitive and affective processes in a human mind? What if molecules behave like humans? What if humans act like molecules? Chemical media are not the only ones described by reaction-diffusion equations. It is not uncommon that aggregates of higher complexity, even crowds of people (particularly in extreme situations of panic or excitement), act analogously to laws of physics and chemistry. What if we think on crowds as solutions of reagents? Moods would possibly diffuse but will they interact? What patterns of precipitates or dissipative structures would they form? For example, when fronts of combatants collide and engage in severe fighting, they may leave (possibly just in a naive computational model) corpses behind (figure 3.11a). Could we construct a Voronoi diagram with the help of fighting crowds? This is a possibility.

Let us consider ant-inspired mobile finite automata, inhabiting a two-dimensional lattice. Each automaton can move, pick up, and drop pebbles. Ideally, we wish to identify those nodes of the lattice that are the edges of the Voronoi cells of the labeled nodes, or data points. Every automaton is given a color corresponding to one of the labeled nodes. Automata start their walks at the nodes of the given set, which is a seed for the lattice subdivision. Automata carry pebbles. When automata of different colors meet at a node, they become agitated and therefore drop their pebbles.

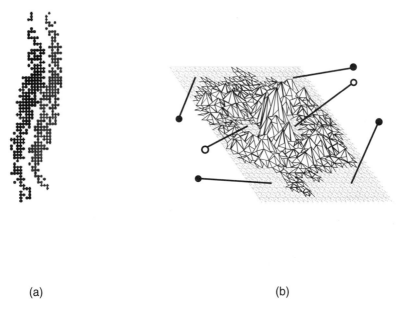

(a)   (b)

Figure 3.11
Computation with spreading and reacting crowds. (*a*) Collision of two fronts of virtual combatants. Simulated in ISAAC software (Ilachinski 1997). (*b*) Pebble-built Voronoi diagram of five lattice nodes, constructed in a lattice swarm model; data nodes are marked by pins; closed Voronoi cells are indicated by pins with hollow heads. (Modified after Adamatzky 2001.)

When this process has run its course, the number of pebbles of each color at each node of the lattice indicates the membership degree of this node in the set of edge nodes of the Voronoi diagram (figure 3.11b).

What if we use doxastic or affective components instead of chemicals? Are there any particulars in development of cognitive or emotional reactors? We can easily extract ten abstract reagents that constitute the "material" base of a chemistry of the mind. They are knowledge, ignorance, delusion, doubt, and disbelief, (all of which are derivatives of belief); and happiness, sadness, anger, confusion, and anxiety, (which are primitive types of emotions). Analyzing binary interactions of doxastic and affective reagents, one can derive several realistic scenarios of reaction development in "conscientiousness solutions" (Adamatzky 2001a, 2001b). Some sets of reactions exhibit quite dull behavior, others are more interesting. Thus, for example, the following set of reactions show rich oscillating behavior in an affective liquid-reaction filled with emotions:

Figure 3.12
Diffusion of a doubt δ in a one-dimensional layer of knowledge (shown by dots). The doubt reacts with the knowledge and a misbelief (μ) is produced. Ignorance (ι) and delusion (ε) emerge as byproducts of the diffusion and reaction. Certain norms are applied, see Adamatzky, 2001a for details.

ANGER + HAPPINESS → CONFUSION + HAPPINESS + ANGER

ANGER + CONFUSION → CONFUSION

HAPPINESS + CONFUSION → ANGER + HAPPINESS.

In this context, two types of reactor vessels are worth investigating: stirred reactors and thin-layer, or nonstirred, reactors. Depending on the particular architecture of the parachemical reactions and relations between doxastic and affective components, the system's behavior exhibits spreading of phase and diffusive waves, formation of domain walls, pseudochaotic behavior, and generation of ordered patterns. A simple case of one-dimensional reaction and diffusion of doxastic (i.e., derived from belief) components is shown in figure 3.12.

References

Adamatzky, A. 1998. Universal dynamical computation in multi-dimensional excitable lattices. *Int. J. Theor. Phys.* 37: 3069–3108.

Adamatzky, A. 2000. Collision-based computing in biopolymers and their automata models. *Int. J. Modern Phys.* C11: 1321–1346.

Adamatzky, A. 2000a. Hot choosy sand: Reflection of grain sensitivity on pattern morphology. *Intern. J. Modern Phys.* C11: 47–68.

Adamatzky, A. 2001. *Computing in Nonlinear Media and Automata Collectives*. Bristol: IoP Publishing.

Adamatzky, A. 2001a. Space-time dynamic of normalized doxatons: Automata models of pathological collective mentality. *Chaos Solitons Fractals* 12: 1629–1656.

Adamatzky, A. 2001b. Pathology of collective doxa. Automata models of collective belief. *Appl. Mathematics Computation.* 112: 195–228.

Adamatzky, A., ed. 2002. *Collision-Based Computing*. London: Springer-Verlag.

Adamatzky, A., and B. De Lacy Costello. 2002a. Experimental reaction-diffusion pre-processor for shape recognition. *Phys. Lett. A* 297: 344–352.

Adamatzky, A., and B. De Lacy Costello. 2002b. Reaction-diffusion path-planning in a hybrid reaction-diffusion and cellular-automaton processor. *Chaos, Solitons & Fractals*. In press.

Adamatzky, A., and C. Melhuish. 2000. Parallel controllers for decentralized robots: Toward nano design. *Kybernetes* 29: 733–745.

Adamatzky, A., and C. Melhuish. 2002. Phototaxis of mobile excitable lattices. *Chaos Solitons Fractals* 13: 171–184.

Adamatzky, A., O. Holland, N. G. Rambidi, and A. Winfield. 1999. Wet artificial brains: Towards the chemical control of robot motion by reaction-diffusion and excitable media. *Lecture Notes Comput. Sci.* 1674: 304–313.

Adamatzky, A., B. De Lacy Costello, C. Melhuish, and N. Ratcliffe. 2002. Effective reactions of Belousov-Zhabotinky medium. Unpublished.

Astrov, Y. A., and H.-G. Purwins. 2001. Plasma spots in a gas discharge system: Birth, scattering, and formation of molecules. *Phys. Lett. A* 283: 349–354.

Banzhaf, W., P. Dittrich, and H. Rauhe. 1996. Emergent computation by catalytic reactions. *Nanotechnology* 7: 307–314.

Bartnik, E. A., and J. A. Tuszynski. 1993. Theoretical models of energy transfer in two-dimensional molecular assemblies. *Phys. Rev. E* 48: 1516–1528.

Bartnik, E. A., K. J. Blinowska, and J. A. Tuszynski. 1991. The possibility of an excitonic fast and nearly lossless energy transfer in biomolecular systems. *Phys. Lett. A* 159: 67–72.

Bartnik, E. A., K. J. Blinowska, and J. A. Tuszynski. 1992. Analytical and numerical modelling of Scheibe aggregates. *Nanobiology* 1: 239–250.

Berlekamp, E. R., J. H. Conway, and R. L. Guy. 1982. *Winning Ways for your Mathematical Plays, Vol. 2: Games in Particular*. New York: Academic Press.

Blittersdorf, R., A. Müller, and F. W. Schneider. 1995. Chemical visualization of Boolean functions: A simple chemical computer. *J. Chem. Educ.* 72: 760–763.

Blum, H. 1967. A transformation for extracting new descriptors of shape. In *Models for the Perception of Speech and Visual Form*, ed. W. Wathen-Dunn. Cambridge: MIT Press.

Blum, H. 1973. Biological shape and visual science. *J. Theor. Biol.* 38: 205–287.

Bode, M., and H.-G. Purwins. 1995. Pattern formation in reaction-diffusion systems—Dissipative solitons in physical systems. *Physica D* 86: 53–63.

Bücher, H., and H. Kuhn. 1970. Scheibe aggregate formation of cyanine dyes in monolayers. *Chem. Phys. Lett.* 6: 183–185.

Chopard, B., and M. Droz. 1999. *Cellular Automata: Modeling of Physical Systems*. Cambridge: Cambridge University Press.

Delorme, M., and J. Mazoyer. 2002. Signals on cellular automata. In *Collision-Based Computing*, ed. A. Adamatzky. London: Springer-Verlag.

Epstein, I. R., and K. Showalter. 1996. Nonlinear chemical dynamics: Oscillations, patterns, and chaos. *J. Phys. Chem.* 100: 13132–13147.

Forinash, K., M. Peyrard, and B. Malomed. 1994. Interaction of discrete breathers with impurity modes. *Phys. Rev. E* 49: 3400–3411.

Forinash, K., T. Cretegny, and M. Peyrard. 1997. Local modes and localizations in multicomponent lattices. *Phys. Rev.* 55: 4740–4756.

Fredkin, E., and T. Toffoli. 1982. Conservative logic. *Int. J. Theor. Phys.* 21: 219–253.

Hjelmfelt, A., and J. Ross. 1993. Mass—Coupled chemical systems with computational properties. *J. Phys. Chem.* 97: 7988–7992.

Hjelmfelt, A., E. D. Weinberger, and J. Ross. 1991. Chemical implementation of neural networks and Turing machines. *Proc. Natl. Acad. Sci. USA* 88: 10983–10987.

Ilachinski, A. 1997. Irreducible semi-autonomous adaptive combat (ISAAC): An artificial-life approach to land warfare. *CNA Res. Memo* 91-61.10.

Jakubowski, M. H., K. Steiglitz, and R. Squier. 2002. Computing with solitons: A review and prospectus. In *Collision-Based Computing*, ed. A. Adamatzky. London: Springer-Verlag.

Kenkre, V. M. 1983. Theoretical methods for the analysis of exciton capture and annihilation. In *Organic Molecular Aggregates: Electronic Excitation and Interaction Processes*, ed. P. Reineker, H. Haken, and H. C. Wolf, 193–201. Heidelberg: Springer-Verlag.

Kennedy, B., C. Melhuish, and A. Adamatzky. 2001. Biologically inspired robots. In *Electroactive Polymer (EAP) Actuators as Artificial Muscles—Reality, Potential, and Challenges*, ed. Y. Bar-Cohen. Washington, DC: SPIE Press.

Krinsky, V. I. 1984. Autowaves: Results, problems, outlooks. In *Self-Organization: Autowaves and Structures Far from Equilibrium*, ed. V. I. Krinsky, 9–19. Heidelberg: Springer-Verlag.

Kuhnert, L., K. L. Agladze, and V. I. Krinsky. 1986. Image processing using light-sensitive chemical waves. *Nature* 337: 244–247.

Langton, C. G. 1990. Computation at the edge of chaos: Phase transitions and emergent computation. *Physica D* 42: 12–27.

Laplante, J. P., M. Pemberton, and J. Ross. 1995. Experiments on pattern recognition by chemical kinetics. *J. Phys. Chem.* 99: 10063–10065.

Liehr, A. W., M. Bode, and H.-G. Purwins. 2001. The generation of dissipative quasi-particles near Turing's bifurcation in three-dimensional reaction-diffusion systems. In *High Performance Computing in Science and Engineering 2000*, ed. E. Krause. and W. Jäger. Heidelberg: Springer-Verlag.

Marek, M., and H. Ševčíková. 1984. Electrical field effects on propagating pulse and front waves. In *Self-Organization: Autowaves and Structures Far from Equilibrium*, ed. V. I. Krinsky, 161–163. Heidelberg: Springer-Verlag.

Masia, M., N. Marchettinib, V. Zambranoa, and M. Rustici. 2001. Effect of temperature in a closed unstirred Belousov-Zhabotinsky system. *Chem. Phys. Lett.* 341: 285–291.

Mazoyer, J. 1999. Computation on cellular automata. In *Cellular Automata. A Parallel Model*, ed. M. Delorme and J. Mazoyer. Boston: Kluwer Academic Publishers.

Miller, J. F. 2000. Evolvable hardware: Some directions to the Future. Invited talk at the second NASA/DOD Workshop on Evolvable Hardware, Palo Alto, Calif., July. On-line. Available at ⟨http://www.cs.bham.ac.uk/~jfm/eh00/sld001.htm⟩.

Miller, J. F., and M. Hartmann. 2001. Evolving messy gates for fault tolerance: Some preliminary findings. In *Proceedings of the Third NASA/DOD Workshop on Evolvable Hardware (EH '01)*, ed. D. Keymeulen, A. Stoica, J. Lohn, and R. Zebulum, 116–123. New York: IEEE Computer Society.

Miller, J. F., A. Thompson, P. Thomson, and T. C. Fogarty, eds. 2000. *Proceedings of the Third International Conference on Evolvable Systems: From Biology to Hardware*, Edinburgh, 17–19 April. Berlin: Springer.

Moebius D., and H. Kuhn. 1979. Energy transfer in monolayers with cyanine dye Scheibe aggregates. *J. Appl. Phys.* 64: 5138–5141.

Nolte, H. J. 1975. A model of the optically active scheibe-aggregate of pseudoisocyanine. *Chem. Phys. Lett.* 31: 134–139.

Park, J. K., K. Steiglitz, and W. P. Thurston. 1986. Soliton-like behaviour in automata. *Physica D* 19: 423–432.

Rambidi, N. G. 1992. An approach to computational complexity: Nondiscrete biomolecular computing. *Computer* 25: 51–54.

Rambidi, N. G., and D. S. Chernavskii. 1991. Toward a biomolecular computer: 1. Ways, means, objectives. *J. Mol. Electron.* 7: 105–114.

Rambidi, N. G., and D. Yakovenchuk. 1999. Finding path in a labyrinth based on reaction-diffusion media. *Adv. Mater. Opt. Electronics.*

Rambidi, N. G., A. V. Maximychev, and A. V. Usatov. 1994. Molecular image processing based on chemical reaction systems: 1. Implementation of Blum-type algorithms. *Adv. Mater. Opt. Electronics.* 4: 191–201.

Rambidi, N. G., A. V. Maximichev, and A. V. Usatov. 1994a. Molecular image-processing devices based on chemical reaction systems: 2. Implementation of Blum-type algorithms. *Adv. Mater. Opt. Electronics.* 4: 191–201.

Rambidi, N. G., E. P. Grebennikov, A. I. Adamatzky, A. G. Devyatkov, and D. V. Yakovenchuk. 2002. *Biomolecular Neural-Network Devices* (in Russian). Moscow: Radiotekhnika.

Schenk, C. P., A. W. Liehr, M. Bode, and H.-G. Purwins. 1999. Quasi-particles in a three-dimensional three-component reaction-diffusion system. In *High Performance Computing in Science and Engineering 1999. Transactions of the High Performance Computing Center*, ed. E. Krause and W. Jäger. Stuttgart.

Ševčíková, H., and M. Marek. 1986. Chemical waves in electric field: Modeling. *Physica D* 21: 61–77.

Steiglitz, K., I. Kamal, and A. Watson. 1988. Embedded computation in one-dimensional automata by phase coding. *IEEE Trans. Comput.* 37: 138–145.

Steinbock, O., A. Toth, and K. Showalter. 1995. Navigating complex labyrinths: Optimal paths from chemical waves. *Science* 267: 868–871.

Steinbock, O., P. Kettunen, and K. Showalter. 1996. Chemical wave logic gates. *J. Phys. Chem.* 100: 18970–18975.

Tabata, O., H. Hirasawa, S. Aoki, R. Yoshida, and E. Kokufuta. 2002. Ciliary motion actuator using self-oscillating gel. *Sensors Actuators A* 95: 234–238.

Toffoli, T., and N. Margolus. 1991. Programmable matter. *Physica D* 47: 263–272.

Tolmachev D., and A. Adamatzky. 1996. Chemical processor for computation of Voronoi diagram. *Adv. Mater. Opt. Electronics* 6: 191–196.

Toth, A., and K. Showalter. 1995. Logic gates in excitable media. *J. Chem. Phys.* 103: 2058–2066.

Toyozawa, Y. 1983. Localization and delocalization of an exciton in the phonon field. In *Organic Molecular Aggregates: Electronic Excitation and Interaction Processes*, ed. P. Reineker, H. Haken, and H. C. Wolf, 90–106. Heidelberg: Springer-Verlag.

Yoshida, R., T. Yamaguchi, and H. Ichijo. 1996. Novel oscillating swelling-deswelling dynamic behaviour for pH-sensitive polymer gels. *Mater. Sci. Eng.* C4: 107–113.

Ziegler, J., P. Dittrich, and W. Banzhaf. 1997. Towards a metabolic robot controller. In *Information Processing in Cells and Tissues*, eds: M. Holcombe and R. Paton, 305–318. New York: Plenum Press.

4 Chemical-Based Computing and Problems of High Computational Complexity: The Reaction-Diffusion Paradigm

Nicholas G. Rambidi

4.1 Several Initial Remarks on von Neumann versus non–von Neumann Computing

A vast variety of engineering projects—keystones for industry—were developed in the 1940s and 1950s and initiated the development of digital von Neumann computing devices. The mathematical and computational basis of these projects could be reduced to problems of rather low (polynomial) computational complexity. The character of the computational complexity of problems inherent in practical projects was of decisive importance in choosing which paradigm would be used in elaborating the computing techniques under development.

In the early 1940s, nearly simultaneously with the advent of the von Neumann paradigm, McCulloch and Pitts (1943) offered a radically different approach to designing information processing devices. According to them, a computational system can be designed to be, in a sense, analogous to the human brain. Simple processors (neurons) are constituent parts of the system, with each being connected to all other processors in some definite manner. Computing capabilities of the system are defined by the predetermined complex structure of the system (that is, by the character of neuron connection), not by the stored program. Problems are solved by the system with a very high degree of parallelism. At the same time, the character of the dynamics inherent in the system defines the storage of information and the information processing capabilities of the system.

McCulloch and Pitts (1943) used two fundamental principles of information processing by biological entities in deriving the basis of this neural net approach. They are:

• An "all or none" mode of a single neuron activity—that is, a nonlinear dynamic mechanism

• A very high degree of parallelism of neural connections in a neural net

Computer designers have been repeatedly rederiving this paradigm during the last several decades. Nonetheless, it is only recently that the neural net approach has been turned into a practical tool for designing methods of information processing for problems of high computational complexity.

In the late 1980s, Michael Arbib (1989, 1994) suggested an expansion of contemporary concepts of computation to further mimic the style of the brain. In his article, "The brain as a metaphor for sixth generation computing" (Arbib 1994), he argued: "This style depends on constant interaction of concurrently active systems, many of which express their activity in the interplay of spatio-temporal patterns in manifold layers of neurons" (107).

The remarkable features of Arbib's approach consist of several important points:

1. The brain is an action-oriented computer. Central to the action-oriented view is that the system (human, animal or computer-robot) must be able to correlate action and the results of its interaction in a such a way as to build up an internal "model" of the world.

2. The brain has a hierarchical multilevel organization. The extremely important point is that no one-level model is able to describe brain functions.

3. The brain is not a serial information processing system.

Arbib's ideas were the basis behind the renewed interest in neural net devices—more precisely, the interest in complex versions of semiconductor computer architecture that have enabled researchers to greatly increase the level of computer parallelism. Arbib argued: "It is only in the last few years that there has been a dramatic reawakening of interest in the technological implications of neural computing—in no small part because the developments of VLSI and computer networking had led computer scientists to explore how problem solving can be distributed across a network of interacting, concurrently acting processors" (Arbib, 1989, 186).

The basic starting point for the following discussion is the suggestion that consistent and straightforward implementation of basic biological information processing principles into computing would lead to information processing devices fundamentally different from von Neumann ones in their architectures and dynamics and based on new technological principles. These devices would not compete with future digital semiconductor techniques but rather supplement them, greatly increasing the capabilities of the "information industry."

The problems discussed in this chapter have a biological background. There are, however, many systems in chemistry, physics, and biology with similar behavioral characteristics. This includes tissues of living organisms, assemblies of primitive microorganisms, biological membranes and other biological assemblies, sets of coupled biochemical and chemical reactions with nonlinear kinetics, and so on. The terms *biomolecular system* and *biomolecular computing* will be used below for all these entities when general problems are discussed.

This chapter was designed to discuss in detail one of the attempts to elaborate non–von Neumann information processing means—that is, a set of pseudobiological paradigms; more precisely, to discuss the important subset that could be called the *reaction-diffusion paradigm.*

Two basic points are of great importance for the following discussion. They are:

• A detailed understanding of the notion of complexity and its significance in information processing

• The nature of the information processing in biological entities—that is, general principles of their data storage and transformation

4.2 Complexity: Structural, Behavioral, and Computational

The world around us is complex. This is the reality that defines our knowledge of the different phenomena we face every day. Complexity shows up in absolutely diverse fields of human activity, beginning from complicated engineering designs and continuing up to sophisticated economic and social problems.

Stafford Beer, former President of the U.S.A. General System Research Society, considered complexity as an integral property of the real world (Beer 1970). He declared that understanding complexity has become the problem of the century—just as the skill to process metals was essential for our ancestors.

According to Casti (1979), the concept of complexity embraces three basic aspects (italics added): "*Static complexity* represents essentially the complexity of the subsystems that realize the system, *dynamic complexity* involves the computational length required by the subsystems' interconnection to realize the process, and *control complexity* represents a measure of computational requirements needed to keep the system behaving in a prescribed fashion" (44).

Following Casti (1979), let us consider three basic hypostases of the complexity inherent in biomolecular systems capable of information processing. Given the biological background of the problems discussed, let us use the following terms:

• *Structural complexity* of the system (static)

• *Behavioral complexity* that determines the spatiotemporal evolution of the system performing an information processing operation (dynamic)

• *Computational complexity* of an algorithm describing information processing operations performed (control)

Several approaches to the quantitative definition of complexity are now in use. The notion of algorithmic complexity seems to be the most adequate for estimating the complexity of the evolution of a dynamic system (Yudin and Yudin 1985; Ming and Vitanyi 1993).

Suppose there is some system that transforms input information $x \in X$ into output information $y \in Y$ according to some program p. Here, X and Y are sets of x and y values. According to Yudin and Yudin (1985), the structure of the system is defined as a description of its operational (hardware) characteristics—that is, function $\phi(p|x) = y$, that can be used by program p. It is essential that this description does not depend on the choice of input data.

The algorithmic complexity of the process performed by a system having the structure $\phi(p|x) = y$ (that is, its behavioral complexity) is defined as the minimal length of the assumed program $l(p)$ from some set of programs S, that describe the process adequately:

$$K_\phi(y|x) = \begin{cases} \min l(p) : \phi(p|x) = y \\ \infty : \forall p \in S \ \phi(p|x) \neq y \end{cases} \tag{4.1}$$

Given the definition of the system structure, it is possible to introduce the notion of the structural complexity of the system itself as complexity $K_\phi(y|x)$ under fixed values of $x = x_0$:

$$K_\phi(y_0|x_0) = \begin{cases} \min l(p) : \phi(p|x_0) = y_0 \\ \infty : \forall p \in S \ \phi(p|x_0) \neq y_0 \end{cases} \tag{4.2}$$

Numerical estimations of algorithmic behavioral and structural complexity are not used in this chapter. All examples discussed below are chosen such that the high (or low) degree of behavioral complexity is evident.

The behavioral complexity in a reaction-diffusion medium is considered to be high. It is determined by nonlinear dynamics inherent in the medium that lead to different spatiotemporal modes, depending on the state of the medium and control stimuli. In any case, the behavior of the medium is much more complicated than the behavior of a semiconductor electronic circuit (YES or NO mode).

The computational complexity of an algorithm describing the behavior of a system can be expressed as the dependence of computational capabilities (resources) that are necessary to simulate system behavior (i.e., a specific system characteristic called the *problem size*).

Several types of so-called complexity functions are used for quantitative estimation of computational complexity. The most known among them are:

• Time complexity function (Klir 1985)

$$t_A(n) = \max_{|x|=n} t_A(x) \tag{4.3}$$

that is, the number of time steps necessary for algorithm A to solve individual problem x determined by the length of the word $|x|$ equal to n.

• Space complexity function (Klir 1985)

$$S_A(n) = \max_{|x|=n} S_A(x) \tag{4.4}$$

where $S_A(x)$ is a number of memory cells necessary for algorithm A.

The algorithm for solving a problem is called polynomial (P type) if the complexity function is polynomially dependent on the problem size. Otherwise, if the complexity function is exponentially dependent on the problem size, the problem is defined as intractable. Several types of these problems having different complexity are known (NP, NP-complete, and so on).

The computational complexity of a particular problem can differ according to the type of machine used to solve it. The problem may scale differently for each type of machine. As an example, let us consider a two-dimensional contour enhancement operation performed by a digital von Neumann machine and a reaction-diffusion machine. Let us choose as the problem size the linear dimensions of an image (the number of points along each axis necessary for performing this operation without contour distortions).

For a digital computer, this operation is equivalent in the general case to a large number of primitive binary operations performed on a two-dimensional array of variables. The complexity function should be proportional to the square of the problem size.

On the other hand, contour enhancement in the case of a reaction-diffusion medium is a primitive operation. It is performed in all points of the medium simultaneously, therefore the complexity function does not depend on problem size.

In what follows, we attempt to:

• Give examples and discuss the high behavioral complexity of biomolecular systems based on nonlinear dynamic mechanisms

• Speculate on the assumption that the high behavioral complexity of biomolecular media is in close correlation with their capabilities in solving problems of high computational complexity

• Give examples of complex computations performed by biomolecular media

4.3 Behavioral Complexity of Biomolecular Systems

Diverse and important examples of high behavioral complexity are shown by biomolecular and biological systems at different levels of their organization and structure.

Complex oscillatory processes in a human brain are known to occur at the tissue level. Heart rhythm disturbances and sudden-death phenomenon can be determined by pathological modes of myocardium excitation (Winfree 1994). Complex dynamic regimes lead to a ordered spatial evolution at the level of cell assembly—for instance, in the formation of nonuniform circular cell distributions in thin layers of dictyostellum discoideum media (Prigogine 1980). Oscillating modes in concentration levels were found for diverse chemical and biochemical reactions in biological membranes and cells (i.e., at the supramolecular level; Goldbetter 1997). Finally, complex dynamics can be considered as the origin of collective excitations in biomacromolecules at the molecular level (Davydov 1984).

One of the basic points in understanding an information processing system is the correlation between its structural and behavioral complexity (Nicolis 1986). It is quite often assumed (e.g., in the case of electronic technical systems) that behavioral complexity should increase proportionally to increasing structural complexity. Nevertheless, the correlation between structural and behavioral complexity is not straightforward. Increased complexity of the system structure does lead in many cases to more complicated behavior, but at the same time, some very simple systems (for instance, two oscillators with nonlinear coupling) are known that demonstrate complex behavior in spite of the simplicity of their structure.

Regrettably, there are no general theoretical approaches to explain what the structure (and other characteristics) of a system should be to provide predetermined complexity of the behavior. Based on experimental experience and theoretical considerations, two basic principles could be stated that determine high behavioral complexity of the system:

• Nonlinear mechanisms in the system dynamics
• A multilevel structural organization with interaction between different levels

Nonlinear biochemical enzymatic systems and chemical oscillators represent striking examples of very complex behavior based on primitive structures. Thin layers of these reagents demonstrate different complex modes of behavior, such as concentration oscillations, waves of switching between different states, traveling concentration pulses, stable dissipate structures, and so on (Field and Burger 1985).

Two examples of temporal evolution of a Belousov-Zhabotinsky system are shown in figure 4.1.

The remarkable feature of such biomolecular systems is that they are capable of fulfilling functions adequate for information processing operations of high computational complexity. Aside from the fantastic intellectual capabilities of a neural system, let us mention the processes of information replication performed by RNA molecules, the recognition at the molecular level inherent in enzyme molecules, and so on.

This feature of biomolecular systems lies behind the basis of the pseudobiological information processing paradigm that is an important alternative to the presently unique von Neumann approach in contemporary digital computing.

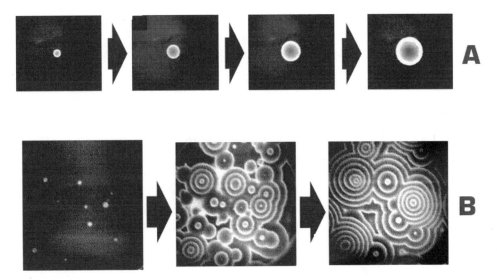

Figure 4.1
Two modes of a Belousov-Zhabotinsky reaction in thin (pseudo two dimensional layers of the reagent. (*A*) A process of trigger wave spreading corresponding to the switching of the medium from one stable state to another; (*B*) an emission of circular waves from point-wise sources and their further evolution. Here and in the following figures gray arrows show steps of the image transformation by the reaction-diffusion medium, black arrows correspond to input of an initial image into medium.

4.4   General Principles of Information Processing Inherent in Biomolecular and Simple Biological Entities

The information processing inherent in biomolecular and simple biological entities is based on principles radically different from the von Neumann paradigm and opposite to them in the main.

In the process of reproduction, DNA (together with messenger RNA and the rest of a cell's information transfer mechanism) provides a biological system with stability. At the same time, the possibilities of modifying this information provide a biological system with the ability to adapt under changing external stimuli. Molecular recognition processes ensure directed information transfer in a biomolecular system and therefore exclude the random search of variants.

Biological information processing systems have a very high level of parallelism exceeding immensely any possible degree of parallelism in contemporary digital semiconductor devices. Extremely important is the ability to use as information processing primitives many complex logical operations equivalent to a large number of binary ones. The nonlinear mechanisms of information processing are responsible for the complex responses that biomolecular and simple biological systems have in regard to external stimuli, and which are equivalent to solving problems of high computational complexity. It is the existence of nonlinear mechanisms within the system that seems to be the basic fundamental in determining the success of information processing in problems of high computational complexity.

Let us try to substantiate this assumption.

Grossberg (1988) has elaborated a nonlinear neural network model that enables one to understand a great variety of different information processing phenomena such as: perception, cognitive information processing, cognitive-emotional interactions, goal-oriented motor control, and robotics. Grossberg (1976) mentioned the functional similarity between these neural networks and reaction-diffusion media. This similarity was also shown in experiments on Belousov-Zhabotinsky-type media.

Similar results for the case of image processing at the level of practical calculations was obtained by a number of authors (see section 4.5 of this chapter).

The second fundamental that gives the system the ability to solve computationally complex problems is its multilevel organization. Nicolis (see, for instance, 1986) has discussed the main principles and details of this organization in detail.

From these considerations, it can be said that both the behavioral complexity of the system and its ability to solve problems of high computational complexity are determined by the same fundamentals as that of a reaction-diffusion system. Therefore the degree of behavioral complexity could be a decisive point in determining the choice of a system capable of solving computationally complex problems.

It is known (Field and Burger 1985) that the dynamics of distributed nonlinear chemical systems that display sufficiently complicated behavior can be described by a system of nonlinear differential equations of the type:

$$U_i(r, t) = F[U_1(r, t), U_2(r, t), \ldots, U_N(r, t)] + \sum_{j=1}^{N} \Delta[D_{ij} U_j(rt)] \tag{4.5}$$

where $U_i(r, t)$ is the concentration of the ith component of reaction proceeding in the system, A is a control parameter, D_{ij} are diffusion coefficients, and $N = 1, 2, 3, \ldots, N$.

The behavior of this system is determined by the complicated nonlinear kinetics of reactions at each spatial point r_k, described by functions

$$F[U_1(r, t), U_2(r, t), \ldots, U_n(r, t)]$$

and also by diffusion of reaction components.

At the same time, such an excitable system can be considered as a realization of a neural network where:

• Each point of the medium is a primitive microprocessor.

• The dynamics of microprocessors can be characterized by complicated chemical reactions produced by external excitations.

• Short-range interactions between primitive processors occur (in principle, each microvolume is coupled with all others by diffusion, but because of a rather low spreading speed, these interactions proceed with a delay proportional to the distance between microvolumes).

In the general form, homogeneous neural nets can be described by a system of integro-differential equations (Masterov et al. 1988):

$$
U_i(r,t) = -\frac{U_i(r,t)}{t_i} + G[-T_i - A + Z_i]
$$

$$
= -\frac{U_i(r,t)}{t_i} + G\left\{ -T_i - A + \sum_{m=1}^{N} \int \Phi_m[r, x, t, U_1, U_2, \ldots, U_N] U_m(r,t)\, dx \right\} \qquad (4.6)
$$

where $G[-T_i - A + Z_i]$ is the response function for elements of ith type upon activation by Z_i, T_i is the shift in function G, and Φ_m is the function of spatial coupling between active elements.

These integrodifferential equations cannot generally be represented by the above system of kinetic differential equations (see Vasilev et al. 1987). Under some assumptions, however, both of these models prove to be adequate.

Based on these considerations, it is natural to broaden the boundaries of the pseudobiological paradigm in comparison with McCulloch and Pitts's original approach (1943) and in particular:

• To pass from discrete neural networks to distributed information processing media

• To pass to systems with much more complicated nonlinear dynamics than in the case of neural networks usually under discussion

• To look for systems possessing multilevel organization

Different separate attempts to do the above are known. We feel the most effective way is to use the unique properties of reaction-diffusion media that comply with the above-mentioned demands.

During recent decades, two basic implementations of the reaction-diffusion paradigm have been developing. The first of these is numerical simulations. In this case, solving systems of reaction-diffusion equations presents an opportunity to perform image processing operations—to generate textures and so on. The second is an attempt to design "hardware" information processing means capable of performing different operations of high computational complexity. Both of these strategies are discussed below.

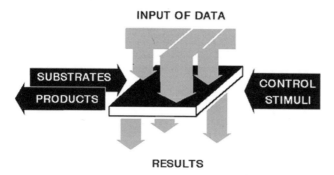

Figure 4.2
Schematic representation of a biomolecular reaction-diffusion processor.

4.5 A Biomolecular Reaction-Diffusion Processor: Basic Principles

The conception of a medium that is able to carry out continuous chemical information processing forms the basis of implementing the reaction-diffusion paradigm.

The principal scheme of a biomolecular computer (see Rambidi, Chernavskii, and
Krinsky 1993) is shown in figure 4.2.

1. *Input of information.* The macro-micro interface unit transforms an information
input (some distribution of external physical stimuli) into a corresponding distribution of molecular components. The most widely known example is a medium
containing photosensitive molecules subject to photochemical reactions under a predetermined spatial distribution of light radiation. As a result, the intensity of light
radiation is converted into a distribution of reaction product concentrations. The
resources of such interface units would be significantly increased by using a set of
molecules sensitive to the radiation in different frequency ranges, by using a combination of different physical stimuli, and so on.

2. *Information processing.* The information processing capabilities of a medium
should be determined by the composition of molecular components in the processor
medium.

The main methodology for choosing the medium is determined by the following
rules:

• Molecular forms released as a result of information input should represent the initial information for a chemical processing system—that is, for a set of coupled
chemical reactions.

• The general scheme of the reaction set (and also their substrates and products) should be chosen in a way that is adequate for the information processing task at hand.

3. *Output of results.* The micro-macro interface for the information processing medium should be a system capable of measuring the distribution of molecular component concentrations corresponding to the final result of the computation. The most convenient versions of such units seem to be different spectrometric systems capable of measuring the spatial distribution of molecular concentrations with appropriate spatial and temporal resolution.

4. *Control and power supply.* The power supply of the biomolecular processor should be of a chemical nature. It is necessary to input continuously (in general) the substrates of the chemical reactions used and to remove the products of these reactions. The control of the processor and data input can be carried out by physical or chemical stimuli affecting the system. Suggested methods are:

• Electromagnetic, mostly visible light radiation

• Local electrical fields

• Local input of controlling molecules or ions

• And so on

The fundamental and most important feature of the reaction-diffusion processor conception is that a reaction-diffusion biomolecular computer is an instance machine (Zauner and Conrad 1996; Rambidi 1997)—that is, the opposite extreme of a universal computer—and it represents an information processing device that encodes a single problem instance in its structure.

There are two basic properties typical for an instance machine:

• The physical structure of the machine is specific for a single problem instance.

• The temporal evolution of the machine leads, under conditions predetermined by the problem under solution, to a state or structure that can be interpreted as a solution of this problem.

A biomolecular processor based on nonlinear dynamic mechanisms is the instance machine. Given a single problem, its solution is determined by an appropriate state of the medium (composition, temperature) and control stimuli.

It should be noted that the definitions of both universal and instance machines are not sharply delimited and in some cases the boundaries between them are rather diffuse.

It is not so difficult to design a reusable instance machine based, for example, on a flow reactor in which nonlinear chemical processes proceed. Moreover, it is possible to change the character of the problem solution after resetting this device by changing the state of the medium or control stimuli. These features are definite steps to universality. Nevertheless, a universal computer is, after reprogramming, the same machine, whereas an instance computer would be more naturally viewed as a different machine (Rambidi 1997).

It should be stressed that the instance machine conception is an important step in understanding the nature of biocomputing. Based on theoretical and experimental investigations performed during the last decade, it presents the further development of Conrad's pioneer guiding principles (Conrad 1985).

The next point important for understanding the essence of the reaction-diffusion means is the neural network architecture of the information processing medium. It is possible to outline a number of structural features that would determine the information processing characteristics of the medium:

1. Cells (figure 4.3), small by comparison with the diffusion length, can be considered as primitive processors representing chemical systems having point-wise kinetics. If these cells are to be considered as independent, trigger and oscillatory regimes should be inherent.

$$\dot{U}_i(r,t) = f_i[U_1(r,t), U_2(r,t)...U_N(r,t)]$$

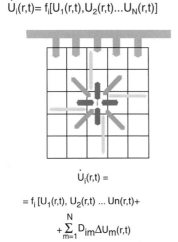

$$\dot{U}_i(r,t) =$$

$$= f_i[U_1(r,t), U_2(r,t)...Un(r,t)+$$

$$+ \sum_{m=1}^{N} D_{im}\Delta U_m(r,t)$$

Figure 4.3
Schematic representation of neural network architecture of reaction-diffusion medium.

Diffusion length is determined as in Field and Burger (1985):

$$l_D = (DT)^{1/2} \tag{4.7}$$

Here, D is an average diffusion coefficient, and T is a characteristic time of the dynamic process.

In common parlance, the diffusion length is the distance where total intermixing of reaction components has taken place because of diffusion.

2. Cells are coupled because of diffusion. This coupling determines a number of complicated dynamic modes that are displayed in thin layers and in a volume of the medium.

3. Changing the composition and temperature of the medium can provide control of excitable medium regimes. One powerful variant is based on using media containing light-sensitive components. In this case, the composition of the medium can be easily changed by light illumination, with the degree of change being controlled by the amount of light exposure.

4. Generally speaking, each cell is connected to each other cell of the medium due to diffusion coupling. This interaction is carried out with a time delay proportional to the distance between cells, and the strength of the interaction decreases proportionally to this distance.

The above model, representing a system of cells coupled by diffusion, does not take into account that the media are uniform distributed systems. A more adequate model should be invariant to infinitesimal shifts of the cell system along the surface of the medium.

Given these features of reaction-diffusion media, a comparison between the dynamic and information processing characteristics of such media and those of neural networks seems to be of substantial value. The most important points seem to be:

• How adequate are the responses of excitable media and neural networks to predetermined external excitation?

• What conclusions can be made about structural characteristics of the media (first, what is the real range of interaction between cells) based on this comparison?

Different approaches to describe such pseudoplanar neural networks with lateral connections are known, starting with the pioneer work by McCulloch and Pitts (1943). A comprehensive review of neural net models offered in the 1970s and 1980s has been done by Grossberg (1988).

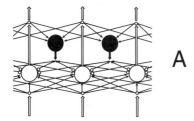

A

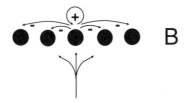

B

Figure 4.4
Schemes of neural networks (*A*) Pozin's feedback network containing excitatory (white circles) and inhibitory (black circles) neurons. (*B*) Grossberg's shunting on-center off-surround feedback network.

In the late 1960s, Pozin (1970) and his coworkers performed a series of investigations based on a neural net model described by the kinetic equation:

$$x_i = -ax_i + F(p_i) + I_i \qquad (4.8)$$

Here, x_i is the potential of the ith neuron, $F(p_i)$ is a sigmoidal function depending on the algebraic sum of signals coming from outputs of other neurons.

$$p_i = \sum_j s_{ij} x_j \qquad (4.9)$$

s_{ij} is a function characterizing the coupling of ith and jth neurons, I_i is an input (external stimulus) of ith neuron.

This model (figure 4.4) represents a neural network having sigmoidal feedback, containing both excitatory and inhibitory inputs. More exactly, the distribution of excitatory and inhibitory signals was set by individual coupling functions $g(x)$, depending on the distance between neurons in the network surface. Extended one- or two-dimensional signals acting on the neural network were considered. It was assumed that the dimensions of input signal features were large compared with interneuron distances. Neural networks were therefore considered as continuous homogeneous media.

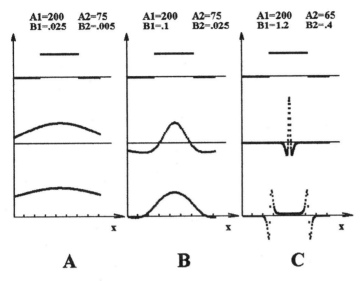

Figure 4.5
Responses of a neural network to external excitation calculated based on Pozin's model and representing: broadening of an input image (*A*), its sharpening (*B*), and contour enhancement (*C*). The upper level of the figure shows the shape of an input distribution, responses of the network are shown at the lower level, shapes of $g(x)$ function (see text) are between them.

The main result obtained in the investigation (Pozin 1970) was that the signal input (for instance, a rectangular wave) into the neural network could be sharpened or broadened; also that the contour of the signal could be enhanced depending on the shape of the coupling function. (Numerical simulations of these effects performed using techniques in Pozin 1970 are shown in figure 4.5).

The simulation represents folding of a rectangular intensity distribution and a function of the form:

$$g(x) = A1 \exp(-x^2/B1) - A2 \exp(-x^2/B2) \tag{4.10}$$

This function depends on four adjustable constants: A1, A2, B1, and B2 (see figure 4.5).

Later, Yakhno and Colleagues (see, for instance, Nuidel and Yakhno 1989; Belliustin et al. 1991) continued this line of investigations and used it for a detailed analysis of image processing operations.

In the late 1960s, Grossberg launched a detailed investigation of neural networks. During the last two decades, Grossberg and his collaborators have analyzed different aspects of neural network activity—the image processing capabilities investigated by

Grossberg (Grossberg 1973, 1976, 1988) and Ellias and Grossberg (1975) are mentioned below.

Based on psychobiological and neurobiological data, Grossberg concluded that shunting on-center off-surround feedback networks (see figure 4.4) display a number of remarkable image features.

Neural networks of this type are described by kinetic equations of the type:

$$x_i = -ax_i + (B - x_i)[I_i + f(x_i)] - x_i\left[J_i + \sum_{j \neq i} f(x_j)\right] \qquad (4.11)$$

Here, the main notations coincide with notations of equation (4.8):

$f(x_i)$ is a feedback nonlinear signal.

I_i and J_i are stimuli acting on excitatory and inhibitory neurons.

Grossberg has shown that shunting on-center off-surround feedback networks posses the key properties of:

· Solving the noise-saturation dilemma

· Normalizing or conserving their total activity

· Being capable of absolutely stable short-time memory

These neural networks proved to be capable of quenching (sharpening) or amplifying (broadening) the noise of input signals, or of enhancing a signal's contour or the most intense fragments depending on the shape of the $f(x)$ function (figure 4.6).

Grossberg (1976) has also noted a dynamic analogy between shunting on-center off-surround feedback neural nets and reaction-diffusion systems, which were used by Gierer and Meinhardt (1972) for the description of the process of biological pattern formation. Later, Masterov, Rabinovich, Tolkov, and Yakhno (Masterov et al. 1988) showed the analogy between the reaction-diffusion equations and the neural net integrodifferential equations.

Thus different theoretical considerations show that common information processing capabilities of neural networks and reaction-diffusion media should be primarily manifested in: storing information in short-term memory; and performing such operations as sharpening or broadening input signals and enhancing the contour of an input picture or its most intense fragments.

Given the information processing properties of reaction-diffusion systems, one may picture some realizable versions of such systems. Their structure defines two general types of design solutions, differing in that the levels of information processing may be spatially combined or spatially separated. In spatially combined systems, the

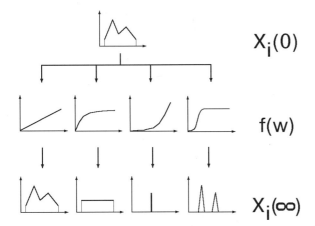

$X_i(0)$

$f(w)$

$X_i(\infty)$

Figure 4.6
Responses of an on-center off-surround feedback neural network to arbitrary chosen external excitation depending on the shapes of $f(w)$ function (see details in text).

successive levels (stages) of information processing are materialized as a set of consecutive dynamic processes (chemical reactions) that proceed in the same volume, the reaction products of some levels being reaction substrates for the following levels. In spatially separated devices, processes of different levels are localized in certain supramolecular domains.

Let us now consider mostly one-level information processing methods. It is easy to construct a variety of devices of different structures using a volume of a liquid Belousov-Zhabotinsky reagent having a preselected shape. It amounts to a three-dimensional network of elementary processors combined into a specific integral system. Control of both the system and the input-output of data proved to be, in this case, too complicated a problem. Therefore a pseudo two-dimensional system using a thin layer of Belousov-Zhabotinsky reagent will be discussed below.

Information processing devices with these capabilities can be designed using complex nonlinear media as a basis (Rambidi, Chernavskii, and Krinsky 1993).

Construction of biomolecular information processing devices is a problem of great complexity because of tremendous technical and material difficulties. Prior simulation of information processing capabilities therefore proves to be urgent to avoid useless, costly, and laborious attempts.

Theoretical methods are powerful tools for the investigation of nonlinear biomolecular system dynamics. Nevertheless, it often happens that commonly used mathematical models do not prove to be fully adequate to mimic processes under investigation because of the high structural and dynamic complexity of the system. Moreover, these models lead often to immense difficulties in analytical handling of the equations describing the model and to cumbersome numerical calculations.

One of the most straightforward ways to simulate information processing primitive operations of biomolecular devices based on complex nonlinear dynamics is via experimental modeling. In this case, Belousov-Zhabotinsky-type excitable media are promising tools because of the close similarity between the dynamics of these media and those of known biomolecular systems.

4.6 Amazing Belousov-Zhabotinsky Media

Two remarkable events in the early 1950s proved the starting points for intense investigations in a new field between physics, chemistry, and biology where systems far from equilibrium demonstrate different and complicated modes of behavior. Chronologically, they were:

1. The discovery of periodic regimes in catalytic reactions of citric acid oxidation by Belousov (Field and Burger 1985; Kapral and Showalter 1995)

2. Publication of the paper "The Chemical Basis of Morphogenesis" by Alan Turing (1952), who first discussed the problem of self-organization in systems far from equilibrium

Later, Zhabotinsky (1964) performed extensive study of the Belousov reaction and developed a very convenient modified version.

The history of the field of oscillating systems is complicated and dramatic (see, for details, Field and Burger 1985; Kapral and Showalter 1995). Different chemical and biological systems have been discovered that demonstrate complicated modes of behavior based on nonlinear dynamic mechanisms. Well-stirred chemical systems have provided examples of behavior based on point-wise kinetics. Using continuous-flow stirred-tank reactors (CSTR) has enabled researchers to demonstrate bistability, different types of temporal oscillations, and chaotic behavior (Field and Burger 1985).

Very sophisticated regimes were discovered using unstirred reactors in thin films of a reagent. These included trigger and other types of traveling waves, as well as different spiral structures (Kapral and Showalter 1995).

Finally, the design of a continuous-flow unstirred gel reactor has allowed experiments to be carried out, proving the actual existence of stable dissipative structures that were predicted by Turing some forty years ago (Kapral and Showalter 1995).

Among these different chemical oscillators, Belousov-Zhabotinsky-type media play a principal role. The dynamics of these media are complex enough to demonstrate diverse and complicated behavior (see two important examples in figure 4.1) and thus have became invaluable model systems for excitable media, providing deep insights into the properties of nonlinear dynamic chemical and biological systems.

The Belousov-Zhabotinsky-type reaction (Field and Burger 1985) is a catalytic oxidation of some organic substance (mainly malonic acid) by potassium bromate or some other oxidizing agent. In the original system, a chemical reaction was found that mimicked the predator-prey population periodicity. The system switches periodically from steady state I to steady state II and vice versa. Such a system is usually self-oscillatory, but under appropriate conditions, the inhibitor bromide can be kept above its critical value, and oscillations will not start. Decreasing the bromide concentration at a small spot for a short while (by touching it with a silver wire, or by an equivalent photochemical reaction) will start the autocatalytic process, with chemical waves propagating outward, like ripples in water.

The overall equations of the Belousov-Zhabotinsky reaction catalyzed by metal ions (Ce, Fe, Ru, and some other metals) (Field and Burger 1985) are:

At the beginning of the process:

$$2\,BrO_3^- + 3\,CH_2(COOH)_2 + 2\,H^+ \rightarrow 2\,BrCH(COOH)_2 + 3\,CO_2 + 4\,H_2O$$

After some time:

$$2\,BrO_3^- + 2\,CH_2(COOH)_2 + 2\,H^+ \rightarrow Br_2\,CHCOOH + 4\,CO_2 + 4\,H_2O$$

But detailed consideration shows that the Belousov-Zhabotinsky reaction includes a set of intermediate stages. The widespread model of the reaction was suggested by Field, Koros, and Noyes (FKN model; Field and Burger 1985). It consists of eleven stages based on several intermediate components.

These media are stable, nonhostile reagents. Furthermore, the temperature range and temporal operation scale of the medium dynamics are convenient for investigation with available physical methods.

B-Z type media based on a light-sensitive catalyst (Kuhnert 1986, 1986b; Kuhnert, Agladze, and Krinsky 1989) are convenient for investigation purposes. The catalyst in the course of reaction changes its electronic state when the medium goes from one stable state to another. As a consequence, the reagent changes its color (from red to blue and vice versa). Therefore it is easy to visualize the process and to observe its spatiotemporal evolution.

The basic important feature of light-sensitive excitable media is that they store input information during a rather long period of time. The periodical process of stored

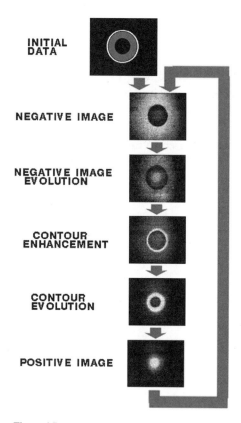

Figure 4.7
Scheme of basic periodic process of image transformation performed by reaction-diffusion medium.

image transformation (figure 4.7) begins after projecting an image onto a thin layer of the medium (Kuhnert, Agladze, and Krinsky 1989; Rambidi and Maximychev 1997).

This process represents a combination of three interlaced primitive responses to the stimulus by light (figure 4.8):

· Contour enhancement of image fragments
· Alternation of negative and positive images of an input picture
· Disappearance of small features of the picture

The first of these predominates at relatively low medium acidity values and high exposures of light radiation. The second process is revealed at high acidity levels and low light exposures.

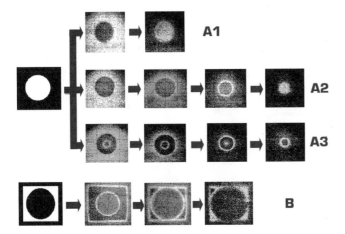

Figure 4.8
Temporal evolution of simple images in thin layers of a light-sensitive Belousov-Zhabotinsky medium depending on the state of the medium (A1–A3 correspond to different acidities of the media) and on the character of the medium illumination (*A* and *B* are positive and negative images). Initial images are at the left side of the figure.

The results, which will be discussed in sections 4.7 and 4.8, were obtained using the experimental setup shown in figure 4.9.

The reaction-diffusion medium was a thin (0.5–1.5 mm), flat nonstirred reagent layer placed in a reaction vessel in which a spatiotemporal oscillating process proceeded. The initial concentrations of the reagent components were: $KBrO_3$: 0.3 M, H_2SO_4: 0.6–0.3 M, malonic acid: 0.2 M, KBr: 0.05 M. Light-sensitive catalyst $Ru(bpy)_3Cl_2$ was used.

The specific feature of this setup was a computer-controlled Sanyo PLC-510M LCD video projector (VGA compatible, 270 ANSI lumens). The high uniformity of the background intensity of this projector improved the reliability of the experiment. Moreover, the computer-controlled projector was indispensable for the elaboration of the technique suitable for finding the shortest paths in complex labyrinths (see below).

An excitation of a thin planar layer of the medium by light radiation was used for the input of initial information. The direction of light was normal to the surface of the medium. The distribution of light intensity on the surface (that is, an image of the labyrinth under processing) determined the initial image stored in the medium.

4.7   Image Processing by Belkousov-Zhabotinsky-Type Media

Wave algorithms in image processing have been discussed in literature beginning from the late 1960s (see, for instance, Pratt 1978). They were "prairie fires" and some other versions that were promising for efficient determination of shape description due to the high parallelism inherent in them.

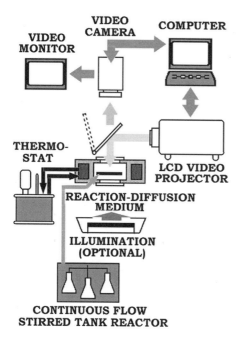

Figure 4.9
Schematic representation of optical and digital video system for investigation of information processing by reaction-diffusion media.

The next step in the further development of wave-image processing approaches was based on the unique properties of reaction-diffusion systems. Both high parallelism and nonlinear dynamic mechanisms that increased behavioral complexity were the basis behind the elaboration of image processing methods.

The foundations of information processing by chemical light-sensitive reaction-diffusion media were laid in pioneering studies performed by Lothar Kuhnert (1986, 1986b), which were followed by the paper "Information processing using light-sensitive waves," published by Kuhnert, Agladze, and Krinsky (1989). This was an important study that determined the physical and chemical principles inherent in information processing by reaction-diffusion media. At the same time, the information processing basis of this work remained meager. Detailed investigations of information processing capabilities in chemical light-sensitive reaction-diffusion media were performed in the beginning of the 1990s (see Rambidi and Maximychev 1997 and references therein). It became clear as a result of these investigations that fundamental differences exist between:

- Image processing of positive and negative images of initial pictures
- responses of the medium to the light excitations and information processing operations performed by the medium based on these responses
- information processing of black-and-white pictures, pictures having several levels of brightness, and halftone pictures

Let us define the positive image of a picture as the image corresponding to a typical picture inherent to human surroundings. If the notion of "typical picture" is uncertain (e.g., the case of geometrical figures; see, for instance, figure 4.10), let us define the positive image as a dark figure on a light background. Black-and-white and halftone pictures will be used below. Images of these pictures could be considered as a set of optical density values $D(i)$ corresponding to each point of the picture $(0 < D(i) < D(\infty)$, where $D(\infty)$ is the maximum value of the optical density). The negative image of the picture is defined as a set of inverted density values $(D_i^N = D_\infty - D_i)$. Adobe Photoshop software was used for the positive-negative transformations.

There were two reasons why this work was performed recently. The first of these was the advent of new experimental techniques during the last decade that have proved to be indispensable for the investigations of complex reaction-diffusion dynamics. The designing of reaction-diffusion media optimal for solving a problem under investigation forms the basis of this technique. The most remarkable features of this technique lie in employing modern polymeric materials as specialized matrices for the medium and immobilization of separate chemical components of the reaction-diffusion system. As a result, improved techniques gave us the opportunity to sufficiently increase the reliability of data in comparison with the data of Kuhnert, Agladze, and Krinsky (1989) and that of subsequent investigations (Rambidi and Maximychev 1997).

Understanding that the experimental data formerly obtained was incomplete and even somewhat incompatible was the second reason why this work was performed recently. New important regimes of image processing by reaction-diffusion media have been found as a result of investigations based on the improved technique, enabling one to explain qualitatively the whole set of the experimental data using the simple FKN model (Field and Burger 1985).

There are four basic points that determine the character of the image processing by light-sensitive reaction-diffusion media (see details in Rambidi and Maximychev 1997). They are:

- The composition of the Belousov-Zhabotinsky reagent

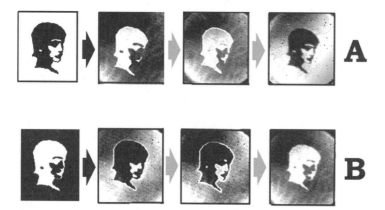

Figure 4.10
Processing positive (A) and negative (B) black and white pictures by a Belousov-Zhabotinsky medium. Here and in following figures black arrows correspond to input of the initial picture, grey ones show transformation of the image by the medium. The sequences of images (A and B) in this figure and in figures 4.3 and 4.5 correspond to one period of Belousov-Zhabotinsky medium oscillation. This period was about 20–30 sec. Time intervals between separate images throughout of each period were 3–5 sec.

- Positive or negative versions of the initial picture
- The optical contrast of the picture
- Exposure in the process of initial picture input into the medium

The Case of a Black-and-White Picture

The negative image of the initial picture is revealed after its input into the medium. After that, the following stages of image evolution can generally be observed:

- Contour enhancement
- Spatial evolution of the contour (the shrinkage of the contour or its spreading, see Rambidi and Maximychev 1997)
- Appearance of the positive image of the input picture

(Some of the above steps are optional, depending on operational conditions.)

Basic stages of picture evolution for positive and negative images of the input picture are shown in figure 4.10.

This process can be qualitatively explained based on the simplest FKN model for stirred Belousov-Zabotinsky-type medium (see, for instance, Field and Burger 1985).

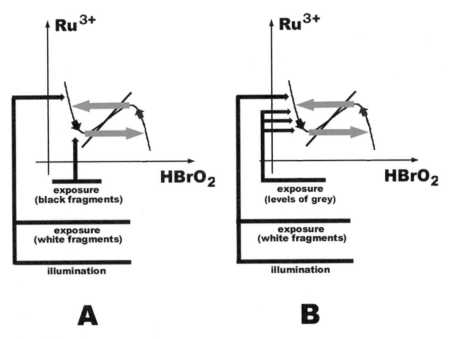

Figure 4.11
Schematic representation of image processing mechanism inherent in a light-sensitive Belousov-Zhabotinsky medium functioning in oscillating mode. Null clines and mechanisms of image transformation are given for cases of black and white (*A*) and half-tone (*B*) pictures. See also explanations in the text.

According to this model, the medium can be described by two ordinary differential equations (ODE) corresponding to activator and inhibitor dynamics. Stationary states of these equations could be characterized by a set of null clines. Light-sensitive Belousov-Zhabotinsky media functioning in oscillating mode were used for the investigation of the discussed image processing capabilities. The null clines corresponding to this mode are shown in figure 4.11. One of them (S-type) corresponds to inhibitor ODE, while the other corresponds to activator ODE. The main feature of this oscillating mode is that null clines have no common stable point.

In a Belousov-Zhabotinsky-type reaction proceeding in oscillating mode, the color of the reagent changes between orange (high concentration of Ru^{2+} and low concentration of Ru^{3+}) and fluorescent bluish (high concentration of Ru^{3+} and low concentration of Ru^{2+}). A black-and-white video camera was used to record the medium evolution (using a blue filter to increase the contrast of the image). The color of the records input into computer memory thus varied from black to white (high and low concentrations of Ru^{2+}, see figure 4.11).

The typical procedure of the experiment was as follows:

First, the medium was illuminated by white light to remove traces of previous experiments. The illumination initiated the photochemical reactions, which sharply increased the concentration of Ru^{3+} (light color). At the same time, the inhibitor ($HBrO_2$) concentration was expected to decrease according to the FKN model. After that, a picture under consideration was projected onto the surface of the medium. As a result:

• The concentration of Ru^{3+} remained high in the areas of the medium where white fragments of the initial picture were projected (the upper part of the left null cline branch).

• The concentration of Ru^{3+} decreased and concentration of Ru^{2+} increased in the areas of the medium where black fragments of the picture were projected (the lower part of the left null cline branch).

A faint positive image of the input picture appeared, usually just after switching off the exposure. At that point, an oscillating Belousov-Zhabotinsky-type process began in the medium. The character of the medium evolution could be described as moving points corresponding to concentrations in exposed areas along null clines toward unstable foci (see figure 4.11). The basic feature of this movement was the tendency to decrease concentration of Ru^{3+} in white exposed fragments and to increase concentration of Ru^{3+} in black exposed fragments of the medium (here the point jumps to the right branch of the null cline and moves upward). Therefore the image of the input picture turned into a negative one. In the process of the following evolution, a negative image would turn into a positive one, and so on.

Basic responses of a Belousov-Zhabotinsky medium to light excitation and image processing operations based on these responses have already been discussed in detail earlier (Rambidi and Maximychev 1997). Image processing operations performed by active chemical media have proved to be similar to human visual capabilities. There are two main sets.

The first can be defined as "description of the general features of an object." This set includes such primitive operations as concentration on the general outline of an image, removing small immaterial features, "addition to the whole" operations, and, in particular, restoration of an image with defects.

The second set of image processing operations can be determined as "switching to the details of an image." It includes contour enhancement, segmentation (i.e., division of an image into simple parts), image skeletonizing, and italicizing small features of an image.

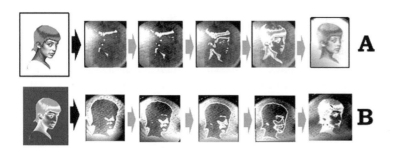

Figure 4.12
Processing positive (*A*) and negative (*B*) half-tone pictures by a Belousov-Zhabotinsky medium. See also caption to figure 4.10.

In this case, the main factors controlling the character of the image evolution are the negative or positive form of the initial picture, and exposure of the light excitation. These two factors are important to control the contour-enhancement mode. Decreasing pH and increasing exposure determine conditions for revealing this mode (see details and examples in Rambidi and Maximychev 1997).

We mention here that basic features of image processing by Belousov-Zhabotinsky media were first discussed in Kuhnert, Agladze, and Krinsky (1989).

The Case of a Halftone Initial Picture
The transformation of positive and negative pictures is shown in figure 4.12. The halftone picture is transformed first by the reaction-diffusion medium into a black-and-white form.

The positive input picture is transformed into its negative black-and-white image step by step—beginning from its darkest fragments. The contour enhancement mode then appears and in the end of the transformation period, a halftone positive image is observed.

In the case of a negative input picture, the main part of the brightest fragments is revealed simultaneously as a black-and-white positive image at the very beginning of the image evolution. After that, more and more dark fragments are enhanced step by step in positive black-and-white forms of the input picture.

This complicated evolution of a halftone image has not been observed before. Although the simple FKN model does not explain all details of the image evolution, it is possible to conclude only that fragments of different brightness should appear simultaneously step by step in the process of image evolution.

When the picture is projected on the layer of Ru-based Belousov-Zhabotinsky reagent, the information on brightness of the picture is introduced into the medium. It is stored as a spatial distribution of the reaction component's concentrations. In this case, the section of the null cline corresponding to different levels of gray spreads along its left branch (figure 4.11.). In the process of the image evolution in the medium (moving along the null cline), the darkest fragments of the stored image emerge first and then step by step all others with less concentration of Ru^{+3}. This process virtually visualizes information about the brightness of the initial picture, transforming it from a spatial into a temporal form.

All control factors that determine the processing of black-and-white pictures work in the case of halftone images. But one more factor is important in this case—the optical contrast within the input picture. For instance, changing the contrast of the initial negative picture gives the opportunity to enhance the contour of the whole picture (figure 4.13, c1) and its separate parts (figure 4.13, c2)

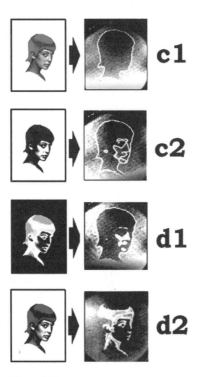

Figure 4.13
Different variants of half-tone picture processing: c1, contour enhancement (low contrast of the initial picture); c2, contour enhancement (high contrast of the initial picture); d1, enhancement of the basic shape of the initial picture; d2, enhancement of details of the initial picture.

Information processing modes of chemical reaction-diffusion media open new ways that seem to be important for practical applications.

There is a great variety of responses of Belousov-Zhabotinsky media to the photochemical input of pictures having several levels of brightness and halftone pictures. These responses allow one to solve many image processing and image recognition problems. Let us consider several examples:

The processing of a negative initial picture leads to enhancement of the basic picture shape (figure 4.13, d1), while the processing of a positive picture gives the possibility to accentuate fine features of the picture (figure 4.13, d2).

The consecutive enhancement of fragments with different levels of brightness is an important feature of the image processing. The evolution of a picture with five levels of brightness in a reaction-diffusion medium is shown in figure 4.14. Numbers in the initial picture of this figure correspond to relative optical densities (0 for white and 100 for black). The separate enhancement of all fragments of the picture indicates an effective enough transformation function of the medium (level of darkness versus consecutive enhancement).

The interpretation of aerial and satellite pictures is one of the most widespread and important problems among different image processing tasks. In practical terms, it comes down to dividing the picture into fragments with specific levels of brightness. It was shown earlier that reaction-diffusion media prove to be promising instruments for solving this problem (Rambidi and Maximychev 1997). The new experimental technique elaborated broadens these possibilities of reaction-diffusion media.

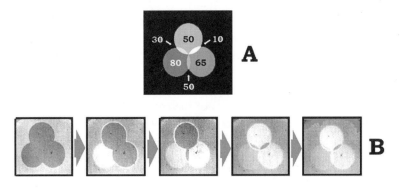

Figure 4.14
Enhancement of picture fragments having different brightness by a Belousov-Zhabotinsky medium. *A* and *B* are the initial picture and subsequent results. Numbers in the initial picture correspond to relative optical densities of the image fragments. See also caption to figure 4.10.

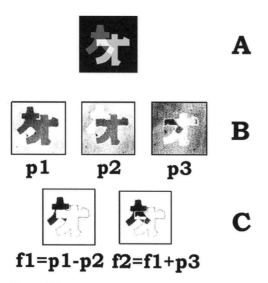

Figure 4.15
The restoration of individual components of the picture where components overlap. Initial picture (*A*), evolution of the overlapped picture in the reaction-diffusion medium (*B*), and image processing operations that restore an overlapped component (*C*).

The consecutive enhancement of fragments with different levels of brightness enables one to restore individual components of the picture where these components overlap. This process is shown in figure 4.15. The whole overlapped figure (p1), then the fragment having lower darkness (p2), and finally the overlapped part of the picture (p3) appear consecutively in the course of the image evolution. Using standard image processing operations performed by a conventional digital computer gives the opportunity to restore the second component of overlapped picture based on these experimental data (f1, f2).

Figure 4.16 shows the situation of "how many original spots are on the skin of a cat." There are two sets of spots: original spots of the cat (p), and additional spots introduced from outside (p1). In the course of processing the negative image of the picture (n1), the following stages are observed: the whole overlapped picture, then the whole assembly of the spots, and finally the spots from the outside only. It enables one to extract an original image from "rubbish" pictures.

It should be noted that the processes of the temporal image evolution can be rather successfully described by solutions to the reaction-diffusion equations. For instance, Balkarey, Evtichov, and Elinson (1991) calculated the process of contour enhance-

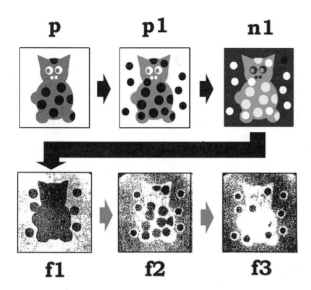

Figure 4.16
How many spots are on the skin of a cat. Original initial picture (p), initial picture together with additional spots statistically distributed (p1), and the negative image of the total picture (n1) are at the top of the figure. Below are: the whole overlapped picture (f1), the whole assembly of spots (f2), and spots introduced from outside (f3).

ment and some other features. The amplifying of small features and spoiled image restoration were demonstrated by Price, Wambacq, and Oosterlinck (1990).

All results discussed above were obtained using light-sensitive Belousov-Zhabotinsky-type media. (In Jinguji et al. 1995, the formation and propagation of rectangular chemical waves are studied.)

Other chemical reaction systems were used by Adamatzky and Tolmachev (Tolmachev and Adamatzky 1996; Adamatzky and Tolmachev 1997) to perform information processing operations. The reaction between palladium chloride and potassium iodide in a thin layer of agar gel made it possible to compute Voronoi diagrams (Tolmachev and Adamatzky 1996). The formation of Prussian blue in agar gel was used for computation of planar shape skeletons (Adamatzky and Tolmachev 1997).

4.8   More Complicated Problem: Finding the Shortest Path in a Labyrinth

The problem of searching for a path in a labyrinth determined by certain conditions is one of the most prevalent contemporary problems of high computational complexity.

There have been a variety of attempts to find effective algorithms for solving this problem (see, for instance, Adamatzky 1996 and references to it).

Proposals to use reaction-diffusion media for solving labyrinth problems have been discussed for the last decade and a half (see, for instance, Conrad et al. 1989; Babloyantz and Sepulchre 1991; Pérez-Muñuzuri, Pérez-Villar, and Chua 1993; Steinbock, Toth, and Showalter 1995; (Adamatzky 1996; Agladze et al. 1997; Muñuzuri and Chua 1998), relying extensively on the extremely high parallelism of such systems. The most important attempt was an experimental work by Steinbock, Toth, and Showalter (1995), who investigated the navigation of a complex labyrinth based on using the trigger wave processes of Belousov-Zhabotinsky media. Conclusions on the practical applicability of these reaction-diffusion systems has, until now, been pessimistic (Agladze et al. 1997) because of the very low velocity of trigger waves in these media.

Let us define a labyrinth as an object whose topological properties can be associated with a finite oriented graph. This means that the object should be composed of an arbitrary number of vertices and edges connecting them. Let us divide vertices into four classes: starting points that are entrances into the labyrinth (the power of the vertex is equal to 1), intermediate points (the power is ≥ 2), deadlocks and target points (the power of these vertices is equal to 1).

The graphs with the simplest structure are trees (figure 4.17). They have one starting point and an arbitrary number of branches and target points. Multigraphs containing cyclic combinations of edges are more complicated. In this case, at least two routes might be determined to exist between the chosen starting and target points.

The basic principles for using light-sensitive reaction-diffusion media to solve labyrinth problems will be discussed below for the case of relatively simple graphs, the target being to find the shortest path between a starting point and a chosen target point. Three principal points are assumed:

Hybridity
Any information processing system based on reaction-diffusion mechanisms and capable of solving labyrinth problems should be of a hybrid type. It should be a combination of a reaction-diffusion medium with a universal digital computer. This architecture enables the efficient performance of operations of high computational complexity (parallel spreading of a wave along all pathways of labyrinth, etc.) with fast digital processing of any intermediate data.

Let us make some remarks on how to design an effective computational procedure for finding paths in a labyrinth. Given the computational nature of the procedure, the labyrinth should be stored in memory as an image (in the simplest case, as a

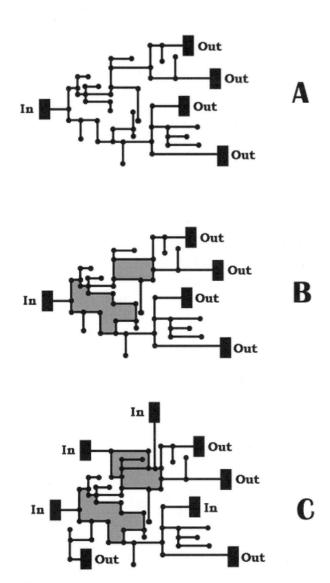

Figure 4.17
Labyrinth structures of different complexity. (*A*) Simple tree-type labyrinth. (*B*) Tree-type labyrinth containing cycles (filled with gray color). (*C*) Complicated labyrinth containing cycles and arbitrary numbers of starting and target points.

black-and-white image—e.g., a black picture of the labyrinth on a white background). Suppose that only the starting point of the labyrinth has been defined and
that a procedure is to be designed that would give the opportunity to record consecutive steps of the spreading wave. When the wave spreads along the path of the
labyrinth, the color changes to that of the background. A more sophisticated procedure could be developed that enables one to follow the wave front and to determine
the point where the black labyrinth path would disappear. In this case, it is impossible to distinguish between deadlocks and target points.

Therefore, to find a path in a labyrinth, both starting point and target points
should be defined. More precisely, certain features should be included in the labyrinth image to mark target points and to help to determine when a wave would reach
it.

Suppose now that the starting point and target points are known. Suppose also
that a trigger wave spreads along the labyrinth beginning from its starting point.
Eventually, the wave would reach the target point nearest to the starting point. After
that, other target points would be successfully determined.

It is easy to see that in this case, only the relative lengths of paths could be determined and not the paths themselves. This technique shows the principal feature of a
computational procedure for finding paths in a labyrinth based on wave processes
inherent in nonlinear reaction-diffusion media.

The spreading of the wave through a labyrinth is a parallel operation of high
computational complexity. A reaction-diffusion medium is able to perform this operation effectively, and consecutive steps of it could be stored in the memory of a
digital computing system.

It will be shown below that a computational digital procedure of low computational complexity could be outlined that is capable of finding paths in a labyrinth and
is based on the set of data stored in computer memory that describe the spreading
wave through the labyrinth.

Image Storage
The most important problem is how to store a labyrinth of arbitrary structure in the
reaction-diffusion medium for its further processing. Steinbock, Toth, and Showalter
(1995) solved this problem by cutting out rectangular regions of the membrane where
ferroin catalyst was immobilized. This procedure allowed the realization of a variety
of geometries and provided an effective two-dimensional system. Steinbock, Kettunen, and Showalter (1995, 1996) prepared a reaction-diffusion system by printing
an object image on the surface of a membrane, and using a solution of Belousov-

Zhabotinsky catalyst instead of ink. These methods, however, are not good enough for a computing device that should be capable of fast reorganization of labyrinth images in the course of its processing and of operative changing labyrinths of different structure (see below).

A light-sensitive B-Z reagent seems an appropriate candidate medium because of the ability of light-sensitive excitable media to store input information for a rather long period of time (Kuhnert, Agladze, and Krinsky 1989). The initial labyrinth image and steps of its further transformation in the medium (that is, spreading wave evolution) can be detected by a video camera and stored in a digital computer memory. After this, finding the shortest paths in a labyrinth can be reduced to image processing operations.

Organization

The main and decisive point of the problem under consideration is how to organize a wave process capable of spreading in a parallel mode through all possible paths of a labyrinth.

Two kinds of traveling processes inherent in interaction-diffusion systems are known (Reusser and Field 1979). The first of these represents the propagation of trigger waves due to the interaction between the chemical reaction and the diffusion of reaction components. The velocity of the trigger waves is very low (~ 0.05 mm/sec). The second of these, the so-called phase waves, propagate independently of diffusion along a phase gradient in an oscillatory medium. These phase waves are fast, but difficult to control.

The remarkable property of Ru-catalyzed Belousov-Zhabotinsky media is the possibility to control phase processes in the medium by light radiation (see also Agladze, Obata, and Yoshikawa 1995).

The actual picture projected on the surface of the medium is a combination of the chosen black-and-white image (initial labyrinth image) and the arbitrary halftone diffuse-light background produced by the optical system.

If the background is uniform, the input image emerges in the medium and changes simultaneously in a process of its evolution from one state to another at all points of the image. If the background is not uniform, an additional uncontrolled light component adds to the input image and the process of the image emergence becomes more complicated (figure 4.18).

The dynamics of the Belousov-Zhabotinsky reaction is controlled by the concentration of Br^- ions produced in the initial photochemical process occurring in the input of an initial image. Therefore the moment when an image emerges at a point

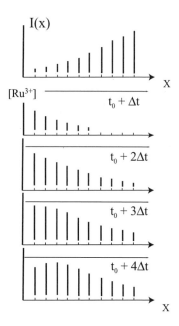

Figure 4.18
Principal scheme explaining the initiation of a light-induced phase wave. Non-uniform light background $I(x)$ is in the upper part of the figure. Temporal evolution of catalyst concentrations at different points of the medium is in the basic part of the figure.

of the medium (and the subsequent evolution of that image) is determined by the total exposure produced by the initial image and the uncontrolled nonuniform background.

This effect is revealed in the experiment as additional waves spreading along the image under investigation (figure 4.18). Let us define this effect as light-induced phase waves.

Suppose that the self-oscillating mode of a Belousov-Zhabotinsky reaction is chosen for solving labyrinth problems when negative and positive images of input picture alternate in the process of temporal image evolution produced by the medium. Suppose also that the quality of the optical system is high enough and the uncontrolled background is negligibly small. In this case, both the negative and positive images emerge in the process of the input picture evolution simultaneously at all their points.

Let us further suppose that the controlled nonuniform background of some pre-determined shape is superimposed on an initial labyrinth image (figure 4.19). This

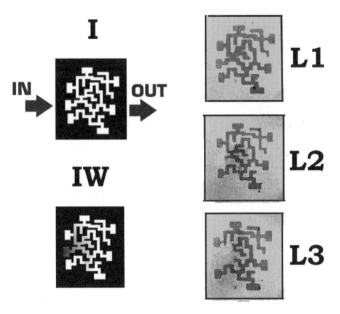

Figure 4.19
The initial labyrinth image (I), a non uniform background superimposed on the initial labyrinth image (IW), and first stages of the labyrinth evolution (phase wave spreading) in a Belousov-Zhabotinsky medium (L1–L3).

combined picture is used instead of the initial image. Then a light-induced phase wave controlled by the shape of the background will spread through the medium.

The procedure for finding the shortest paths in a labyrinth consisted of two basic stages. The first was the excitation of the phase wave at a chosen point of the labyrinth and recording the consecutive steps of the wave spreading through the labyrinth. The images of the labyrinth corresponding to these steps were stored in the computer memory. The second stage was the numerical processing of these images to determine the shortest path between starting and target points of the labyrinth.

Let us begin discussing the technique by investigating the case of the simplest linear treelike labyrinth, having one starting and several target points. The initial labyrinth picture is shown in figure 4.20.

Let a predetermined nonuniform and monotonically decreasing background be superimposed at a chosen point of the initial labyrinth picture. After projecting this combined picture on the surface of the Belousov-Zhabotinsky reagent, its negative image appears in the medium. At first, an image of the initial labyrinth emerges

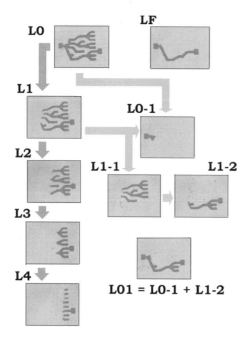

Figure 4.20
Finding the shortest path in a simple tree-type labyrinth. L0 is an initial image of the labyrinth in the Belousov-Zhabotinsky medium, L1–L4, some consecutive steps of its evolution in the process of the wave spreading; LF, the image of the shortest path in the labyrinth; L0-1, the pathway which the wave has passed during the first step of its spreading; L1-1, the result of Paint Bucket operations for L1 image; L1-2, the result of subtraction from the L1 image of parts unconnected with the target point (see details in text).

(black image on the white background). After that, a spreading wave appears, changing consecutively from black to the background color along the labyrinth pathway.

The time necessary to spread this wave through the labyrinth depends on the gradient of the superimposed background intensity. It is easy to make it rather quick (about 3–5 sec) and shorter than the lifetime of the negative image state when it evolves from a negative to a positive state.

The wave spreading in the labyrinth, beginning from the starting point of the labyrinth to its target points, is shown in figure 4.20. Because this process lasts for about 3–5 seconds, it is easy to record consecutive steps of this dispersal with a video camera and store these records in computer memory. Some of these records are shown in figure 4.20.

Finding the shortest path between the starting point and the target point was then performed using numerical image processing of stored records.

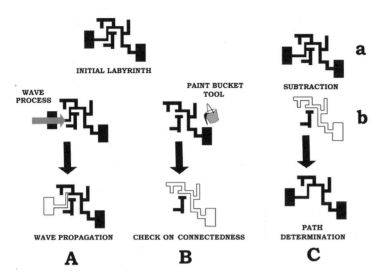

Figure 4.21
Basic steps of the procedure for finding the shortest paths in a labyrinth. (*A*) Wave propagation. (*B*) Check for connectedness. (*C*) Removal of deadlocks (subtraction of *B* and *A*).

Proposals have already been made on how to use a wave propagating through a labyrinth for finding minimal paths (Pérez-Muñuzuri, Pérez-Villar, and Chua 1993; Agladze et al. 1997; Muñuzuri and Chua 1998; see also references to Muñuzuri and Chua 1998). A different procedure estimated to be more effective computationally was used in this work.

In the process of the wave spreading through the labyrinth, when it passes over a branching point, it is divided into two (or more) fragments (figure 4.21). One of these is connected with the output, but the other one is not. It is easy to find the fragment connected with a target point of the labyrinth if a backward wave is initiated in the medium at this point. As a result, fragments connected with a target point change their color (from black to the color of labyrinth background) while the color of the nonconnected fragment remains unchanged.

If the complexity of the labyrinth is not too high, it is possible to change this auxiliary reaction-diffusion process by numerical processing images of the labyrinth stored in the memory of the computer. The technique is to fill black fragments with the background color ("paint bucket" operation), initiated at the target point of the labyrinth. Subtracting the resultant image from the initial labyrinth image enables one to remove fragments not connected with the output.

All image processing operations used for the implementation of the procedure discussed can be effectively performed by means of Adobe Photoshop 5.0 software.

Successive repetition of this procedure at every branching point gives the opportunity to exclude all blind channels (and paths to other possible target points) and to determine the path from the starting to the target point.

Two important remarks should be made about the procedure suitable for finding minimal paths in linear treelike labyrinths:

First, the advantage of the above procedure is that there is no need to determine through human intervention where a branching point occurs. The shortest path can be found in this case as a result of reiterated steps that consecutively process records of the spreading wave.

The sequence of operations for each step is as follows (assuming that record processing begins from L1; see figure 4.20):

• Subtraction of record L1 from the initial image of the labyrinth L0 to determine the pathway that the wave traversed going from initial to target points (L0-1)

• Filling fragments of L1 connected with a target point with background color (L1-1)

• Subtraction of L1-1 from L1—that is, rejection of parts not connected with a target point (L1-2, subtraction of any fragment from the background intensity should result in a zero level of intensity)

• Addition of L0-1 and L1-2 to determine the subsequent image of the labyrinth (L01), which is used at the next step instead of L0

• Changing L0 to L01

Each instantaneous image, after processing, is as follows:

• The same as the previous instantaneous image of the labyrinth if the wave has not passed over a branching point

• A changed instantaneous image where some parts of the labyrinth are rejected if the wave has passed over a branching point

The second important remark is that changing the backward wave via a paint bucket operation to determine parts of the labyrinth not connected with a target point is not absolutely correct, because the paint bucket operation is not carried out in parallel. It is possible to use this, however, if the complexity of the labyrinth is not very high and the time of labyrinth processing is not too long.

The procedure discussed is simple and effective in the case of linear treelike labyrinths where all possible pathways from a starting point to target points have nearly the same direction that coincide with the direction of the spreading wave. In a general case, however, this procedure should be changed because light-induced phase waves will spread along the gradient of the background intensity and not necessarily along the pathways of a labyrinth that can change direction significantly.

Changing the procedure offered allows us to elaborate the technique into something suitable for more complicated labyrinths.

This "step-by-step" technique is based on dividing the labyrinth into linear treelike parts and on the reiterative processing of each of them. An individual step of this technique would consist of the following operations:

· Determination of the labyrinth pathway direction at a chosen starting point

· Excitation of a phase wave at a chosen starting point that would spread along the gradient of the background intensity (which coincides in this case with the labyrinth pathway direction) and recording consecutive steps of the spreading

· Rejection of possible blind pathways

· Determination of pathway turning points

The "individual" step ends at a pathway turning point, which is considered as a starting point for the next step.

The most important part of this step-by-step technique is the determination of the pathway turning points. The results shown below were obtained by using visual control of the process of finding paths in a labyrinth. At the same time, algorithms could be offered for the implementation of this technique. (We are presently developing a computerized version of how to carry out the step-by-step procedure without a human being as an operator; this work will be published elsewhere.)

This main idea of moving step by step along a labyrinth pathway (as used here) is analogous to a numerical simulation approach successfully developed by Muñuzuri and Chua (1998) for finding the shortest paths in an arbitrary complex labyrinth.

An example of finding the shortest path in a labyrinth based on the technique discussed is shown in figure 4.22.

The important feature of this case is that the labyrinth under investigation is of a multigraph type containing a cyclic combination of edges. Therefore the path between starting and target points, after using the step-by-step technique, contains some remaining part of this cycle (see figure 4.22, LF1). But this will disappear (see figure 4.22, LF2) if the step-by-step technique is repeated over and over, with the shortest path obtained (figure 4.22, LF1) becoming the new labyrinth.

Several points should be made about the practical implementation of this algorithm and for the estimation of its efficiency. The main operational feature of the

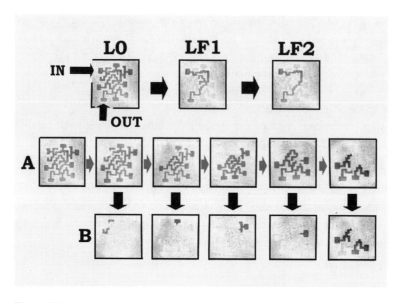

Figure 4.22
Finding the shortest path in an arbitrary labyrinth. L0 is the initial image of the labyrinth in the Belousov-Zhabotinsky medium; (*A*) stages of its evolution; LF1 and LF2 are images of the shortest paths (see details in text); (*B*) results of Paint Bucket operations.

Ru-based Belousov-Zhabotinsky system is that it is highly sensitive to small variations in experimental conditions. The quality of the optical system used for the input of initial data should therefore be high, with the reaction vessel being thereafter thoroughly shielded from outside light radiation.

The quality of images produced by the Belousov-Zhabotinsky medium is determined by the constant thickness of the medium layer at all points. Two methods of medium formation satisfying this condition have been elaborated (Rambidi, Kuular, and Machaeva 1998; see below).

Let us make some remarks on the efficiency of the technique discussed above.

When a wave goes over a branching point, some part of the labyrinth is removed as a result of the procedure used. The more complicated the labyrinth is, the larger the parts that will be rejected in the process of finding the shortest paths. Therefore, the remarkable feature of this technique is that its efficiency becomes higher as the complexity of the labyrinth increases.

Using a step-by-step procedure significantly increases the time necessary to find the shortest paths in a labyrinth. The efficiency of the procedure depends on the operational time of the reaction-diffusion medium and on the number of labyrinth turning points in this case. Nevertheless, it is sufficiently higher than the efficiency of procedures using trigger waves (Steinbock, Toth, and Showalter 1995; Agladze et al. 1997). The time necessary for processing a labyrinth of average complexity is about 5 minutes, assuming a cycle time of the medium of about 40 seconds. This time is less by an order of magnitude in comparison with that of the "trigger wave procedure" (Steinbock, Toth, and Showalter 1995). Another important feature is that the operational time is linear with the number of the labyrinth pathway turning points.

4.9   Recognition Capabilities of Coupled Reaction-Diffusion Systems

During recent decades, most of the experimental and theoretical investigations on reaction-diffusion systems have been devoted to systems wherein the reaction medium was assumed to be continuous. But many interesting phenomena can be observed in cases of discrete reaction-diffusion media, particularly in systems that can be considered as a set of subsystems.

Coupled reaction-diffusion dynamic regimes in such systems have been investigated by different research groups (see, for instance, Stuchl and Marek 1982; Laplante and Erneux 1992; Dechert et al. 1996, and references in them). The following discussion will be from the point of view of designing information processing systems. Let us consider a system built of the simplest chemical elements (subsystems) that have only one state variable:

$$dx_i/dt = f(x_i) \tag{4.12}$$

Because this is a one-dimensional system, the only attractors that are present are fixed points. They may be stable or unstable.

There are three possible cases of the system dynamics that are described by this equation (figure 4.23). Two of these are cases when the system has one fixed point; the third has three fixed points. A simple analysis of stability shows that if $f(x)$ has only one zero, the fixed point is stable. If $f(x)$ has three zeros, there are two fixed points where $df(x)/dx < 0$ are stable and the third where $df(x)/dx > 0$ is unstable. This is the case of a bistable system that could be in two different states.

Let us consider a network consisting of systems of the type shown in equation 4.12, which are coupled by diffusion, mass transfer (pumping), or some other stimulus. If all $f(x)$ have only one zero, the network has only one stable state, which is homogeneous. If $f(x)$ has three zeros, however, then the network may have up to 2^N steady states. Thus each element in the network can, in principle, have two states, and the patterns of the network are given by different distributions of states corresponding to each element in the network.

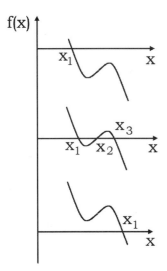

Figure 4.23
Different cases of nonlinear dynamics in distributed one-dimensional systems.

There have been several experimental examples of stationary structure manifestations in coupled reaction-diffusion systems. Let us consider in more detail one of these reported by Laplante and Erneux (1992). They investigated a system of sixteen stirred-tank reactors arranged in a linear geometry. Each reactor was coupled to its next neighbors by mass exchange. The chlorite-iodine reaction

$$5\,ClO_2{}^- + 2\,I_2 + 2\,H_2O \rightarrow 5\,Cl^- + 4\,IO_3{}^- + 4\,H^+$$

was used as a reaction medium. This is a bistable system whose states depend on flow rates. At low rates, only high iodine states exist. At intermediate flow rates, the autocatalytic mechanism results in a bistable state of either low or high iodine concentrations. The state of each reactor was determined visually by adding starch to the reactor inflow. Two 16-channel peristaltic pumps (for chlorite and iodide reagents) were used to feed each reactor with an identical flow of reagents.

Two more sixteen-channel peristaltic pumps implemented mass transfer. Reactors were split into two groups, odd and even, to avoid experimental drawbacks. The principal scheme of reactor interconnections is shown in figure 4.24.

Laplante and Erneux (1992) investigated two different cases of network dynamics. In the first of these, reactor 1 was fed with a chlorite solution only (asymmetrical boundary conditions). Then a wave of switching from high iodide concentration to

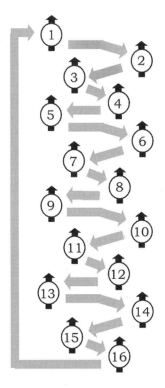

Figure 4.24
Physical configuration of the continuous flow stirred tank reactor. Black arrows correspond to feeding of each reactor, gray arrows show reactor coupling. See details in the text.

low was observed in the process of network evolution after switching on the reactor coupling.

If the boundary condition was symmetrical (that is, reactor 1 and 16 were fed simultaneously with chlorite solution only) several different stationary structures were observed depending on coupling flow rates (figure 4.25).

Ross and his coworkers (see, for instance, Hjelmfelt, Weinberger, and Ross 1991, 1992; Hjelmfelt and Ross 1992; Hjelmfelt, Schneider, and Ross 1993; Hjelmfelt and Ross 1995) made a decisive step in understanding the importance of coupled reaction-diffusion systems for information processing. They used the network architecture of these systems to theoretically consider the possibilities of implementing a Turing machine (Hjelmfelt, Weinberger, and Ross 1991), finite-state machines (Hjelmfelt, Weinberger, and Ross 1992), and Hopfield-type neural networks (Hjelmfelt and Ross 1992).

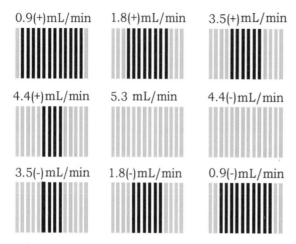

Figure 4.25
Scheme of stationary structures in assembly of 16 coupled reactors obtained under symmetrical boundary conditions. Black blocks correspond to high iodine concentrations, grey blocks to low iodine concentrations. Exchange rates are shown in each plate ("+" means that the structure was obtained when exchange rate increased, "−" corresponds to a decrease of the exchange rate.)

It was shown by and Colleagues Ross (Hjelmfelt, Schneider, and Ross 1993; Hjelmfelt and Ross 1995) that chemically implemented neural networks display pattern-recognition capabilities. They used a bistable chemical medium based on the following reaction:

$$2\ IO_3^- + 5\ H_3AsO_3 + 2\ H^+ \rightarrow I_2 + 5\ H_3AsO_4 + H_2O$$

The processing elements of neural networks are called neurons. Each neuron has two states (like those of McCulloch and Pitts 1943) determined by the state variable x. For ith neuron, $x = 0$ and $x = 1$ correspond to "not firing" and "firing" states. Therefore a typical Hopfield network is unimodal (i.e., it has only one excited state).

Neurons in the net are coupled and the strength of connections is determined by matrix T. Here T_{ij} is the strength of connection between ith and jth neurons. Matrix T is symmetrical in the case of a Hopfield neural net ($T_{ij} = T_{ji}$). It has zero diagonal elements ($T_{ii} = 0$). The differences between neural nets are determined by the architecture of connections that are given in the T matrix.

The initial distribution of neuron states in the network could be defined as the initial pattern. This pattern is transformed by the network in a process of its evolution according to rules defined by matrix T.

A number of patterns could be stored in a neural network. One of the most well-known ways to do it is the so-called Hebbian rule:

Suppose that patterns that should be stored are:

$$V^\mu = \{V_1^\mu, \ldots, V_N^\mu) \qquad \mu = 1, 2, \ldots, M \tag{4.13}$$

Then for binary vectors, the Hebbian rule is defined as:

$$T_{ij} = \sum_\mu (2V_i - 1)(2V_j - 1) \tag{4.14}$$

It means that:

• Two elements T_{ij}, which are in the same state in the majority of the stored patterns, are connected with a strength that depends on the number of patterns in which these elements have the same state.

• Elements that are in opposite states in the majority of the stored patterns are unconnected.

In the case of chemical neural networks, Ross and his coworkers (Hjelmfelt, Schneider, and Ross 1993; Hjelmfelt and Ross 1995) used a modified Hebbian rule to store patterns, where the connection strength between elements i and j was defined as

$$T_{ij} = \lambda\theta\left\{\sum_\mu (2R_i^\mu - 1)(2R_j^\mu - 1)\right\} \tag{4.15}$$

where R_i^μ and R_j^μ are activities of systems i and j in the pattern μ, λ is a coupling constant—that is, the strength of reagent flow (in the case of chemical networks)—and:

$$\theta\{x\} = x \qquad \text{if } x \geq 0$$

$$\theta\{x\} = 0 \qquad \text{if } x < 0$$

It was shown (Hjelmfelt and Ross 1993) that this modified rule generates stable states corresponding to the stored patterns.

The theoretical approach developed by Ross and his coworkers proved to be a basis for experimental implementation (Laplante et al. 1995). A set of eight continuous-flow stirred-tank (CSTR) reactors was used to store three patterns. Mass transfer coupled this network of CSTRs. The matrix of connections as calculated according to equation 4.15 is shown in figure 4.26.

Suppose that the states of CSTRs when coupling is switched off are set according to some patterns. After switching on coupling, two opportunities are possible:

• The network of CSTRs will have a homogeneous distribution of states if the input pattern is far in phase space from any stored pattern.

• one of the stored patterns is recalled if the input pattern is "near" to the stored one.

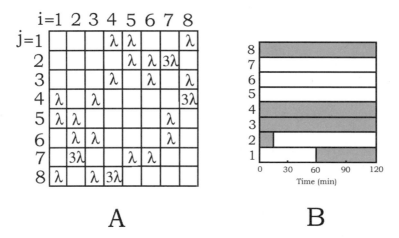

A   B

Figure 4.26
Matrix of connections for a chemical network having recognition capabilities (*A*; see text) and the process of recognition of a 10110001 pattern beginning from a 01110001 distribution (*B*).

The performance of this chemical network was tested with three different sets of patterns having a variety of initial conditions (small differences in comparison with stored patterns). The efficiency of recalling stored patterns proved to be quite good, but the time needed proved to be about 60 minutes (see figure 4.26).

The investigation of chemical network recognition capabilities performed by Laplante and coworkers (Laplante et al. 1995) was the first where pattern recognition has been experimentally proved. It is necessary, however, to mention that the setup used by them was too cumbersome to be an efficient operating device.

There are other possibilities for designing multilevel systems that have recognition capabilities. A chemical system, based on electrical coupling of subsystems (Dechert et al. 1996) seems to be promising. In any case, the opportunities of this approach are far from exhausted. New, more powerful devices could be designed in the near future.

4.10   Numerical Modeling: From the Generation of Button Textures up to Pattern Formation in Ecological Systems

The variety of reaction-diffusion simulations performed during recent decades has been extremely broad. It should not be forgotten that the first fundamental work in this field was the article by Alan Turing entitled "The chemical basis of morphogenesis" (1952). It contained simulations of the differentiation processes in living entities based on nonlinear kinetic equations describing a set of coupled chemical reactions. This article was also one of the first examples showing that nonlinear dynamic mechanisms could be responsible for the high behavioral complexity of a biological system.

This biological research using reaction-diffusion simulations covers a wide range of problems beginning from models of biological pattern formation such as giraffe or zebra patterns up to applications in population dynamics.

In the early seventies, Gierer and Meinhardt (1972) used a reaction-diffusion approach to elaborate a theory of biological pattern formation. This approach was later further developed (Murray 1981; Meinhardt and Klinger 1987), particularly by Meinhardt and Klinger, who offered a model for pattern formation on the shells of mollusks. A similar technique was used for purely practical purposes, such as for computer graphics. It gave the opportunity to generate different reaction-diffusion textures for picturesque buttons, specific art painting, and so on (Turk 1991; Witkin and Kass 1991). It should be mentioned that the high behavioral complexity of reaction-diffusion media as revealed in textures seems to be a basis of the human sense of beauty.

Also very important were repeated approaches to simulate regimes inherent in Belousov-Zhabotinsky and other reaction-diffusion media. This enabled the calculation of different reaction-diffusion patterns including evolution of breathing spots, spiral and labyrinthine patterns (see, for instance, Hagberg and Meron 1994; Haim et al. 1996).

Simulations of reaction-diffusion regimes in three-dimensional media have been the standard method up to now because to obtain experimental information is extremely difficult. The simulations seem to indicate that increasing the structural complexity of the system by going from two to three dimensions leads to a large increase in behavioral complexity of the medium (Winfree and Strogatz 1983, 1984).

Simulating the image processing capabilities of reaction-diffusion systems has been another remarkable field of interest for different research groups. Yakhno and Colleagues (Nuidel and Yakhno 1989; Belliustin et al. 1991) used a set of integro-differential equations that describe media having short-range nonlocal interactions. They found out that their simulations were capable of describing a number of image processing operations (figure 4.27). They embrace:

· Contour enhancement

· Transformation of halftone images into high-contrast ones

· Image skeletonizing

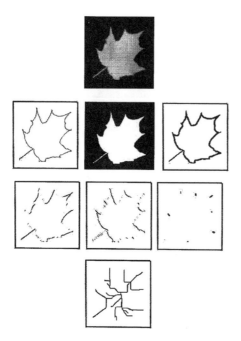

Figure 4.27
Numerical simulation of image processing operations based on the reaction-diffusion equation. Initial half-tone picture is shown in upper part of the figure. Results of simulation which can be different due to diverse choice of coupling functions (see text): enhancement of thin and thick contours, contrast enhancement, enhancement of lines having different slope and corners of the image, and skeleton of the image.

• Extraction of lines having a given direction
• Calculation of invariant features

Some of these results were obtained a little earlier by Price, Wambacq, and Oosterlinck (1990).

These simulations are in good correspondence with experimental results conforming at the theoretical level, thus confirming the close correlation between the behavioral complexity of a system and its ability to solve problems of high computational complexity.

The development of cellular automata techniques has also been an important part of numerical simulations of reaction-diffusion media. Between different realizations of this technique, two directions of investigations should be mentioned:

Tyson and his coworkers (Gerhardt, Schuster, and Tyson 1990; Weimar, Tyson, and Watson, 1992) succeeded in simulating complicated modes of Belousov-

Zhabotinsky-type media. Markus and Hess (1990) have also offered a very interesting isotropic cellular automaton model for modeling excitable media.

Adamatzky (1994, 1995, 1996b) used cellular automata calculations to analyze important characteristics of reaction-diffusion media and the potentialities of their practical use.

Let us mention also that many attempts have been made during the last decade to use nonlinear dynamic ideas for explaining the behavior of complex systems inherent in different fields of human activity (neurobiology, ecology, economics, and so on). Many of these have been covered in the book *Interdisciplinary Approaches to Nonlinear Complex Systems* (Haken and Mikhailov 1993).

4.11   What Next: Toward a Biomolecular Computer?

Prediction of the future seems to be quite often more of a complacent pastime than an activity producing useful results. Too many presently unknown factors might dramatically change contemporary, seemingly reliable tendencies. Let us try therefore to consider the state of the art in the field of information processing capabilities of reaction-diffusion systems. Let us discuss the new experimental and theoretical accomplishments that have occurred in this field during the last several years that might change approaches of design and increase greatly the information processing potentialities in reaction-diffusion systems.

An attempt was made above to demonstrate that reaction-diffusion systems are capable of effectively implementing image processing operations, labyrinth problems, and recognition capabilities—the most widely-known problems of high computational complexity.

The very remarkable feature of the last several years has been that different research groups have begun to use a reaction-diffusion approach to solve diverse practical problems. Sendiña-Nadal and Colleagues (Sendiña-Nadal et al. 1998) experimentally and theoretically investigated percolation thresholds based on chemical light-sensitive excitable media. Light excitation enables one to create a number of sites of predetermined shape and size. Spreading a planar wave front in this medium gave the opportunity to observe different percolation thresholds. The system investigated (Sendiña-Nadal et al. 1998) is similar to the situation found in experiments of disordered semiconductors. Using similar techniques, Sendiña-Nadal and Colleagues (Sendiña-Nadal et al. 1998b) also studied wave propagation in a medium with disordered excitability.

Yoshikawa and his coworkers (Yoshikawa, Motoike, and Kajiya 1997; Yamaguchi et al. 1998; Motoike and Yoshikawa, 1999) found that unidirectional signal transmission with an excited propagating wave can be generated by a chemical diode—a spatially asymmetric connection between excitable fields separated by a diffusion field. They discovered that such a diode function could be created both in an actual experiment (with a Belousov-Zhabotinsky medium) and in computer simulations. These investigations open the way to design a massively parallel computational medium.

One should emphasize that fundamental experimental accomplishments are the basis of the substantial progress of the last several years, greatly increasing the reliability of experimental data. The decisive step toward experimental implementation of the information processing capabilities inherent in these media had been made by Kuhnert and Colleagues (Kuhnert 1986, 1986b; Kuhnert, Agladze, and Krinsky 1989), who originally suggested the use of light-sensitive reaction-diffusion Belousov-Zhabotinsky media for information processing.

The reliability of data has improved greatly during the past decade. Two basic achievements are behind this improvement: the advent of continuous-flow unstirred reactors and the use of polymer matrices, in which the reaction-diffusion phenomena can proceed. The use of polymer materials in reaction-diffusion systems as an indispensable component has proved to be a design solution of very great importance.

Many useful ways of using polymer materials for investigating chemical oscillators are known (for details, see Rambidi, Kuular, and Machaeva 1998). Nevertheless, the design of information processing devices based on reaction-diffusion systems faces a number of additional problems: The investigation of information processing operations is based on the visualization of processes occurring in these systems. Therefore a high-quality level of detection of the structures arising in such processes is necessary.

Let us discuss the main potentialities of using polymer materials in reaction-diffusion systems, with a view to their information processing applications (Rambidi, Kuular, and Machaeva 1998).

1. There are several main techniques that depend strongly on the peculiarities of the input and output of initial data to and from the system and the methods of control. Optical methods have been, until now, the basic tools for the input and output of information to and from reaction-diffusion media and for the control of medium functioning. Projecting an image under investigation—that is, a nonuniform spatial light intensity distribution onto the surface of the medium—causes the formation of a nonuniform spatial distribution in the system components and provokes the beginning of the subsequent system evolution.

Two main factors determine the adequacy of conversion of an input light picture to a molecular distribution corresponding to this picture. The first of these is the uniformity of the primary light intensity distribution used for the input of data. If the distribution is nonuniform, it is equivalent to an additional nonuniform background that is superimposed on the image under processing. The degree of light uniformity should be rather high because the sensitivity of the medium to changes in light intensity has proved to be significant.

The second factor is the constancy of the medium layer thickness. If the thickness is nonuniform (figure 4.28), the stages of image evolution do not proceed simultaneously at different points of the image under processing. This effect hampers image processing by reaction-diffusion media.

2. Using polymer materials as inert matrices in which the reaction-diffusion proceeds greatly improves the quality of images in the media. A flat two-dimensional layer of

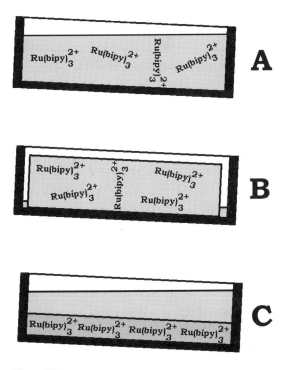

Figure 4.28
Different realizations of light-sensitive polymer based reaction-diffusion media: a thin flat layer of liquid medium (A), a liquid medium in a polymer matrix, for instance in thin flat layer of polyacrylamide gel (B), a system where a catalyst is immobilized on a solid support (C).

a polymer usually contains 80–90 percent water in the polymer framework. This water can be replaced easily by a solution of the reaction-diffusion medium. As a result, this system (polymer plus reagent) seems to be of low sensitivity to mechanical forces (vibrations and so on), hydrodynamic effects, and surface evaporation. Moreover, it proves to be practically insensitive to the inclinations of the system layer with respect to the Earth's vertical—that is, the thickness of the medium layer becomes constant.

3. Polymer media are very convenient for designing spatially nonuniform versions of reaction-diffusion systems. They enable one to design predetermined spatial gel structures and to determine, as a result, the mode of functioning of the reaction-diffusion system.

Let us mention only two of the most simple and naive examples. Immobilization of the catalyst in the Belousov-Zhabotinsky reaction onto the surface of a solid carrier transforms the system into a pseudo-two-level system. In this case, the reaction components are in the liquid phase but the reaction itself proceeds at the boundary of the phases.

Steinbock and coworkers (Steinbock, Kettunen, and Showalter 1996) used a simple two-level system for the implementation of chemical wave logic gates. They plotted a drawing of the gate onto the surface of a membrane placed on the agarose polymer layer. All other components of the Belousov-Zhabotinsky reaction were in the volume of the gel. The wave proceeding in the gel switched the logic states of the device.

4. A polymer matrix could control the mode of a reaction-diffusion system designed on the basis of this matrix. Kazanskaya and Colleagues (Kazanskaya et al. 1996; Eremeev, Kukhtin, and Kazanskaya 1998) elaborated two different systems of this kind. The first one consisted of polymer membrane containing a photosensitive component—spiropyrane. When the spiropyrane is incorporated into the polymer membrane, its potential changes upon UV irradiation of the membrane surface. The ionophore nonactin was introduced into the membrane to couple the membrane photoresponse with urea hydrolysis catalyzed by urease. The urea hydrolysis proceeded in another polymer matrix combined with a photosensitive membrane.

The second system was a two-level spatially combined one. It consisted of a thermosensitive polymer matrix saturated by urease. Enzyme activity was a function of temperature near the point of reversible collapse of the gel.

Further investigations in this field seem to give the opportunity to design complicated systems capable of performing complex logical functions.

5. Finally, possibilities exist to design chemical nonlinear dynamic systems wherein the polymer is used as one of the components of the chemical process. This could

provide an opportunity to create a predetermined structure in the gel matrix at some stages of the dynamic process. This structure of the gel will determine the mode of subsequent processes in the matrix. In some sense, this seems to be the analogue of long-term memory organization.

The above-discussed various design solutions based on polymer materials are currently at different levels of understanding and implementation.

Let us mention that further progress of experimental technique should lie in the basis implementing the above possibilities. Recently, new phenomena were investigated that seem to be quite promising for elaborating more effective information processing devices.

Toth, Gaspar, and Showalter (1994) performed a detailed study of signal transmission through capillary tubes. Possibilities of controlling the shape of the wave front based on light excitations of the reaction-diffusion medium were offered by Sendiña-Nadal and Colleagues (Sendiña-Nadal et al. 1997).

The coupling of chemical oscillators was studied (Miyakawa et al. 1995; Miyakawa and Mizoguchi 1998) in systems formed by immersing cation exchange beads loaded with ferroin in the Belousov-Zhabotinsky reagent. Cation exchange beads of about 500 μm in diameter were used.

Other investigations of sufficient interest should be mentioned:

• Formation of scroll waves in photosensitive media (Amemiya et al. 1998)

• Wave propagation along the line of a velocity jump (Steinbock, Zykov, and Muller 1993)

• Splitting of autowaves in an active medium (Muñuzuri, Pérez-Villar, and Markus 1997)

• Some works concerning interactions of spiral waves (Ruiz-Villarreal et al. 1996; Muñuzuri, Pérez-Muñuzuri, and Pérez-Villar 1998)

All these examples show that the last several years have been quite successful in further progress of experimental techniques. Some of these studies, moreover, seem to be important for constructing a new generation of information processing devices.

Based on the previous discussion, one should also conclude that multilevel systems will be an important source for further progress in this field. It was stressed above that nonlinear mechanisms and multilevel architecture are two basic features of a complex system with increased behavioral complexity.

The last point that should be considered in discussing future potentialities of the reaction-diffusion paradigm is the information processing nature of reaction-diffusion systems. This point is very important for choosing the fields where this paradigm should be the most effective.

In the late 1980s, Conrad (1989) discussed in detail the analogy and lack of analogy between information features of the brain and that of digital von Neumann computers. In the background of this analysis lies the trade-off principle formulated by Conrad (1985):

"A system cannot at the same time be effectively programmable at the level of structure, amendable to evolution by variation and selection, and computationally efficient" (464).

Proceeding from the trade-off principle, Conrad paid attention just to those differences between the information features of the brain and von Neumann computers that are of fundamental significance (figure 4.29). He concluded that according to

🖥	?	☺
PROGRAMMED FROM OUTSIDE	SELF-ORGANIZING	SELF-ORGANIZING
STRUCTURALLY PROGRAMMABLE	STRUCTURALLY NON-PROGRAMMABLE	STRUCTURALLY NON-PROGRAMMABLE
SEQUENTIAL USE OF RESOURCES	HIGHLY PARALLEL	MASSIVELY PARALLEL
DISCRETE DYNAMICS	CONTINUOUS AND DISCRETE DYNAMICS	DISCRETE AND CONTINUOUS DYNAMICS
HIGHLY CONSTRAINED	HIGHLY INTERACTIVE	HIGHLY INTERACTIVE
HORIZONTAL FLOW OF INFORMATION	VERTICAL INFORMATION FLOW	VERTICAL INFORMATION FLOW

Figure 4.29
Brain [☺] machine - [🖥] - reaction-diffusion processor [?] analogies-disanalogies.

these differences, von Neumann computers could not pass the Turing test (Turing 1950)—namely, that the intellect of the brain differs appreciably from the possible degree of von Neumann computer intellect.

Conrad (1989) stressed that information processing devices based on principles of information processing at the molecular level should possess information features extremely similar to the information features of the brain. Therefore it seems reasonable to consider information features of reaction-diffusion systems that can now be designed utilizing contemporary laboratory technology (Rambidi 1994).

Let us choose as such devices a reaction-diffusion system using Belousov-Zhabotinsky media. Let us consider the basic information features of this device.

First, there is a high degree of organization inherent in molecular media of this type. These media display gradualism (i.e., small changes of active medium composition), which, within definite limits, lead only to small quantitative and not qualitative changes of system dynamics.

Also, Belousov-Zhabotinsky media have other necessary characteristics for displaying adaptive behavior, as according to Ashby (1960). Among these is the nature of the interaction of the system with the environment, feedback organization, and so on. Therefore we can conclude that it could really be possible to create a device that is capable of learning, has multilevel architecture, and has a high degree of behavioral complexity.

It is easy to see that the lack of structural programmability, a high degree of parallelism, mixed continuous and discrete dynamics, and highly developed couplings between elements of the medium are typical in reaction-diffusion means (see figure 4.29). Even simple reaction-diffusion systems display a vertical flow of transmission and processing information. Also, even in a simple system, the following can be determined:

• The level of macro-micro type transformation of information (in particular, photochemical transformation of a light two-dimensional picture into pseudo-two-dimensional distribution of reaction components)

• Dynamics at the molecular level implementing a definite information process

• The level of micro-macro information transformation (i.e., physicochemical reading information)

Unlike the digital von Neumann computer, the reaction-diffusion device is not a rigid, structurally predetermined system. Its dynamics depends on the composition and control stimuli variations. It enables implementation of rather effective control of the dynamics.

In general, a detailed comparison of the information features of the brain, the digital von Neumann computer, and reaction-diffusion media leads to the conclusion that there is a sufficiently greater analogy between features of reaction-diffusion media and the brain. From the considerations discussed above, it seems to follow that it is the complicated nonlinear dynamics that determines the information features inherent in reaction-diffusion biomolecular devices. At the same time, the surprising resemblance of features of the brain and simple enough reaction-diffusion systems that determine the general principles of information processing (self-organization, high parallelism, vertical flow of information, etc.) is striking.

The brain is immeasurably richer in its functions than a specialized reaction-diffusion device. The completeness of solving intellectual problems by brain exceeds all that can be reached nowadays by any "man-made" device. Nevertheless, the analogy of information processing features seems to be the evidence that there exists a set of logical operations inherent in reaction-diffusion systems that are optimal and whose mechanisms are close to the analogous mechanisms of the brain.

References

Adamatzky, A. I. 1994. Constructing a discrete generalized Voronoi diagram in reaction-diffusion media. *Neural Netw. World* 6: 635–643.

Adamatzky, A. I. 1995. Computation of discrete convex hull in homogeneous automata networks. *Neural Netw. World* 3: 241–254.

Adamatzky, A. I. 1996. Computation of shortest path in cellular automata. *Math. Comput. Modelling* 23: 105–113.

Adamatzky, A. I. 1996b. On the particle like waves in the discrete model of excitable medium. *Neural Netw. World* 1: 3–10.

Adamatzky, A., and D. Tolmachev. 1997. Chemical processor for computation of skeleton of planar shape. *Adv. Mater. Opt. Electron.* 7: 135–139.

Agladze, K., S. Obata, and K. Yoshikawa. 1995. Phase shift as a basis of image processing in oscillating chemical medium. *Physica D* 84: 238–245.

Agladze, K., N. Magome, R. Aliev, T. Yamaguchi, and K. Yoshikawa. 1997. Finding the optimal path with the aid of chemical waves. *Physica D* 106: 247–254.

Amemiya, T., P. Kettunen, S. Kadar, T. Yamaguchi, and K. Showalter. 1998. Formation and evolution of scroll waves in photosensitive excitable media. *Chaos* 8: 872–878.

Arbib, M. A. 1989. Schemas and neural networks for sixth generation computing. *J. Parallel Distributed comput.* 6: 185–216.

Arbib, M. A. 1994. The brain as a metaphor for sixth generation computing. In *Computing with Biological Metaphors*, ed. Ray Paton, 107–123. London: Chapman and Hall.

Ashby, W. R. 1960. *Design for a Brain*. London: Chapman and Hall.

Babloyantz, A., and J. A. Sepulchre. 1991. Target and spiral waves in oscillatory media in the presence of obstacles. *Physica D* 49: 52–60.

Balkarey, Y. I., M. G. Evitkhov, and M. I. Elinson. 1991. Autowave media and neural networks. *Proc. SPIE* 1621: 238–249.

Beer, S. 1970. Managing modern complexity. *Futures* 2: 245–257.

Belliustin, N. S., S. O. Kuznetsov, I. V. Nuidel, and V. G. Yakhno. 1991. Neural networks with close nonlocal coupling for analyzing composite image. *Neurocomputing* 3: 231–246.

Casti, J. 1979. *Connectivity, Complexity, and Catastrophe in Large-Scale Systems.* New York: John Wiley and Sons.

Conrad, M. 1985. On design principles for a molecular computer. *Commun. ACM* 28: 464–480.

Conrad, M. 1989. The brain-machine disanalogy. *BioSystems* 22: 197–213.

Conrad, M., R. R. Campfner, K. G. Kirby, E. N. Rizki, G. Schleis, R. Smalz, and R. Trenary. 1989. Towards an artificial brain. *BioSystems* 23: 175–218.

Davydov, A. S. 1984. Solitons in molecular systems (in Russian). Kiev: Naukova Dumka.

Dechert, G., K.-P. Zeier, D. Lebender, and F. W. Schneider. 1996. Recognition of phase patterns in a chemical reactor network. *J. Phys. Chem.* 100: 19043–19048.

Ellias, S. A., and S. Grossberg. 1975. Pattern formation, contrast control, and oscillations in the short-term memory of shunting on-center off-surround networks. *Biol. Cybern.* 20: 69–98.

Eremeev, N. L., A. V. Kukhtin, and N. F. Kazanskaya. 1998. *BioSystems* 45: 141–149.

Field, R. J., and M. Burger, eds. 1985. *Oscillations and Traveling Waves in Chemical Systems.* New York: Wiley-Interscience.

Gerhardt, M., H. Schuster, and J. J. Tyson. 1990. A cellular automaton model of excitable media including curvature and dispersion. *Science* 247: 1563–1566.

Gierer, A., and H. Meinhardt. 1972. A theory of biological pattern formation. *Kybernetik* 12: 30–39.

Goldbetter, A. 1997. *Biochemical Oscillations and Cellular Rhythms.* Cambridge: Cambridge University Press.

Grossberg, S. 1973. Contour enhancement, short term memory, and constancies in reverberating neural networks. *Stud. Appl. Math.* 52: 217–257.

Grossberg, S. 1976. On the development of feature detectors in the visual cortex with applications in learning and reaction-diffusion systems. *Biol. Cybern.* 21: 145–159.

Grossberg, S. 1988. Nonlinear neural networks: Principles, mechanisms, and architectures. *Neural Networks* 1: 17–61.

Hagberg, A., and E. Meron. 1994. From labyrinthine patterns to spiral turbulence. *Phys. Rev. Lett.* 72: 2494–2497.

Haim, D., G. Li, Q. Quyang, W. D. McCormick, H. L. Swinney, A. Hagberg, and E. Meron. 1996. Breathing spots in a reaction-diffusion system. *Phys. Rev. Lett.* 77: 190.

Haken, H., and A. Mikhailov, eds. 1993. *Interdisciplinary Approaches to Nonlinear Complex Systems.* Berlin-Heidelberg: Springer Verlag.

Hjelmfelt, A., and J. Ross. 1992. Chemical implementation and thermodynamics of collective neural networks. *Proc. Natl. Acad. Sci. USA* 89: 388–391.

Hjelmfelt, A., and J. Ross. 1993. Mass-coupled chemical systems with computational properties. *J. Phys. Chem.* 97: 7988–7992.

Hjelmfelt, A., and J. Ross. 1995. Implementation of logic functions and computations by chemical kinetics. *Physica D* 84: 180–193.

Hjelmfelt, A., E. D. Weinberger, and J. Ross. 1991. Chemical implementation of neural networks and Turing machines. *Proc. Natl. Acad. Sci. USA* 88: 10983–10987.

Hjelmfelt, A., E. D. Weinberger, and J. Ross. 1992. Chemical implementation of finite-state machines. *Proc. Natl. Acad. Sci. USA* 89: 383–387.

Hjelmfelt, A., F. W. Schneider, and J. Ross. 1993. Pattern recognition in coupled chemical kinetic systems. *Science* 260: 335–337.

Jinguji, M., M. Ishihara, T. Nakazawa, and H. Nagashima. 1995. Formation and propagation of rectangular chemical waves in the Belousov-Zhabotinsky reaction. *Physica D* 84: 246–252.

Kapral, R., and K. Showalter, eds. 1995. *Chemical Waves and Patterns*. Boston: Kluwer Academic Publishers.

Kazanskaya, N., M. Kuchtin, M. Manenkova, N. Repetilov, L. Yarysheva, O. Arzhakova, A. Volynskii, and N. Bakeyev. 1996. FET sensors with robust photosensitive polymer membranes for detection of ammonium ions and urea. *Biosens. Bioelectron.* 11: 253–256.

Klir, G. J. 1985. Complexity: Some general observations. *Syst. Res.* 2: 131–140.

Kuhnert, L. 1986. A new optical photochemical memory device in a light-sensitive chemical active medium. *Nature* 319: 393–394.

Kuhnert, L. 1986b. Photochemische Manipulation von chemischen Wellen. *Naturwissenschaften* 73: 96–97.

Kuhnert, L., K. I. Agladze, and V. I. Krinsky. 1989. Image processing using light-sensitive chemical waves. *Nature* 337: 244–247.

Laplante, J. P., and T. Erneux. 1992. Propagation failure and multiple steady states in an array of diffusion coupled flow reactors. *Physica A* 188: 89–98.

Laplante, J.-P., M. Pemberton, A. Hjelmfelt, and J. Ross. 1995. Experiments on pattern recognition by chemical kinetics. *J. Phys. Chem.* 99: 10063–10065.

Markus, M., and B. Hess. 1990. Isotropic cellular automaton for modelling excitable media. *Nature* 347: 56–58.

Masterov, A. V., M. I. Rabinovich, V. N. Tolkov, and V. G. Yakhno. 1988. Studies of regimes of autowaves' and autostructures' interaction in neural-net-like media (in Russian). In Collective dynamics of excitations and structure formation (in Russian), ed. V. G. Yakhno, 89–104. Gorkyi: Institute of Applied Physics of the USSR Academy of Sciences.

McCulloch, W. J., and W. Pitts. 1943. A logical calculus of the ideas immanent in nervous activity. *Bull. of Math. Biophys.* 5: 115–133.

Meinhardt, H., and M. Klinger. 1987. A model for pattern formation on the shells of mollusks. *J. Theor. Biol.* 126: 63–89.

Ming, L., and P. Vitanyi. 1993. *An Introduction in Kolmogorov Complexity and Its Applications*. New York: Springer Verlag.

Miyakawa, K., and M. Mizoguchi. 1998. Responses of an immobilized-catalyst Belousov-Zhabotinsky reaction system to electric fields. *J. Chem. Phys.* 109: 7462–7467.

Miyakawa, K., T. Okabe, M. Mizoguchi, and F. Sakamoto. 1995. Synchronization in the discrete chemical oscillation system. *J. Chem. Phys.* 103: 9621–9625.

Motoike, I., and K. Yoshikawa. 1999. Information operations with an excitable field. *Phys. Rev. E* 59: 5354–5360.

Muñuzuri, A. P., and L. O. Chua. 1998. Shortest-path-finder algorithm in a two-dimensional array of nonlinear electronic circuits. *Int. J. Bifurcation Chaos* 8: 2493–2501.

Muñuzuri, A. P., V. Pérez-Villar, and M. Markus. 1997. Splitting of autowaves in an active medium. *Phys. Rev. Lett.* 79: 1941–1944.

Muñuzuri, A. P., V. Pérez-Muñuzuri, and V. Pérez-Villar. 1998. Attraction and repulsion of spiral waves by localized inhomogeneities in excitable media. *Phys. Rev. E* 58: R2689–R2692.

Murray, J. D. 1981. A pre-pattern formation mechanism for animal coat markings. *J. Theor. Biol.* 88: 161–199.

Nicolis, J. S. 1986. *Dynamics of Hierarchical Systems: An Evolutionary Approach*. Heidelberg: Springer Verlag.

Nuidel, I. V., and V. G. Yakhno. 1989. Possible architecture principles of parallel information processing in bioelectronics. *Studia Biophysica* 132: 137–144.

Pérez-Muñuzuri, V., V. Pérez-Villar, and L. O. Chua. 1993. Autowaves for image processing on a two-dimensional CNN array of excitable nonlinear circuits: Flat and wrinkled labyrinths. *IEEE Trans. Circuits Syst.* 40: 174–181.

Pozin, N. V. 1970. Modeling neural net structures (in Russian). Moscow: Nauka.

Pratt, W. K. 1978. *Digital Image Processing*. New York: John Wiley and Sons.

Price, C. B., P. Wambacq, and A. Oosterlinck. 1990. Image enhancement and analysis with reaction-diffusion paradigm. *IEEE Proc.* 137: 136–145.

Prigogine, I. 1980. *From Being to Becoming: Time and Complexity in the Physical Sciences*. San Francisco: W. H. Freeman.

Rambidi, N. G. 1994. Biomolecular computing: From the brain-machine disanalogy to the brain-machine analogy. *BioSystems* 33: 45–54.

Rambidi, N. G. 1997. Biomolecular computer: Roots and promises. *BioSystems* 44: 1–15.

Rambidi, N. G., and A. V. Maximychev. 1995. Molecular image processing devices based on chemical reaction systems: 3. Some operational characteristics of excitable light-sensitive media used for image processing. *Adv. Mater. Opt. Electron.* 5: 223–231.

Rambidi, N. G., and A. V. Maximychev. 1997. Towards a biomolecular computer: Information processing capabilities of biomolecular nonlinear dynamic media. *BioSystems* 41: 195–211.

Rambidi, N. G., D. S. Chernavskii, and V. I. Krinsky. 1993. Information processing and computing devices based on biomolecular nonlinear dynamic systems. In *Molecular Electronics and Molecular Electronic Devices*, ed. K. Sienicki, 85–153. Ann Arbor: CRC Press.

Rambidi, N. G., T. O.-O. Kuular, and E. E. Machaeva. 1998. Information processing capabilities of reaction-diffusion systems: 1. Belousov- Zhabotinsky media in hydrogel matrices and on solid supports. *Adv. Mater. Opt. Electron.* 8: 163–171.

Reusser, E. R., and R. J. Field. 1979. The transition from phase waves to trigger waves in a model of the Zhabotinsky reaction. *J. Am. Chem. Soc.* 101: 1063–1071.

Ruiz-Villarreal, M., M. Gomez-Gesteira, C. Souto, A. P. Muñuzuri, and V. Pérez-Villar. 1996. Long-term vortex interaction in active media. *Phys. Rev. E* 54: 2999–3002.

Sendiña-Nadal, I., M. Gómez-Gesteira, V. Pérez-Muñuzuri, V. Pérez-Villar, J. Armero, L. Ramirez-Piscina, J. Casademunt, F. Sagués, and J. M. Sancho. 1997. Wave competition in excitable modulated media. *Phys. Rev. E* 56: 6298–6301.

Sendiña-Nadal, I., D. Roncaglia, D. Vives, V. Pérez-Muñuzuri, M. Gómez-Gesteira, V. Pérez-Villar, J. Echave, J. Casademunt, L. Ramírez-Piscina, and F. Sagués. 1998. Percolation thresholds in chemical disordered excitable media. *Phys. Rev. E* 58: R1183–R1186.

Sendiña-Nadal, I., A. P. Muñuzuri, D. Vives, V. Pérez-Muñuzuri, J. Casademunt, L. Ramírez-Piscina, J. M. Sancho, and F. Sagués. 1998b. Wave propagation in a medium with disordered excitability. *Phys. Rev. Lett.* 80: 5437–5440.

Steinbock, O., V. S. Zykov, and S. C. Muller. 1993. Wave propagation in an excitable medium along a line of a velocity jump. *Phys. Rev. E* 48: 3295–3298.

Steinbock, O., P. Kettunen, and K. Showalter. 1995. Anisotropy and spiral organizing centers in patterned excitable media. *Science* 269: 1857–1860.

Steinbock, O., A. Toth, and K. Showalter, 1995. Navigation complex labyrinths: Optimal paths from chemical waves. *Science* 267: 868–871.

Steinbock, O., P. Kettunen, and K. Showalter. 1996. Chemical wave logic gates. *J. Phys. Chem.* 100: 18970–18975.

Stuchl, I., and M. Marek. 1982. Dissipative structures in coupled cells: Experiments. *J. Chem. Phys.* 77: 2956–2963.

Tolmachev, D., and A. Adamatzky, 1996. Chemical processor for computation of Voronoi diagram. *Adv. Mater. Opt. Electron.* 6: 191–196.

Toth, A., V. Gaspar, and K. Showalter. 1994. Signal transmission in chemical systems: Propagation of chemical waves through capillary tubes. *J. Phys. Chem.* 98: 522–531.

Turing, A. M. 1950. Computing machinery and intelligence. *Mind* 59: 433–460.

Turing, A. M. 1952. The chemical basis of morphogenesis. *Philos. Trans. R. Soc. Lond. Biol. Sci.* 327: 37–72.

Turk, G. 1991. Generating textures on arbitrary surfaces using reaction-diffusion. *Comput. Graph.* 25: 289–298.

Vasilev, Y. A., Y. M. Romanovsky, D. S. Chernavsky, and V. G. Yakhno. 1987. *Autowave Processes in Kinetic Systems.* Berlin: Verlag der Wissenschaften.

Weimar, J. R., J. J. Tyson, and L. T. Watson. 1992. Third generation cellular automaton for modeling excitable media. *Physica D* 55: 328–339.

Winfree, A. T. 1994. Electrical turbulence in three-dimensional heart muscle. *Science* 266: 1003–1006.

Winfree, A. T., and S. H. Strogatz. 1983. Singular filaments organize chemical waves in three dimensions: II. Twisted waves. *Physica D* 9: 65–80.

Winfree, A. T., and S. H. Strogatz. 1984. Organizing centers for three-dimensional chemical waves. *Nature* 311: 611–615.

Witkin, A., and M. Kass. 1991. Reaction-diffusion textures. *Comput. Graph.* 25: 299–308.

Yamaguchi, T., T. Kusumi, R. R. Aliev, T. Amemiya, T. Ohmori, M. Nakaiwa, K. Urabe, S. Kinugasa, H. Hashimoto, and K. Yoshikawa. 1998. Unidirectionality of chemical diode. *ACH-Models Chem.* 135: 401–408.

Yoshikawa, K., I. Motoike, and K. Kajiya. 1997. Design of an excitable field towards a novel parallel computation. *IEICE Trans. Electron.* E80-C: 931–934.

Yudin, D. B., and A. D. Yudin. 1985. The number and the thought (in Russian). 26–35. Moscow: Znanie.

Zauner, K.-P., and M. Conrad. 1996. Parallel computing with DNA: Toward the anti-universal machine. Paper presented at the fourth International Conference on Parallel Problem Solving from Nature, Berlin.

Zhabotinsky, A. M. 1964. Periodic processes of malonic acid oxidation in a liquid phase (in Russian). *Biofizika* 9: 306–311.

5 DNA Computing and Its Frontiers

Carlo C. Maley

5.1 Introduction

This is a great age of discovery for the intersection between biology and computation. Most of the work in this intersection has consisted of the application of computational techniques to the analysis of biological data—so-called computational biology. This chapter is about the opposite endeavor, the application of biological techniques and substrates to computation. In November 1994, Adleman stunned the scientific community when he demonstrated that through the simple annealing of Watson-Crick complementary base pairs, strands of DNA could compute a solution to an instance of the Hamiltonian Path Problem (HPP). In retrospect, there were a number of precursors that presaged Adleman's discovery. Work in formal language theory (Head 1987) had examined formalisms based on DNA manipulations. At the wet benches of biology, artificial selection of RNA had engineered solutions to a number of biological problems (Beaudry and Joyce 1992; Sassanfar and Szostak 1993; Lorsch and Szostak 1994; Stemmer 1994). But it was not until Adleman (1994) that the field of DNA computing was launched. Research in DNA computing is moving quickly, so many of the references in this chapter will be out of date by the time of publication. Thus, rather than give a comprehensive explication of the entire field, I have chosen to try to provide the reader with an understanding of the techniques, approaches, and issues in DNA computing and related research. It is my hope that with these tools you may both assess the potential of the field and perhaps begin to contribute to it yourself. An alternative review can be found in Reif (1998). Păun and coworkers (Păun, Rozenberg, and Salomaa 1998) provide a thorough treatment of the various theoretical formalisms for DNA computing. I have intentionally skewed the discussion of results in this field toward experimental rather than theoretical work. There is no longer any doubt as to the theoretical potential of DNA computing. Yet only the crucible of the laboratory can extract its true potential.

The Sequence That Launched a Thousand Sequences

Adleman has once again reminded us that computation is independent of its medium. He saw that there is computation in the interaction of molecules. His insight was that the sequence-specific binding properties of DNA allow it to carry out massively parallel computation in a test tube. The Hamiltonian Path Problem is a famous NP-complete problem in computer science. The question is, given a graph, a starting node, and an ending node, is there a path through the graph beginning and ending at the specified nodes such that every node in the graph is visited exactly once? Briefly, Adleman's experiment followed these six steps:

0. Create a unique sequence of 20 nucleotides (a 20-mer) associated with each vertex in the graph. Similarly, create 20-mer sequences to represent the edges in a graph. If two vertex sequences v_1 and v_2, were each composed of two 10-mer sequences $x_1 y_1$ and $x_2 y_2$, then an edge, $e_{1,2}$ from v_1 to v_2 was a 20-mer composed of the Watson-Crick complement[1] of y_1 and x_2 ($\overline{y_1 x_2}$). Thus, when put in solution, the edge sequence will bind to the second half of the source vertex and the first half of the destination vertex and serve as a sort of "connector" for binding the vertices together.

1. Generate random paths through the graph by putting many copies of the vertex and edge sequences into a solution and letting them anneal to each other, as shown in figure 5.1. That is, any complementary sequences will bind to each other to form double-stranded DNA. In addition to the simple edge and vertex sequences, two further sequences were added. If $v_{in} = x_{in} y_{in}$ was the starting vertex and $v_{out} = x_{out} y_{out}$ was the terminating vertex, the sequences $\overline{x_{in}}$ and $\overline{y_{out}}$ were added in order to "cap off" sequences starting with v_{in} and ending with v_{out}. The process of annealing resulted in long double strands of DNA with breaks in the "backbone" wherever one vertex (or edge) sequence ended and another began. These breaks were filled in by adding ligase enzyme to the solution, thus forming the covalent bonds between subsequences necessary to construct two coherent single strands of DNA annealed together.

2. Separate out all paths starting with v_{in} and ending with v_{out}. This was done not by actually separating the DNA representing good paths from DNA representing bad paths, but by exponentially replicating the good paths using a polymerase chain reaction (PCR). In this way, the proportion of good paths in the solution far outweighed the proportion of bad paths.

3. Separate out all paths that go through exactly n vertices (where $n = 7$ is the number of vertices in Adleman's graph). This was implemented by separating the strands by their lengths and identifying all 140-mers. Separation by length is typically carried out by gel electrophoresis. Different length strands of DNA move at different rates

---

1. The four nucleic acids that make up DNA combine in "Watson-Crick" complementary pairs. Thus Adenine (A) binds to Thymine (T) while Guanine (G) binds to Cytosine (C). Any sequence of nucleotides, such as TAGCC, has a complementary sequence, ATCGG, that will bind to it so as to form a double strand of DNA.

Ligation

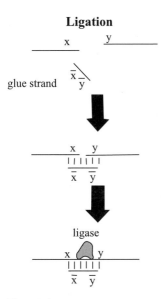

Figure 5.1
In order to connect strand y to strand x a "glue strand" is used to bring the two strands into proximity through annealing. Then a ligase enzyme is added to fuse the two strands together. Here $\bar{x}$ indicates the Watson-Crick complement of sequence x.

through an electrical field in a gel.[2] The section of the gel corresponding to 140-mers was identified, the DNA extracted from the gel, and replicated, or amplified, by PCR. This sequence of gel electrophoresis, extraction, and amplification was repeated several times in order to purify the sample.

4. Separate out all paths that go through all n vertices. This was done by first constructing (for each vertex in the graph) a set of magnetic beads attached to the complement sequence of the vertex. The double-stranded DNA from step 3 was "melted" to reduce it to a solution of single-stranded DNA, and then mixed with the magnetized vertex complement sequence for vertex 1. The sequences binding to these beads were magnetically extracted. They should represent paths that include vertex 1. The process was repeated on the results of the previous extraction for each vertex in the graph. At the end, only those paths that include all seven vertices should remain.

2. For a strand of length $N < 150$, biologists have experimentally found that the distance a DNA strand travels is $d = a - b\,ln(N)$, for some constants a and b.

5. Detect if there are any DNA sequences in the remaining solution. This was done by first amplifying the results with PCR and then using gel electrophoresis to see if anything of the appropriate length is left.

Elegant in design, clumsy in implementation. This is perhaps appropriate for the first steps of a field. Let us consider the amount of time that was necessary to perform this experiment. The time required to create a desired sequence, such as the sequence representing v_1, depends on the enzymes used; however, it is on the scale of hours (Gannon and Powell 1991). There are $O(n^2)$ such sequence generation processes in step 0, where n is the number of nodes in the graph. In many cases, subsequences might be taken from a preexisting DNA library or bought from a vendor. Adleman omits a description of how he obtained the sequences representing the vertices, except to say that the sequences were random. The process of annealing (step 1) requires about 30 seconds (Vahey, Wong, and Michael 1995: 20). Each PCR process (step 3, multiple times, and step 5) takes approximately 2 hours (Vahey, Wong, and Michael 1995: 20). The time required for gel electrophoresis (steps 2 and 5) depends on the gel used and the size and charge of the molecules. For the agarose gel that Adleman used, electrophoresis takes about 5 hours. For a polyacrylamide gel, it takes about 70 minutes (Kaplan, Cecci, and Libchaber 1995). It should also be noted that gel electrophoresis currently requires human intervention to visually identify and extract the desired results. Constructing the magnetic beads bound to premade sequences is a simple annealing operation. Finally, separation using the magnetic beads, which Adleman noted was the most labor-intensive step of the algorithm (performed n times in step 4), requires at a minimum approximately 1 hour using standard techniques (Lönneborg, Sharma, and Stovgaard 1995: 445). The entire experiment took Adleman 7 days of lab work. Adleman asserts that the time required for an entire computation should grow linearly with the size of the graph. This is true as long as the creation of each edge does not require a separate process. But the limiting factor here is the fact that the volume of DNA needed to compute the path grows exponentially with the size of the graph.

Kaplan and coworkers (Kaplan, Cecci, and Libchaber 1995) rightly criticize Adleman for not using a positive or a negative control. This is a serious issue, in part because the only known attempt to replicate Adleman's experiment produced ambiguous results (Kaplan, Cecci, and Libchaber 1995).

Despite all the practical delays of the biological manipulations, the real excitement over Adleman's work comes from the fact that in step 1, a massively parallel computation of all the possible paths through the graph is carried out in $O(1)$ time. With an estimated upper bound of 10^{20} "operations" in step 1 (Adleman 1994), the massive parallelism of DNA computing might be able to make the delays in the other steps seem negligible. In fact, Adleman (1994) makes a series of claims for the promise of DNA computing. DNA computation may outstrip modern silicon computers on three counts:

1. Speed. This should fall out from the massive parallism of the approach, amortized across the slow serial operations.

2. Energy efficiency. Because the molecules actually release energy when they anneal together, there is some hope that computations could be carried out using very little energy.

3. Information density. Packing 10^{20} strands of data into a liter of volume would give us an information density at least five orders of magnitude better than current hard drive technology.

But more immediately, Adleman identified a number of important open questions for the new field:

1. What is the theoretical power of DNA computation?

2. Are there practical algorithms for solving problems with DNA?

3. Can errors be adequately controlled?

4. Gifford (1994) adds: Is there universal computation in naturally occurring systems?

The purpose of this chapter is to introduce the state of the art of DNA computing as well as the related research programs that it has launched. The ships of many proposals have set sail for this new world. Most have not reached the point of implementation in the real world, although some are beginning to establish colonies. It remains to be seen if any will bring back the gold for which they were sent.

Mapping the Known World

The majority of work in DNA computing has taken place in vitro. That is, researchers have sought to manipulate DNA in test tubes and other artificial environments. This is the subject of section 5.2. DNA computing in vitro has no relation to biology or life except that it shares some of the same substrates and tools. A more recent, radical, and less developed approach is to carry out computation within a cell (generally *E. coli*), as described in section 5.3. In a sense, this in vivo form of computation is the old engineering trick of adding a layer of abstraction to our machines so as to give ourselves more powerful tools. Adleman's techniques are a little like machine code. The researcher must explicitly, and laboriously, drive each operation to change the state of the computation. Computation in a cell might be more like an assembly language. The cell can provide some of the nitty-gritty work to manipulate the computation, while the researcher need only provide an appropriate environment for the cells.

Within the world of in vitro DNA computation, I will discuss in section 5.2 the kinds of manipulations of DNA that have been discussed in the literature. This will provide a sketch of the tools that we have at hand. I will then show how various subsets of these tools have been proposed as the bases for computing with DNA. This is still an area of great ferment, for the choice of computational model will probably determine whether or not DNA computing will ever outperform its silicon brother. The end of section 5.2 reports on some of the daunting practical obstacles that will face any colonists to this new world. Section 5.3 discusses computation in cells. Finally, section 5.4 attempts to summarize the current state of the field and makes some predictions for its future.

5.2   The New World of DNA Computing

Adleman (1994) demonstrated one particular type of algorithm in DNA called "generate and test." To do this, he had to utilize a handful of techniques from molecular biology, including the construction of sequences of DNA, their hybridization, ligation, polymerase chain reaction, sequence separation, and gel electrophoresis (each of which is described below). But there are many other tools for manipulating DNA and these can be used to implement algorithms beyond the simple brute force approach of generate and test. Which tools and algorithms will turn out to be best for DNA computing is still an open question.

Tools of the Trade

Researchers in DNA computation have plundered molecular biology for tools with which to manipulate and analyze DNA. Luckily, both natural and artificial resources in this new world are abundant. Over the last few billion years, Nature has invented a vast diversity of molecules designed to interact with DNA. Furthermore, the last few decades have witnessed dramatic advances in the technology of molecular biology. There are probably many natural manipulations of DNA that have yet to be discovered. Similarly, there are probably many enzymes and other tools that are known to biologists but have yet to be applied to the endeavor of DNA computation. What follows is a description of those tools and techniques that have been discussed within, and in some cases applied to, DNA computation.

Anneal. This is probably the most basic operation used in DNA computing. Single-stranded complementary DNA will spontaneously form a double strand of DNA when suspended in solution. This occurs through the hydrogen bonds that arise when complementary base pairs are brought into proximity. This is also called "hybridization."

Melt. The inverse of annealing is "melting." That is, the separation of double-stranded DNA (dsDNA) into single-stranded DNA (ssDNA). As the name implies, this can be done by raising the temperature beyond the point where the longest double strands of DNA are stable. Because the hydrogen bonds between the strands are significantly weaker than the covalent bonds between adjacent nucleotides, heating separates the two strands without breaking apart any of the sequences of nucleotides. "Melting" is a bit of a misnomer because the same effect can be achieved by washing the double-stranded DNA in doubly distilled water. The low salt content also desta-bilizes the hydrogen bonds between the strands of DNA and thereby separates the two strands. Heating to an intermediate temperature can be selectively used to melt apart short double-stranded sequences while leaving longer double-stranded sequences intact.

Ligate. Often invoked after an annealing operation, ligation concatenates strands of DNA. Although it is possible to use some ligase enzymes to concatenate free-floating double-stranded DNA, it is dramatically more efficient to allow single strands to anneal together, connecting up a series of single-strand fragments, and then use ligase to seal the covalent bonds between adjacent fragments, as in figure 5.1.

Polymerase extension. Polymerase enzymes attach to the $3'$ end[3] of a short strand that is annealed to a longer strand. It then extends the $3'$ side of the shorter strand so as to build the complementary sequence to the longer strand. This is shown in figure 5.2.

Cut. Restriction enzymes will cut a strand of DNA at a specific subsequence. As of 1993, there were over 2,300 different known restriction enzymes that were specific to more than 200 different subsequences. These subsequences are usually on the order of 4–8 nucleotides. Some restriction enzymes will only cleave single-stranded DNA, while others will only cleave double-stranded DNA. Similarly, methylation of the cytosine nucleotides on a strand of DNA interferes with the activity of some restric-

---

3. Nucleotides form chains by connecting the $5'$ position (5th carbon) in the five-carbon sugar ring (the pentose) to the $3'$ position of the pentose in the next nucleotide. This gives a strand of DNA a particular direction with a free $3'$ position at one end of the strand and a free $5'$ position at the other end. The convention is to list the sequence of a DNA strand starting at the $5'$ end and finishing at the $3'$ end.

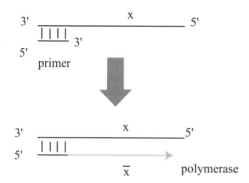

Figure 5.2
Polymerase extension. A polymerase enzyme attaches to the 3′ end of a short primer sequence and constructs the complement ($\bar{x}$) of the longer sequence.

tion enzymes, but not others. Furthermore, some restriction enzymes will cleave a wide range of subsequences of DNA. That is, the specificity of an enzyme relative to its target sequence varies across different enzymes.

Destroy. Subsets of strands can be systematically destroyed, or "digested" by enzymes that preferentially break apart nucleotides in either single- or double-stranded DNA.

Merge. Given two test tubes, combine them, usually by pouring one into the other.

Separate by length. Given a test tube of DNA, split it into two test tubes, one with strands of a particular length, and the other with all the rest. This is done with gel electrophoresis and requires the DNA to be extracted from the gel once the strands of different length have been identified by some form of straining or radioactive tagging.

Reverse chirality. DNA naturally forms two different sorts of double helixes. The most common form has a right-handed chirality and is called B-DNA; however, complementary strands of DNA can also twist around each other in the opposite direction, with left-handed chirality, called Z-DNA. The propensity with which a double strand of DNA forms Z-DNA depends on both the sequences of nucleotides in the strand as well as modifications to those bases (methylation of cytosine's 5 position increases this propensity). Enzymes called topoisomerases can reverse the chirality of a molecule (Seeman et al. 1998).

These basic manipulations can be combined into higher level manipulations. Perhaps the most famous example of a higher level manipulation is polymerase chain reaction (PCR). Composite manipulations include:

Amplify.   Given a test tube of DNA, make multiple copies of a subset of the strands present. This is done with polymerase chain reaction (PCR). PCR requires a beginning and an ending subsequence, called "primers," which are usually about twenty base pairs long, to identify the sequence (called the "template") to be replicated. Copies of these subsequences anneal to the single strands, and polymerase enzymes build the complementary strands, as in figure 5.3. Heat then melts apart the double strands, reducing them to single strands and the process repeats, doubling the number of strands in the test tube each cycle.

Separate by subsequence.   Given a test tube of DNA, split it into two test tubes, one with the sequences that contain the specified subsequence, and the other with the rest. We have already seen how this can be done with magnetic beads and the Watson-Crick complement of the specified subsequence, as in Adleman (1994). This is also sometimes called an "extraction." It can also be implemented by destroying the unwanted strands.

Append.   This adds a specific subsequence to the ends of all the strands. This can be done by annealing a short strand to a longer strand so that the short strand extends off the end of the longer strand. Then the complement of the subsequence that is extending off the end can be added to the longer strand either through the use of a polymerase enzyme, or through the introduction and annealing of that sequence, cemented by ligase, as depicted in figure 5.1.

Mark.   This operation tags strands so that they can be separated or otherwise operated upon selectively. Marking is commonly implemented by making a single strand into a double strand through annealing or the action of a polymerase. It can also mean appending a tag sequence to the end of a strand or even the methylation of the DNA or (de)phosphorylation of the $5'$ ends of the strands.

Unmark.   The complement of the marking operation. Unmark removes the marks on the strands.

Models of Computation

Now that we know some of the basic operations that can be performed on strands of DNA, we have the pressing question of how those operations should be combined to carry out computations. The question of whether or not DNA is capable of universal computation is no longer at issue. A variety of models have been shown to be computationally complete (Beaver 1995; Boneh, Dunworth, and Sgall 1995; Rothemund 1996; Winfree 1996; Csuhaj-Varjú et al. 1996). Of course, we would like the computation to be relatively fast (with few operations that require human intervention),

Polymerase Chain Reaction

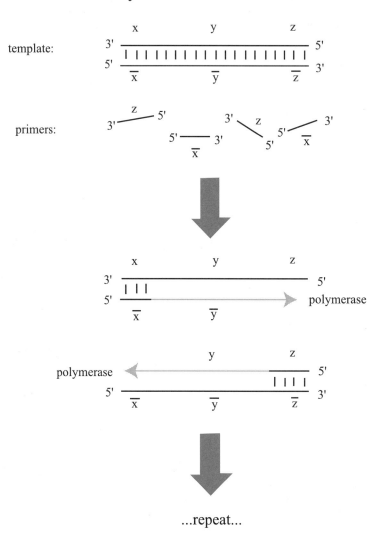

Figure 5.3
Polymerase chain reaction (PCR) follows in cycles of three steps. (1) The double-stranded templates are melted apart. (2) The primers anneal to both strands. (3) A polymerase enzyme extends the primers into replicas of the templates. This is repeated, causing an exponential growth in the number of templates, as long as there are enough primers in the solution to catalyse the reaction. Note that because polymerase attaches to the $3'$ end of a primer we need to use the subsequences $\bar{x}$ and z to get the desired reaction.

error free (or at least error tolerant), and massively parallel. These are the parameters upon which a proposed model of DNA computation must be measured. Ideally, we would like a "one-pot" computation, such that the computation would play out in a single test tube with a minimum number of external manipulations. Although many models have been invented, none have yet proven themselves practical.

Kazic (2000) suggests that trying to force DNA to emulate our traditional notions of computation may be misguided. Chemical reactions are continuous, they can take on an infinite number of states through a stochastic process, and the reactions do not halt. Kazic argues that this makes modern computational theory inadequate to describe molecular computation. On the other hand, much the same could be said for the electrical medium of conventional computing. Computer engineers have developed ways to channel the continuous real world into the discrete world of digital computation (Knight and Sussman 1997).

It is not yet clear whether we will be forced to abandon attempts to make DNA emulate discrete computations, but that has not stopped many people from trying. There are two general classes of computational models for using DNA. "Generate and test" models are based on Adleman (1994) and Lipton (1995). Alternatives to this brute force approach rely on controlling a sequence of chain reactions to construct a solution to a problem.

Generate and Test   The most popular model for using DNA to do computation comes directly out of Adleman's first paper and falls into the category of "generate and test" algorithms (Adleman 1994, 1996; Boneh, Dunworth, and Sgall 1995; Roweis et al. 1998). The technique was refined into a process with two phases (Boneh, Dunworth, and Sgall 1995; Adleman 1996). First, randomly generate all possible solutions to the problem at hand. Second, isolate the correct solution through repeated separations of the DNA into incorrect solutions and potentially good solutions. At the end of this series of separation steps, it may only be necessary to detect if there are any DNA strands left in the set of good solutions. Adleman's step 5 provides one example.

Generating solutions and then isolating the correct one was easily generalized to finding all the inputs of a Boolean circuit that would result in a specified output (Boneh, Dunworth, and Sgall 1995). Lipton (1995) showed how to generate the set of all[4] binary strings of length n in $O(1)$, as long as $n < 64$. Lipton's procedure involves first creating a graph of size $O(n)$ such that a path through the graph is a realization

---

4. I will defer the problem of guaranteeing that all strings are actually generated until the section entitled of Errors and Catastrophes.

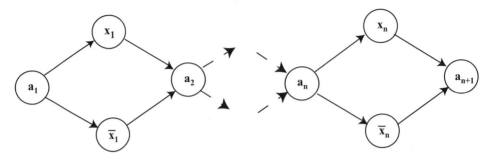

Figure 5.4
Lipton's graph for constructing binary numbers. The vertices and edges are constructed using Adleman's algorithm so that the longest path through the graph will represent an *n*-bit binary number. If the path goes through an $\bar{x}$ then it has a 0 at that position, otherwise it has a 1 at that position.

of a binary number of length *n*. (figure 5.4.) The graph is implemented in the same way as Adleman's (1994). In Lipton's words:

The graph G_n has nodes $a_1, x_1, \overline{x_1}, a_2, \ldots, a_k$ with edges from a_1 to both x_k and $\overline{x_k}$ and from both x_k and $\overline{x_k}$ to a_{k+1} .... The graph is constructed so that all paths that start at a_1 and end at a_{n+1} encode an *n*-bit number. At each stage a path has exactly two choices: If it takes the vertex with an unprimed label, it will encode a 1; if it takes the vertex with a primed label, it will encode a 0. Therefore, the path $[a_1 \, \overline{x_1} \, a_2 \, x_2 \, a_3]$ encodes the binary number 01.[5]

The second phase of solving a Boolean circuit involves repeated separations, with a little molecular bookkeeping to keep track of the progress. The idea is to create an ordering on the gates of the circuit so that the inputs of gate g_i are either inputs to the circuit or outputs of gates g_j where $j < i$. Then, using this ordering, we evaluate the output for the gates, one at a time, given the input values represented in each strand. We append to each strand a bit indicating the value of the output of each gate. This is done in parallel across all the strands, representing all the possible input values. For example, if we are processing gate g_i, then we separate all strands whose inputs to gate g_i would result in the output 1. To these strands we append a sub-sequence representing 1 with a tag identifying it as the output of gate g_i. To all the other strands we append a 0, and then we merge the two sets in order to process the next gate. Selection is done by using magnetic beads attached to the Watson-Crick complement of the subsequences representing the input bit values. This process is

5. Lipton 1995, 543; I have altered the notation to preserve internal consistency.

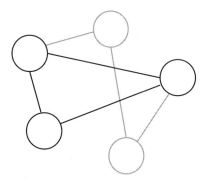

Figure 5.5
An example of a 5-node graph with a 3-node clique shown in black.

simply repeated until the output gate has been processed. Then all strings with a 1 on the end represent input values that make the circuit output a 1.

Ouyang and coworkers (Ouyang et al. 1997) trumped this with an experimental demonstration of a solution to the maximal clique problem. This is another NP-complete graph problem. In this case, the problem is to find the largest subset of nodes of the graph in which every node of the subset (clique) is connected to every other node of the subset, as shown in figure 5.5. Their approach was novel in two ways. First they used "parallel overlap assembly" to generate the potential solutions. Second, they used restriction enzymes to digest and thus remove strands that did not represent cliques. A potential solution was coded as a string of value (v_i) and position (p_i) sequences, one pair for each node (i) in the graph. The value sequences (v_is) could either be 0 (represented by the empty string, or 0 nucleotides) or 1 (represented by a 10-mer sequence). The position sequences (p_is) were represented by unique 20-mer sequences. Parallel overlap assembly is similar to Adleman's annealing step in his procedure, except where his adjacent sequences were fused with ligase. Parallel overlap assembly allows larger gaps between adjacent subsequences to be filled in with polymerase, as depicted in figure 5.6. Strands that do not represent cliques can be removed by digesting strands that include pairs of nodes that are not connected by an edge in the graph. This removal is done once for each missing edge in the graph. At the end of this process, PCR was used to amplify the solutions and then gel electrophoresis revealed the shortest remaining sequence that represented the largest clique in the graph.

An alternative implementation of bit strings allows for the modification of bits. The "sticker model" (Roweis et al. 1998; Adleman et al. 1996) represents a 0 as a

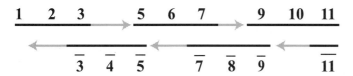

Figure 5.6
Full sequences can be constructed through the combination of short sequences that anneal together and polymerase to fill in the gaps. The grey arrows indicate the activity of polymerase while the numbers and their complements serve to label the sub-sequences. The black lines indicate the input sequences for the process of parallel overlap assembly. PCR will rapidly amplify the fully constructed sequences.

sequence of single-stranded DNA and a 1 as a sequence of double-stranded DNA. The basic structure is a single fixed-length strand representing a string of 0s. Each M-mer interval (where M is about 20 or 30) is unique and encodes a bit position. Thus, to set a bit in all the strands in a test tube, one merely has to add to the test tube a large quantity of the subsequence representing the complement of that bit position. These anneal to the ssDNA and set the bit to 1. A collection of random bit strings can be created by repeatedly splitting the test tube into two test tubes, setting the next bit position in one of the two tubes, and then merging the results. The problem of clearing a single bit position without clearing all the bit positions has not yet been solved and remains a limitation of the sticker model at present.

Adleman (1994) and Lipton (1995) suggested using random encodings to represent information in DNA. But a number of authors have recognized that this can cause problems due to the inadvertent creation of sequences that complement and thus may anneal with each other or themselves (Smith 1995; Deaton et al. 1996; Baum 1998; Hartemink, Gifford, and Khodor 2000). Hartemink and coworkers (Hartemink, Gifford, and Khodor 2000) developed a program SCAN to search for sequences with desired properties to be used for DNA computation. These properties include binding specificity of subsequences to particular locations on a strand, the lack of secondary structure or the formation of dimers (i.e., the sequences should not bind to themselves or others), and different degrees of binding stability in different parts of the strand. The sequences suggested by SCAN proved significantly better than sequences designed by hand (Hartemink, Gifford, and Khodor 2000). Cukras and coworkers (Cukras et al. 2000) solved the knight's problem from chess using RNA rather than DNA.[6] The knight's problem is the question of how many knights can be fit on a chessboard such that no knight can attack another knight in a single

6. The solution and accuracy of their technique was reported to me in a personal communication with Laura Landweber.

move. They first generated all possible 3 by 3 chessboards with knights as strands of RNA. They then destroyed all illegal boards by annealing other RNA strands to the offending positions and using RNase H to cut the double-stranded RNA. In a sample of 44 remaining strands, 43 were legal board configurations and one encoded the maximal (5) solution (Faulhammer et al. 2000).

Liu and coworkers (Liu et al. 2000b) chose to sacrifice some parallelism for ease of manipulation and reduced error rates by binding ssDNA to a gold surface. They "marked" the strands by annealing sequences to them to form dsDNA and then destroyed unwanted ssDNA with an enzyme that selectively digests ssDNA. They used these operations to demonstrate the solution to the 3SAT problem with four variables and four clauses. They first generated all possible Boolean assignments for the four variables as ssDNA attached to the surface. For each clause, they marked the strands that would satisfy the clause and then destroyed the others. Any strands that remained at the end of this process were sequenced by removing them from the surface, tagging them with a fluorescent dye, and annealing them to complementary strands on a surface whose positions and sequences are known. This requires that all possible strands be laid down in specified positions on the final surface. The labor in constructing such an addressable surface may be offset by the possibility of its repeated use. They do not give an algorithm for determining which strands would satisfy a clause. If this has to be done in silicon, there is no clear advantage of solving 3SAT in DNA. At present, the experiment of Liu and coworkers (Liu et al. 2000b) shows that DNA computation can be done on a surface. They have not shown that this is a promising direction for developing truly useful DNA computations.

Smith (1995) raises the important objection that the naive brute force algorithms of generate-and-test methods can never outperform a good algorithm in silicon for the same problem. For example, Lipton (1995) estimates that his technique for solving 3SAT has an upper bound of 70 literals, yet current computers can already solve 2SAT problems with 300 literals (Smith 1995). Bach and coworkers (Bach et al. 1996: 290–299) recognized the importance of a good algorithm and developed an algorithm of the 3-coloring problem[7] that only required the generation of $\Omega(1.89^n)$ potential solutions as compared to the brute force algorithm's $\Omega(3^n)$ space requirements. This remains an important area of open problems. Can we improve the efficiency of DNA algorithms to the point where they can compete with silicon computation?

7. The 3-coloring problem is the problem of determining if the nodes of a graph can be colored such that no neighboring nodes have the same color, given only 3 colors.

Programmed Chain Reactions A fundamentally different approach to DNA computation is not to generate and test all possible solutions but rather to control a cascade of chain reactions that results in the answer to a desired computation. If these cascades can be adequately controlled, the parallelism of DNA computation could be utilized for the solution of a vast number of problems (or subproblems) in parallel. A number of computational models of chain reactions in DNA have begun to be experimentally investigated.

Guarnieri and coworkers (Guarnieri, Fliss, and Bancroft 1996) have developed a procedure to implement the addition of two nonnegative binary numbers through a chain reaction. Furthermore, they have demonstrated the algorithm on pairs of single-bit binary numbers. They implement an addition through a cascade of branches in the chain reaction, which are predicated on the value of the sum in the previous bit position. I have summarized their algorithm in pseudo-C code below:

```
Int number1[n]; / *Binary numbers represented as arrays of
bits. */
Int number2[n];
Carry = 0; /*Keeps track of the carryover from the previous
bit. */
N2=0; /* An intermediary variable to hold carry + number2.*/

For (i= 0; i < n; i++){
If (number2[i] ==0)/*Calculate number2 + carry.*/
     if (carry==0)
          n2= 0;
     else n2 = 1;
     else
     if (carry == 0)
          n2= 1;
     else n2= 2;

if (number1[i] == 0) /*Calculate number1 + n2.*/
     switch (n2) {
          case 0: output(0); carry = 0; break;
          case 1: output(1); carry = 0; break;
          case 2: output(1); carry = 1; break;
     }
     else
     switch (n2)
```

```
            case 0: output(1); carry = 0; break;
            case 1: output(0); carry = 1; break;
            case 2: output(1); carry = 1; break;
      }
}

if (carry == 1) output(1);/*Spit out any carryover.*/
```

Notice that there is no explicit addition operation in the above algorithm, besides my encoding of the iteration. The branching statements are implemented as annealing operations between the number being constructed (the sum of the two input numbers) and a set of possible complements. Once the number being built (the sum) anneals to the appropriate strand, a polymerase enzyme extends the sum. Then the two strands are melted apart and then cooled so that the sum is free to anneal to the next bit position in the sequence. Each value in each bit position has a unique sequence. Then, if the `number2` had a 1 in the 2^3 position, there would be two strands added to the soup: one representing the code `if(carry == 0) n2= 1` and one representing `if(carry == 1) n2 = 2`. Then, if the sum had a string at its $3'$ end, representing the complement $\overline{carry == 1}$ in the 2^2 position, it would bind to the second option and polymerase would add on the string representing n2=2 at the 2^3 position.

The same process follows for the reaction with the 2^3 position in `number1`, but this time, three strings would be present in the test tube representing how to extend the sum under each of the three cases n2= 0,1,2. In this way, the addition operation is actually built into the encoding of the two binary numbers. At the end of the chain reaction, the resulting sum must be sequenced in order to determine the result. The addition of $11 + 11$ $(3 + 3$ in binary) is depicted in figures. 5.7, 5.8, and 5.9. The amount of DNA necessary to implement an n-bit addition is only $O(n)$, although it requires the construction of seven unique subsequences (and their complements) for each bit position.

Guarnieri and coworkers (Guarnieri, Fliss, and Bancroft 1996) point out the worst flaw in this algorithm. The encoding of the output number is different from the encoding of the two input numbers. Thus the output cannot be fed back into the DNA computer for future computation without translating it back into the input format. There are further limitations. As they state from the beginning, this procedure only works for nonnegative numbers. Theoretically, this algorithm should be able to handle different addition operations being carried out in parallel as long as all subsequences representing different bit position branches in the test tube are unique

Addition of 11 + 11: bit 0

Figure 5.7
Addition proceeds from least significant to most significant bit. The numbers in parentheses represent sub-sequences encoding partial sums at each bit position. The numbers without parentheses are the bits of the answer. The sub-sequences are all assumed to include patterns that label the bit position, so that (0) at bit position 0 is a different sequence than (0) at bit position 1. Multiple fragments represent the operands n1 and n2. The addition for bit position 0 is simpler than addition for the other positions because there is no carry bit from a previous computation. Thus at the start, the least significant bit of the "answer" is the same as the least significant bit of n1. This bit is then added to the least significant bit of n2 and the result includes both the least significant bit of the sum of n1 and n2 as well as a pattern representing the presence (or absence) of a carry-over bit. Here there are two options for n2, corresponding to the cases where the least significant bit is either (0) or (1). By introducing (1) to the solution, we create an answer sequence (1) 0 (1), indicating that the least significant bit of the answer is 0 and there is a carry-over bit (1).

Addition of 11 + 11: bit 1

Step A: answer + n1

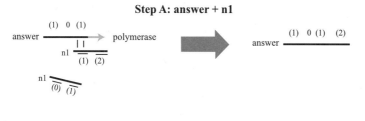

Step B: answer + n2

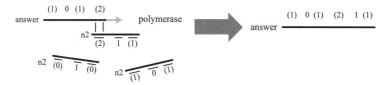

Figure 5.8
For all bit positions other than the least significant bit, addition has to follow in two steps. In step A, the carry-over bit is added to the bit of n1. Then, in step B, the result is added to the bit of n2. Note again that n1 and n2 are both represented as a set of DNA fragments, only one of which will bind to the answer strand in the chain reaction. The 3′ ends of these fragments have been altered to prevent the polymerase extending them.

Addition of 11 + 11: Carry-over

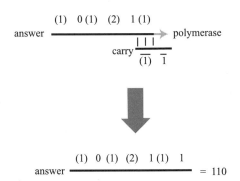

Figure 5.9
Finally, a strand representing the carry-over bit anneals to the answer and completes the process of constructing the answer: 110 (in reverse order), or 6, encoded in binary.

and unlikely to bind to each other. Although it is a "one-pot" computation,[8] it must be driven by temperature cycling. The speed of the cycling is limited in turn by the speed of the annealing reaction and the melting apart of the strands. Because the strand representing the sum may well anneal back again to the last strand that allowed the polymerase to extend the sum, we are not guaranteed that the addition operation will make progress in every temperature cycle. In fact, the strand that will allow progress has fewer base pairs that complement the sum than the last strand that matched it.

Winfree (Winfree 1996) describes a more general approach to computation. They introduced the idea of laying down tiles of DNA to implement blocked cellular automata. After an initial sequence of DNA blocks is constructed with exposed sticky ends along one edge, free DNA blocks from the solution should precipitate out and anneal to matching sticky ends of the growing DNA crystal. The blocks can be designed to implement rules of cellular automata and thus the growth of the crystal can carry out a computation based on the state and input of the initial sequence of blocks (Winfree 1996; Winfree, Yang, and Seeman 1998). Winfree and coworkers (Winfree et al. 1998) dramatically demonstrated that it is possible both to construct two-dimensional blocks of DNA and to control their annealing into crystals in the plane.

8. It is a "one-pot" algorithm in theory. In implementation, Guarnieri, Fliss, and Bancroft added the terminal "carry" strand to the solution after they had carried out the addition on the first bit position of $1 + 1$. So it still remains to be demonstrated how effective a chain reaction will be.

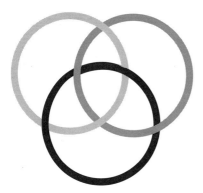

Figure 5.10
An example of three Borromean rings. Removing any one of the three rings will disconnect the other two.

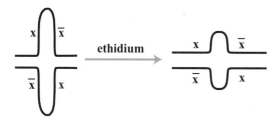

Figure 5.11
The migration of a branch in dsDNA can be controlled through the application of ethidium. In this case the ethidium applies torque to this cruciform and causes intrusion, a reduction of the hairpin bulges.

Seeman's lab has gone even further to construct three-dimensional shapes (cubes and truncated octahedra), raising the possibility of computation through three-dimensional cellular automata (Seeman et al. 1998). Alternatively, they suggest that Borromean rings of DNA could be used to carry out computation. Borromean rings are knots of n rings such that the removal of any single ring will disconnect other rings in the knot. A knot of 3 Borromean rings is shown in figure 5.10. If the closure of a strand of DNA into a ring represented the truth of a logical clause, then a conjunction of clauses could be represented by a Borromean ring. If any one clause were false, the whole would fall apart. Seeman and coworkers (Seeman et al. 1998) also show that information can be stored and manipulated in dsDNA through branch migration, as depicted in figure 5.11.

Khodor and Gifford (2000) have begun to develop a novel approach they call *programmed mutagenesis*. The idea is to place primers that represent rewrite rules

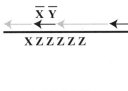

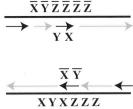

Figure 5.12
Three steps in the programmed mutagenesis of a counter. In the upper strand, the sequence XZZZZZ (representing 1) has an XY rewrite rule annealed to it (there is only a slight mismatch between Z and Y), as well as a standard PCR primer that catalyzes the construction of the template strand shown in the middle. The middle template strand now represents 2. It has the YX rewrite rule annealed to it. Again, X includes only a slight mismatch for annealing to $\overline{Z}$. This causes the polymerization of the third template XYXZZZ which represents 3. The chain reaction will continue until the strand $\overline{XYXYXY}$ (6) has been constructed.

into a PCR reaction and allow these rules to consecutively rewrite the template DNA. The primers not only initiate replication of the template, but the rewrite rules are slight mismatches, which nevertheless anneal to the template and are incorporated into the new strand that is being polymerized. Thus the slight alteration becomes part of the new template for copying. Khodor and Gifford (2000) described an algorithm for constructing a counter that takes as input a sequence XZZZZZ and incrementally replaces the Z subsequences with alternating X and Y subsequences of the same length. This process is depicted in figure 5.12.

An ingenious form of DNA computation, dubbed *whiplash PCR* by Adleman, was introduced by Hagiya and coworkers (Hagiya et al. 1999). In whiplash PCR, computation is carried out within single strands of DNA that anneal to themselves, forming hairpins. Once a hairpin has formed, the presence of polymerase will extend the 3′ end. Control over consecutive reactions is attained by designing subsequences of the form <stop> <new state> <old state>. If the end of the strand has the encoding of <old state> then it will anneal to <old state> and the polymerase will extend the sequence from right to left, adding <new state> to the 3′ end. In fact, it would continue adding the complement of the strand to the end if it weren't for the <stop> sequence. The <stop> sequence is composed of bases whose complements are not available to the polymerase in the test tube. Thus the polymerization stops when it reaches the <stop> sequence. Once the <new state> sequence

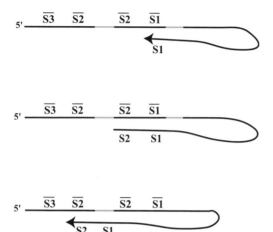

Figure 5.13
Three steps of a whiplash PCR reaction. The top strand shows the starting state (S1) with the 3′ end of the strand annealing to S1 and being extended by polymerase. In the middle strand, polymerase has added S2 to the 3′ end and halts at the stop sequence (shown in grey) because there are no available bases in the solution to construct the complement of the stop sequence. At some point the 3′ end melts away from the strand and then anneals to the beginning of the next transition ($\overline{S3S2}$). This continues until there are no more possible transitions.

has been added to the 3′ end of the strand, there is a nonzero chance that it will melt off of its current position and form a new hairpin by annealing to a new transition sequence, as shown in figure 5.13. Sakamoto and coworkers (Sakamoto et al. 2000) and Winfree (Winfree 2000) generalized this technique to carry out any computation. Sakamoto and coworkers (Sakamoto et al. 2000) implemented a two-transition system and found that the optimal temperatures for the transitions were different.

Conrad and Zauner (Conrad and Zauner 1999) suggest using the methylation of DNA as input channels of a gate, and its resulting chirality (B-DNA or Z-DNA) as the output of logic gates. Sequences that have the desired gate behavior could be evolved. Perhaps with control over sequence-specific methylation, these gates could be "wired up" to form a useful circuit. But for now, this remains a purely theoretical proposal.

Oliver (1996) described a process by which DNA could be made to implement matrix multiplication of Boolean or positive real valued matrices. The critical insight is that an $m \times n$ matrix can be represented by a graph of m source nodes and n sink nodes with edges between every source and sink node that has a positive value. The multiplication of an $m \times n$ by an $n \times p$ matrix is then a matter of computing which of the p sink nodes can be reached from the m source nodes. Oliver suggests encoding an edge from node i to node j as a dsDNA with a unique sequence representing $\langle ij \rangle$ and sticky (single-stranded) ends. The sticky ends then allow $\langle ij \rangle$ to bind to $\langle jk \rangle$. With the addition of ligase, this forms the edges of the product $m \times p$ matrix. Positive real values can be encoded as concentration of edges, with the result that (under appropriate conditions) the concentration of edges in the product matrix are the products of the edge concentrations in the operand matrices. Unfortunately, this approach has not been tested in the laboratory yet.

RNA has the interesting property that when it folds up into a three-dimensional shape, it can exhibit enzymatic activity (Landweber and Kari 2000). The powerful enzymatic activity was recently discovered in DNA as well (Santoro and Joyce 1997). The existence of these ribozymes (RNA) and DNA ribozymes (dioxyribozymes) suggest that it may well be possible to design computational systems wherein nucleic acids are both the data and the programs that manipulate that data (Kurtz et al. 1997).

The Search for the Killer Application   One reason researchers are still floating new proposals of computational models for DNA is that no one has yet found the fountain of youth, the *killer app*, that will justify the value of DNA computation: "A killer app is an application that fits the DNA model; cannot be solved by the current or even future electronic machines; and is *important*" (Landweber, Lipton, and Rabin 1999: 161, emphasis theirs).

Even a solution that merely outperformed current electronic machines—though perhaps not future electronic machines—would probably still be considered a killer app. Boneh and coworkers (Boneh, Dunworth, and Lipton 1995) have made a start with a description of an algorithm for breaking the Data Encryption Standard (DES). This is just a variation on the Boolean circuit satisfiability algorithm. The algorithm only requires one example of a 64-bit sample of plain text and the encryption of that text to find a 56-bit DES key. The algorithm follows in three steps:

1. Generate all possible 56-bit keys.

2. For all keys in parallel, simulate the behavior of the DES circuit given that key and the 64-bit sample of plain text. (A description of such a circuit simulation is given above in the section entitled Generate and Test.) The DES circuit requires only a minor elaboration to handle XOR gates and 64-entry lookup tables. The result of this is to append an encrypted version of the plain text to each strand of DNA representing a key.

3. Use the known encrypted version of the plain text to separate out all those keys that produce that encryption.

Boneh and coworkers (Boneh, Dunworth, and Lipton 1995) use the somewhat more conservative estimate that 10^{17} strands of DNA can fit in a liter of water. Thus (assuming all operations work perfectly, including the generation of the initial keys, all the separation steps involved in simulating the circuit, and extracting the answer strands) such a process can break any encryption algorithm that uses keys less than or equal to 57 bits. This is one bit more than necessary in the case of DES. Boneh and his coworkers claim the algorithm will work in the same amount of time for keys up to 64 bits long. This is predicted on a more optimistic estimate of the ability to manipulate 10^{20} strands of DNA and would probably require more than a liter of water.

Assuming that they can set up a laboratory that can do 32 separations in parallel, a table lookup can be done in one of these parallel separation steps. Their algorithm requires a total of 916 separation steps (128 table lookups, 788 × 3 XOR gates evaluated 3 at a time). With a rough estimate of 1 hour per separation step, and the calculation of 10 separation steps per day, DES could be broken in about 4 months of work. What is worse for those who rely on DES is that once this calculation is made, the results can be used repeatedly to locate other keys given the same pair of plain text and encrypted text under the new key. Adleman and coworkers (Adleman et al. 1996) developed a relatively error-tolerant algorithm for breaking DES using the sticker model and a mere gram of DNA. Yet these algorithms are currently out of our practical reach and may well depend on overly optimistic estimates of error rates.

Baum and Boneh (1996) suggest that rather than focusing on NP-complete problems, DNA might best be suited to dynamic programming problems. Dynamic programming problems generally involve a large number of constraints that must be simultaneously satisfied. This can be approached as a large number of subproblems that might be solved in parallel using the massive parallelism of DNA computation. Baum and Boneh give an algorithm for solving the graph connectivity problem (is there a path from a specified source node to a specified sink node in a graph?) as well as the knapsack problem (given a set of positive integers $b_1, b_2, \ldots, b_n$ and a target integer value B, is there a subset of those integers S such that $\sum_{i \in S} b_i = B$?), but note that DNA computing has difficulty implementing interprocess communication and so might be best at problems with relatively independent subproblems. But it is interesting to note that Blumberg (1999) has developed a model of just such interprocess communication.

Perhaps problems in traditional computer science do not provide the most fertile land of the settlers of DNA computation. Landweber and coworkers (Landweber, Lipton, and Rabin 1999) suggest that applying DNA computing to useful problems in the analysis of DNA itself may well provide the first killer apps. They suggest

DNA fingerprinting, sequencing, and mutation screening as possible applications. They describe a method for translating an unknown input sequence into an encoded sequence with redundancy that can then by manipulated by the DNA tools described in the above section entitled Tools of the Trade. The guiding insight is that the tools of DNA computation are best at manipulating DNA, and so might be best applied to problems in the analysis of DNA. A further example of this is the work of Stemmer. Stemmer (1994) has shown that by removing the TEM-1 β-lactamase gene that confers antibiotic resistance to a strain of *E. coli*, cutting it into many pieces with DNase I, and then reassembling the pieces and reinserting into the *E. coli*, he was able to select for a 32,000-fold increase in antibiotic resistance!

Of Errors and Catastrophes

Many theoretical proposals have floundered on the shoals of practicality. A few studies have begun to quantify the error rates in our tools for manipulating DNA. The results are not encouraging. Failures in a DNA computation can derive from many problems:

Failure to generate the solution.   If, in general, we assume that solution sequences of a generate-and-test algorithm are being created at random, then the problem of how much DNA you need, or how many solutions you need to generate, reduces to the coupon collector's problem. This problem states that if you want to collect the entire set of n different coupons by randomly drawing a coupon each trial, you can expect to make $O(n \log n)$ drawings before you collect the entire set. Similarly, the amount of DNA required to create all 2^n potential binary solutions is actually $O(n2^n)$. This was first noted in Linial and Linial (1995). Bach and coworkers (Bach et al. 1996) show that Lipton's (1995) algorithm for generating random solutions reduces to the coupon collector's problem. Even though there is some bias in the process due to the equal amounts of "0" and "1" added to the test tube, the first 2^{n-1} solutions form in a relatively unbiased fashion. Thus, in order to have a reasonable chance $(1 - \varepsilon)$ of generating all possible solutions under Lipton's algorithm, you need to use $O(n2^n)$ DNA.

Breakage of the DNA in solution.   DNA is not stable in water over long periods of time. It tends to break (hydrolyze). Furthermore, the mechanical shear of passing through a syringe puts a practical limit on sequence length of about 15 Kb (Smith 1995).

Failure of complementary strands to "find" each other.   For two strands to anneal, they must bump into each other in the solution. This failure becomes more likely as problems are scaled up to real-world complexity with an exponential increase in the number of distinct strands in the solution. The time to anneal grows as the square root of the length of the strands and the reciprocal of the concentration of the desired "mates" (Smith 1995).

Failure to properly discriminate in annealing. In the process of exploring DNA computation on a surface, as opposed to in a solution, Liu and coworkers (Liu et al. 2000a) discovered that for a set of 16 different 16-mer sequences, only 9 of the complements could perfectly discriminate between the 16 target sequences at 37 °C; the other 7 even annealed to some incorrect sequences at 40 °C.

Yoshinobu and coworkers (Yoshinobu et al. 2000) examined errors in the process of annealing. They found that an 8-mer sequence could only tolerate a single base mismatch and still successfully anneal. They also noted that G and T readily annealed at a single mismatch locus. Let that be a warning for those who would design sequences for efficient and accurate DNA computations.

Failure of annealing due to secondary structure in the strands. If a strand of DNA (or RNA) has subsequences that complement each other, it will tend to fold up into hairpins and other secondary structures. This can prevent the desired annealing between strands.

Incorporation of incorrect bases during PCR. Polymerization in PCR is not error free. Depending on the polymerase enzyme used, the error can be as low as 7×10^{-7} per base pair (for *Pfu*) and as high as 2×10^{-4} per base pair (for *Taq*) (Cha and Thilly 1995). There is evidence that an alternative process, called the *ligase chain reaction* (LCR), does better than most PCR enzymes (Dieffenbach and Dveksler 1995).

Furthermore, PCR is designed with the assumption that the proportion of primer is far greater than the proportion of template in the solution. If there are a lot of templates, the interactions between the templates can interfere with the PCR (Kaplan, Cecci, Libchaber 1995). Kaplan and coworkers (Kaplan, Cecci, and Libchaber 1996) point out that the DNA computation literature tends to ignore the possibility for undesirable interactions between the various strands during the application of PCR. In particular, if an undesired 3′ end of a strand anneals to the middle of another strand, the polymerase will extend the 3′ end to complement the other strand. In general, this will cause a computational error. They demonstrate the hazards of PCR and those of gel electrophoresis by the production of supposedly "impossibly" long strands, which turned out to be an unanticipated hybridization of two desired strands. Finally, PCR may leave behind partially constructed strands in the solution. These may interfere with future manipulations.

Failure to extract a target sequence from a solution. Both Karp and coworkers (Karp, Kenyon, and Waarts 1995) and Roweis and coworkers (Roweis et al. 1998) replace a single separation with a series of separations. They trade off time and space (number of test tubes) for accuracy. If the separation step divides a set of DNA strands into a "true" test tube and a "false" test tube, the simplest version of this is to repeat the separation step on the "false" test tube, in order to lower the rate of false negatives. A more sophisticated version of this is to do repeated separations on both results, creating an array of test tubes $1, \ldots, n$, where test tube k contains all those strands that have been processed as "true" k times. Thus a DNA strand does a biased random walk across the array. Roweis and coworkers (Roweis et al. 1998) suggest fixing the size of the array and making absorbing boundaries out of the test tubes at the ends. They point out that any DNA strands that reach the boundary test tubes can immediately be used in the next step of the computation. This creates a form of pipelining. By increasing the size of the array and thus the number of separation steps that must be performed, the error rates can be made arbitrarily small.

Khodor and Gifford (1999) took a hard look at sequence separation based on biotinylation, with rigorous controls and measurements. Under ideal conditions, they were able to retrieve only 8–24 percent of the desired strands, although there were few false positives ($<1\%$). This suggests that if sequence separation is called for in an algorithm, there must be many copies present of the desired sequence. Khodor and Gifford also note that if the target sequence is rare relative to the other sequences in the solution, even a small false positive rate will leave the target sequence in the minority in the resulting "positive" vial. These problems have prompted researchers to avoid sequence separation by annealing and instead use restriction enzymes to digest undesired sequences (Ouyang et al. 1997; Amos, Gibbors, and Hodgson 1998; Cukras et al. 2000).

Loss of DNA strands. It is known that DNA can stick to the walls of test tubes when a solution is poured from one tube into another. Khodor and Gifford (1999) found that significant portions of the population of DNA strands were completely lost in the process of sequence separation, appearing in neither the positive nor the negative test tubes after the separation. This implies that a sequence separation step of an algorithm should generally be followed by PCR amplification.

Failure of the split operation. If an algorithm relies on equally dividing the contents of a test tube into two test tubes, there is no guarantee that the copies of a particular sequence in the test tube will be equally divided between the two tubes. Bach and coworkers (Bach et al. 1996) model this with a "probabilistic split" operator and use their analysis to derive bounds on the amount of redundancy they need to find a desired solution with reasonable probability.

Failure to separate by length in a gel electrophoresis. This failure can result from a host of problems. Gels are not perfectly even in their porousness. Strands of DNA can stick to each other, or form secondary structures that affect their movement through the gel. They can also simply impede each other's progress in microscopic traffic jams. It can be extremely hard to separate strands of similar length. After two cycles of electrophoresis and PCR, Adleman had to repeat the electrophoresis four times on the product of the third PCR (Kaplan, Cecci, and Libchaber 1995), each time removing the 120-bp band in an attempt to reduce contamination.

Failure of restriction enzymes. Restriction enzymes might fail to cut the strands at their restriction sites due to lack of time, secondary structure in the strands, or other unknown interferences. Amos and coworkers (Amos et al. 1998) found that they were only able to destroy 2 out of 3 target sequences through the use of restriction enzymes. Their technique was to anneal a primer to the target sequence and then use a restriction enzyme that only cleaves dsDNA. Their failure thus may have been due to problems in annealing of the primer to the target sequence. In contrast, Wang and coworkers (Wang et al. 2000) report 97 percent efficiency of their restriction enzyme.

Failure of ligation due to secondary structure in the strands. Because ssDNA (and RNA) can fold up into complex shapes, these shapes may interfere with the ability of ligase to ligate the ends of two strands.

A Rocky Beginning Kaplan and coworkers (Kaplan, Cecci, and Libchaber 1995) set out to replicate Adleman's original experiment and failed. Or, to be more accurate, they state: "At this time, we have carried out every step of Adleman's experiment, but we have not gotten an unambiguous final result" (2). Adleman himself reported contamination of his 140-bp sample with 120-bp molecules. Kaplan and coworkers used both a positive and a negative control. The positive control was a simple graph with in-degree 1 and out-degree 1 for every node between v_{in} and v_{out}. This formed a single (Hamiltonian) path. The negative control was a graph identical to Adleman's except a single edge was removed, making the HPP unsolvable. They observed smears in their gels where there should have been distinct bands. Even the positive control, with such a simple structure, resulted in many different-length paths, including "impossible" paths longer than the total number of edges in the graph. When they cut out this path and ran it again on the gel, they found bands at 120-bp and 140-bp, suggesting either contamination due to the shorter (faster) strands getting caught in the gel, or "an unusual configuration of 3 strands of partially hybridized DNA" (18). Kaplan and coworkers suggest that incomplete ligation, irregular ligation, heterogeneous sequence-dependent shapes of different paths, paths that break in the gel, temporary binding of proteins to the DNA in the gel, or single strands hanging off the ends may explain the smear.

Kazic (2000) points out that DNA is less stable than other molecules, hybridization is a low-yield reaction, and separation by gel is difficult and complicated by contamination.

5.3   The Old World of DNA Computing

The rich diversity of computational models for DNA shows that nucleic acids are extraordinary flexible media for storing and manipulating information. Perhaps this should come as no surprise in that DNA has been used to store and manipulate information for more than 3 billion years. Adleman has helped to open our eyes to the computational riches that have lain hidden all around us for millennia. This has provoked some researchers to look for computation in the natural dynamics in the interior of cells. It has provoked others to try to engineer those dynamics into cells so as to implement human-crafted cellular computers.

Natural Computation in a Cell

Laura Landweber and Lila Kari have led the effort to identify and understand computational processes in natural organisms, though they are certainly not the only ones who have considered life as the processing of information (e.g., Gánti 1987; Kampis and Csányi 1991; Dawkins 1995). They have focused on gene scrambling in ciliates and the more general phenomenon of RNA editing (Landweber and Kari 2000; Kari and Landweber 2000).

There are more than eight thousand species of ciliates (a form of unicellular eukaryote). Genes in species of the *Osytricha* genus are often broken into many fragments and coded in the genome in permuted order. For example, the gene encoding DNA polymerase α in *O. trifallax* seems to be a scrambled sequence of at least 50 sequences. The process of unscrambling closely resembles Adleman's method of generating paths through his graph (1994). The process of constructing the unscrambled genes involves massive copying of the genome along with annealing and recombination to splice together necessary pieces. Each fragment of a gene ends with a sequence that complements the start of the next fragment in the correctly unscrambled gene; however, there are false matches of these sequences to incorrect positions in a genome. These false matches would likely prevent the construction of an unscrambled gene if the process of annealing were random in these ciliates. Apparently, evolution has developed mechanisms for solving this Hamiltonian path problem, but the details of this have yet to be illuminated (Landweber and Kari 2000). Landweber and Kari (2000), however, have developed a formal description of this process and have shown that it is computationally complete.

RNA editing is found in many eukaryotes, including both protozoa and humans. After a sequence of DNA is transcribed into RNA, the sequence or RNA can undergo significant alterations before it is translated into a sequence of amino acids. These editing operations include insertions, deletions, and substitutions. Such editing operations have already been shown to have the power of a universal Turing Machine (Kari 1996; Beaver 1996). This process is apparently carried out by small "guide RNA" (gRNA) molecules that anneal to the target sequence and catalyze an editing operation. In some cases, the results of one editing operation can trigger the next in a cascade somewhat reminiscent of Khodor and Gifford's programmed mutagenesis (2000). In the case of *Trypanosoma brucei* (a parasite that causes African sleeping sickness), RNA editing creates more than 90 percent of the codons that are translated into amino acids (Landweber and Kari 2000). This technique allows a single sequence in the genome to code for a combinatorial set of amino acid sequences.

Finally, it is interesting to note that information in the cell can be maintained in media beyond just the sequences of nucleic acids in the DNA or RNA. The heritable silencing of genes near the telomeres, which produce mosaic colorings like those of the calico cat, are another form of information storage (Lustig 1998). Unfortunately, we do not yet understand this dynamic enough to harness it for our computing needs.

Artificial Computation in a Cell
There is only a small conceptual jump between recognizing the computational properties of a cell and attempting to harness them (Smith 1995; Knight and Sussman 1997; Eng 2000; Ji 2000; Gardner, Cantor, and Collins 2000; Elowitz and Leibler 2000). There are many desirable properties of cells for the endeavors of DNA computation. Smith (1995) argues that polymerization takes place at least an order of magnitude faster in cells than in vitro. Also, sequences that would be impractically long for in vitro manipulation due to hydrolysis or mechanical shear are protected in the cell by the supercoiling of the DNA.

Knight and Sussman (1997) view the cell as a nice homeostatic environment with its own built-in power source. Their goal is to engineer logic gates into the dynamics of a cell (in this case, *E. coli*). Although in silicon we encode a low voltage as a 0 and a high voltage as a 1, Knight and Sussman have chosen to encode high and low concentrations of gene products as 1 and 0, respectively. Their first step in this en-

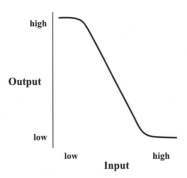

Figure 5.14
The function describing an idealized inverter's mapping of input values to output values. Note that a wide range of low input values maps to a narrow range of high output values. This allows a digital circuit to incrementally remove noise from the system.

deavor is the construction of an inverter. All inverters have the general property that when the input is low, the output is high, and vice versa. A good quality inverter has a wide range of low inputs that will make its output high and a wide range of high inputs that will make its output low, with a steep transition between these states, as depicted in figure 5.14. The wide ranges give us a margin for noise and allow the output to be more pure than the input.

An inverter can be implemented by a constitutive gene with a repressor site. A constitutive gene is a gene that is always active in the absence of a repressor. In addition, to make the gene produce a predictable amount of product, we can add negative feedback by making that gene product a repressor of the gene. Knight and Sussman (1997) explored the dynamics of such a system through simulation. Their simulation included the processes of repressor binding and disassociation for two different repressors (the input and the negative feedback of the output), translation of the gene, and gene product degradations. They found that the desired sigmoidal response of the inverter was surprisingly robust to changes in parameters. They have gone on to simulate a closed circuit of three inverters that should produce oscillations in the gene product concentrations (Knight and Sussman 1997). Elowitz and Leibler (2000) scooped them by not only simulating a three-inverter oscillator, but by actually constructing one in *E. coli*. One surprising result was that the period of oscillations was longer than the period of cell division. This shows that *E. coli* can maintain their state across cell divisions. Similarly, Gardner and coworkers (Gardner, Cantor, and Collins 2000) constructed a flip-flop (bistable state toggle switch) in *E. coli* by inserting two genes whose products mutually repress each other. The repression of either product may be inhibited by external signals so as to change the state of the cell.

Eng (2000) takes a more familiar approach by describing an algorithm for solving 3CNF-SAT (or just 3SAT) in a cell. Let the truth and falsehood of a literal be encoded by the presence of one of two distinct gene products (e.g., gene product x_i and gene product $\overline{x_i}$). Then create the sequence `<reverse of gene` x_i`>` `<promotor>` `<gene` $\overline{x_i}$`>`, where the `<promotor>` sequence is invertible. On the one hand, if the promoter is in the state where transcription is initiated from right to left, gene product x_i will be produced, making the x_i literal true. On the other hand, if the promoter is in the state where transcription is initiated from left to right, gene product $\overline{x_i}$ will be produced, making the x_i literal false. Note that these states are mutually exclusive. Catalyzing the inversion of the promoter changes the truth value of the literal.

Alternatively, one might use the flip-flop of Gardner and coworkers (Gardner, Cantor, and Collins 2000). A disjunction clause of n variables can be represented by a single unique gene with n alternative promoters, one for each literal gene product. A conjunction can be implemented in a variety of ways: through multiple repressor sites (although the maximum number of repressor sites for any one gene is probably fairly small); through a cascade of reactions, each step requiring one of the input gene products, eventually producing an output product; and finally, we might encode the truth of a disjunction clause as the absence of a gene product. In this last case, a disjunction can be implemented by a constitutive (always on) gene with repressor literals. If any disjunction clause is false, it will produce a promoter protein to turn on the gene for the conjunction. If we make this final conjunction gene code for some reporter protein that is easily observed, then we can observe the truth of the encoded Boolean formula given the state of the literals. The entire process begins by randomly inverting the promoters for the literal genes in a large population of transgenic *E. coli* carrying our carefully constructed DNA encoding of the formula. Assuming that host cells can tolerate 1Mbase of foreign DNA and it takes 1Kbase per gene with $2n + m + 1$ genes (for n literals and m disjunction), we could conceivably solve formulas with $2n + m + 1 = 1000$. One liter of solution can hold about 10^{12} cells, and thus we might be able to handle up to $n = 40$ literals (we may have to reset the literals a time or two to generate a truth assignment that satisfies the formula). Of course, in reality both m and n would probably have to be less than 10 due to difficulties in designing the control of the computation. We also have to worry about interfering with the survival of the *E. coli* when we introduce hundreds of gene products to the cells (Eng 2000). Selection will likely excise the foreign DNA unless it is made necessary to the survival of the cells.

5.4   Conclusions

DNA computing still labors under a preponderance of theory. Laboratory experiments have only explored the nearest shoals. All the techniques from the section above, entitled Tools of the Trade, need to be examined with the same kind of rigor that Khodor and Gifford (1999) used to examine the sequence separation procedure. Potential improvements to the techniques should be explored. An efficient computational model should be derived from the least (or tolerably) error-prone manipulations along with algorithms for handling those errors that are unavoidable. This is the rather mundane work that would bring civilization to the hinterlands of current DNA computing. Nevertheless, glory will surely be heaped on she who demonstrates a DNA solution to a problem beyond the ken of silicon computation. This is the fabled fountain of youth for the field: The so-called killer app that will firmly establish DNA computing as more than just a curiosity. Yet no one truly knows if such a killer app exists. The catastrophes of errors may still sink all our hopes.

Meanwhile, one cause for real optimism in the future of DNA computing is its synergy with molecular biology. Almost any advances in techniques in one field will be useful to the other. The work of Seeman and others (Seeman et al. 1998; Gardner, Cantor, and Collins 2000; Elowitz and Leibler 2000) suggest that the major contribution of DNA computation may not even be to the field of computation but rather to the development of nanotechnology. Even if DNA computers never manage to leapfrog traditional silicon computers, they are still bound to be of value. Even if it proves impossible to implement a universal DNA computer—able to run all our software at blazingly fast speeds—the massively parallel nature of DNA computing is sure to be useful for certain practical problems. I take the position that DNA computation is likely to turn out to have a role similar to neural networks. They will be better than traditional methods for some problems, and worse for others. In this way, I expect DNA computation to complement rather than replace our current computational techniques.

Acknowledgments

Significant portions of this chapter have been reproduced from Maley (1998). I would like to thank MIT Press for their generosity in allowing me this freedom. I would also like to thank Erik Winfree and Laura Landweber for helpful comments and discussion. I would like to thank Stephanie Forrest for her patience and support. This work was carried out under her aegis and ONR Grant N00014-99-1-0417. Finally, I would like to thank Marvin Minsky for ushering me down this path.

References

Adleman, L. M. 1994. Molecular computation of solutions to combinatorial problems. *Science* 266: 1021–1024.

Adleman, L. M. 1996. On constructing a molecular computer. In *DNA Based Computers*, ed. R. J. Lipton and E. B. Baum, 1–22. Providence: American Mathematical Society.

Adleman, L. M., P. W. K. Rothemund, S. Roweis, and E. Winfree. 1996. On applying molecular computation to the data encryption standard. In *DNA Based Computers II*. Vol. 44 of *DIMACS: Series in Discrete Mathematics and Theoretical Computer Science*, ed. L. F. Landweber and E. B. Baum, 31–44. Providence: American Mathematical Society.

Amos, M., A. Gibbons, and D. Hodgson. 1998. Error-resistant implementation of DNA computations. In *DNA Based Computers II*. Vol. 44 of *DIMACS: Series in Discrete Mathematics and Theoretical Computer Science*, ed. L. F. Landweber and E. B. Baum, 151–162. Providence: American Mathematical Society.

Amos, M., S. Wilson, D. A. Hodgson, G. Owenson, and A. Gibbons. 1998. Practical implementation of DNA computations. In *Unconventional Models of Computation*, ed. C. Calvde, J. Casti, and M. Dinneen, 1–18. Heidelberg: Springer Verlag.

Bach, E., A. Condon, E. Glaser, and C. Tanguary. 1996. *DNA Models and Algorithms for NP-complete Problems*. New York: IEEE Computer Society Press.

Baum, E. B. 1998. DNA sequences useful for computation. In *DNA Based Computers II*. Vol. 44 of *DIMACS: Series in Discrete Mathematics and Theoretical Computer Science*, ed. L. F. Landweber and E. B. Baum, 235–242. Providence: American Mathematical Society.

Baum, E. B., and D. Boneh. 1996. Running dynamic programming algorithms on a DNA computer. In *DNA Based Computers II*. Vol. 44 of *DIMACS: Series in Discrete Mathematics and Theoretical Computer Science*, ed. L. F. Landweber and E. B. Baum, 77–86. Providence: American Mathematical Society.

Beaudry, A. A., and G. F. Joyce. 1992. Directed evolution of an RNA enzyme. *Science* 257: 635–641.

Beaver, D. 1995. Molecular computing. *Technical Report TR95-001*, Pennslyvania State University, University Park, Penn.

Beaver, D. 1996. A universal molecular computer. In *DNA Based Computers*, ed. E. B. Baum and R. J. Lipton, 29–36. Providence: American Mathematical Society.

Blumberg, A. J. 1999. Parallel computation on a DNA substrate. In *DNA Based Computers III*. Vol. 48 of *DIMACS: Series in Discrete Mathematics and Theoretical Computer Science*, ed. H. Rubin and D. H. Wood, 275–289. Providence: American Mathematical Society.

Boneh, D., C. Dunworth, and R. J. Lipton. 1995. Breaking DES using a molecular computer. *Technical Report CS-TR-489-95*, Princeton University, Princeton, N.J.

Boneh, D., C. Dunworth, and J. Sgall. 1995. On the computational power of DNA. *Technical Report TR-499-95*, Princeton University, Princeton N.J.

Calude, C., J. Casti, and M. Dinneen, eds. 1998. *Unconventional Models of Computation*. Heidelberg: Springer Verlag.

Cha, R. S., and W. G. Thilly. 1995. Specificity, efficiency, and fidelity of PCR. In *PCR primer*, ed. C. W. Dieffenbach and G. S. Dveksler, 37–52. Plainview, N.Y.: Cold Spring Harbor Laboratory Press.

Conrad, M. and K.-P. Zauner. 1999. Design for a DNA conformational processor. In *DNA Based Computers III*. Vol. 48 of *DIMACS: Series in Discrete Mathematics and Theoretical Computer Science*, ed. H. Rubin and D. H. Wood, 290–295. Providence: American Mathematical Society.

Csuhaj-Varjú, E., R. Freund, L. Kari, and G. Păun. 1996. DNA computation based on splicing: Universality results. In *Biocomputing: Proceedings of the 1996 Pacific Symposium*, ed. L. Hunter and T. Klein, 179–190. Singapore: World Scientific Publishing.

Cukras, A. R., D. Faulhammer, R. J. Lipton, and L. F. Landweber. 2000. Chess games: A model for RNA based computation. In *Preliminary Proceedings of the Fourth DIMACS Workshop on DNA Based Computers*, ed. L. Kari, 27–37.

Dawkins, R. 1995. *River out of Eden*. New York: Basic Books.

Deaton, R., R. C. Murphy, M. Garzon, D. R. Franceschetti, and J. Stevens. 1996. Good encodings for DNA-based solutions to combinatorial problems. In *DNA Based Computers II*. Vol. 44 of *DIMACS: Series in Discrete Mathematics and Theoretical Computer Science*, ed. L. F. Landweber and E. B. Baum, 247–258. Providence: American Mathematical Society.

Dieffenbach, C. W., and G. S. Dveksler. 1995. *PCR Primer*. Plainview, N.Y.: Cold Spring Harbor Laboratory Press.

Elowitz, M. B. and S. Leibler. 2000. A synthetic oscillatory network of transcriptional regulators. *Nature* 403: 335–338.

Eng, T. K. 2000. On solving 3CNF-satisfiability with an *in vivo* algorithm. In *Preliminary Proceedings of the Fourth DIMACS Workshop on DNA Based Computers*, ed. L. Kari, 163–171.

Faulhammer, D., A. R. Cukras, R. J. Lipton, and L. F. Landweber. 2000. When the knight falls: On constructing an RNA computer. In *DNA Based Computers V*. Vol. 54 of *DIMACS: Series in Discrete Mathematics and Theoretical Computer Science*, ed. E. Winfree and D. K. Gifford, 1–8. Providence: American Mathematical Society.

Gannon, F., and R. Powell. 1991. Construction of recombinant DNA. In *Essential Molecular Biology*, ed. T. A. Brown, 143–160. Oxford: Oxford University Press.

Gánti, I. 1987. *The Principle of Life*. Budapest: OMIKK.

Gardner, T. S., C. R. Cantor, and J. J. Collins. 2000. Construction of a genetic toggle switch in Escherichia coli. *Nature* 403: 339–342.

Gifford, D. K. 1994. On the path to computation with DNA. *Science* 266: 993–994.

Guarnieri, F., M. Fliss, and C. Bancroft. 1996. Making DNA add. *Science* 273: 220–223.

Hagiya, H., M. Arita, M., D. Kiga, K. Sakamoto, and S. Yokoyama. 1999. Towards parallel evaluation and learning of Boolean μ-formulas with molecules. In *DNA Based Computers III*. Vol. 48 of *DIMACS: Series in Discrete Mathematics and Theoretical Computer Science*, ed. H. Rubin and D. H. Wood, 105–114. Providence: American Mathematical Society.

Hartemink, A. J., D. K. Gifford, and J. Khodor. 2000. Automated constraint-based nucleotide sequence selection for DNA computation. In *Preliminary Proceedings of the Fourth DIMACS Workshop on DNA Based Computers*, ed. L. Kari, 287–297.

Head, T. 1987. Formal language theory and DNA: An analysis of the generative capacity of specific recombinant behaviors. *Bull. Math. Biol.* 49: 737–759.

Ji, S. 2000. The cell as a DNA-based molecular computer. In *Preliminary Proceedings of the Fourth DIMACS Workshop on DNA Based Computers*, ed. L. Kari, 151–162.

Kampis, G., and V. Csányi. 1991. Life, self-reproduction, and information: Beyond the machine metaphor. *J. Theor. Biol.* 148: 17–32.

Kaplan, P. D., G. Cecci, and A. Libchaber. 1995. Molecular computation: Adleman's experiment repeated. Technical report, NEC Research Institute, Princeton, N.J.

Kaplan, P. D., G. Cecchi, and A. Libchaber. 1996. DNA based molecular computation: Template-template interactions in PCR. In *DNA Based Computers II*. Vol. 44 of *DIMACS: Series in Discrete Mathematics and Theoretical Computer Scierce*, ed. L. F. Landweber and E. B. Baum, 97–104. Providence: American Mathematical Society.

Kari, L. 1996. DNA computers, tomorrow's reality. *Bull. Eur. Assoc. Theor. Comput. Sci.* 59: 256–266.

Kari, L., ed. 2000. *Preliminary Proceedings of the fourth DIMACS Workshop on DNA Based Computers*, held at the University of Pennsylvania, 15–19 June 1998. In press.

Kari, L., and L. Landweber. 2000. Computational power of gene rearrangement. In *DNA Based Computers V*. Vol. 54 of *DIMACS: Series in Discrete Mathematics and Theoretical Computer Science*, ed. E. Winfree and D. K. Gifford, 203–213. Providence: American Mathematical Society.

Karp, R., C. Kenyon, and O. Waarts. 1995. Error resilient DNA computation. Research report 95-20, Laboratoire de l'Informatique du Parallélism, Ecole Normale Supérieure de Lyon.

Kazic, T. 2000. After the Turing machine: A metamodel for molecular computing. In *Preliminary Proceedings of the Fourth DIMACS Workshop on DNA Based Computers*, ed. L. Kari, 131–149.

Khodor, J., and D. K. Gifford. 1999. The efficiency of sequence-specific separation of DNA mixtures for biological computing. In *DNA Based Computers III*. Vol. 48 of *DIMACS: Series in Discrete Mathematics and Theoretical Computer Science*, ed. H. Rubin and D. H. Wood, 26–34. Providence: American Mathematical Society.

Khodor, J., and D. K. Gifford. 2000. Design and implementation of computational systems based on programmed mutagenesis. In *Preliminary Proceedings of the Fourth DIMACS Workshop on DNA Based Computers*, ed. L. Kari, 101–107.

Knight, T. F., and G. J. Sussman. 1997. Cellular gate technology. In *Unconventional Models of Computation*, ed. C. S. Calude, J. Casti, and M. J. Dinneen, 257–272. Singapore: Springer-Verlag.

Kurtz, S. A., S. Mahaney, J. Royer, and J. Simon. 1997. Biological computing. In *Complexity Retrospective II*, ed. L. A. Hemaspaandra and A. L. Selman. Singapore: Springer Verlag.

Landweber, L. F., and E. B. Baum, eds. 1998. *DNA Based Computers II*. Vol. 44 of *DIMACS: Series in Discrete Mathematics and Theoretical Computer Science*. Providence: American Mathematical Society.

Landweber, L. F., and L. Kari. 2000. The evolution of cellular computing: Nature's solution to a computational problem. In *Preliminary Proceedings of the Fourth DIMACS Workshop on DNA Based Computers*, ed. L. Kari, 3–13.

Landweber, L. F., R. J. Lipton, and M. O. Rabin. 1999. DNA^{2}DNA computations: A potential "killer app?" In *DNA Based Computers III*. Vol. 48 of *DIMACS: Series in Discrete Mathematics and Theoretical Computer Scierce*, ed. H. Rubin and D. H. Wood, 161–172. Providence: American Mathematical Society.

Linial, M., and N. Linial. 1995. Letters to *Science*. *Science* 268: 481.

Lipton, R. J. 1995. DNA solution of hard computational problems. *Science* 268: 542–545.

Lipton, R. J., and E. D. Baum, eds. 1996. *DNA Based Computers*. Vol. 27 of *DIMACS: Series in Discrete Mathematics and Theoretical Computer Science*. Providence: American Mathematical Society.

Liu, Q., A. G. Frutos, L. Wang, A. J. Thiel, S. D. Gillmor, T. Strother, A. E. Condon, R. M. Corn, M. G. Lagally, and L. M. Smith. 2000a. Progress towards demonstration of a surface based DNA computation: A one-word approach to solve a model satisfiability problem. In *Preliminary Proceedings of the Fourth DIMACS Workshop on DNA Based Computers*, ed. L. Kari, 15–25.

Liu, Q., L. Wang, A. G. Frutos, A. E. Condon, R. M. Corn, and L. M. Smith. 2000b. DNA computing on surfaces. *Nature* 371: 31–36.

Lönneborg, A., P. Sharma, and P. Stougaard. 1995. Construction of a subtractive cDNA libary using magnetic beads and PCR. In *PCR Primer*, ed. C. W. Dieffenbach and G. S. Dveksler, 439–452. Plainview, N.Y.: Cold Spring Harbor Laboratory Press.

Lorsch, J. R., and J. W. Szostak. 1994. In vitro evolution of new ribozymes with polynucleotide kinase activity. *Nature* 371: 31–36.

Lustig, A. J. 1998. Mechanisms of silencing in *Saccharomyces cerevisiae*. *Curr. Opin. Genetics Dev.* 8: 233–239.

Maley, C. C. 1998. DNA computation: Theory, practice, and prospects. *Evolutionary Comput.* 6: 201–229.

Oliver, J. S. 1996. Computation with DNA-matrix multiplication. In *DNA Based Computers II*. Vol. 44 of *DIMACS: Series in Discrete Mathematics and Theoretical Computer Science*, ed. L. F. Landweber and E. B. Baum, 113–122. Providence: American Mathematical Society.

Ouyang, Q., P. D. Kaplan, S. Liu, and A. Libchaber. 1997. DNA solution of the maximal clique problem. *Science* 278: 446–449.

Păun, G., G. Rozenberg, and A. Salomaa. 1998. *DNA computing: New Computing Paradigms*. Heidelberg: Springer-Verlag.

Reif, J. 1998. Paradigms for biomolecular computation. In *Unconventional Models of Computation*, ed. C. Calude, J. Casti, and M. Dinneen, 72–93. Heidelberg: Springer Verlag.

Rothemund, P. W. K. 1996. A DNA and restriction enzyme implementation of Turing machines. In *DNA Based Computers*. Vol. 27 of *DIMACS: Series in Discrete Mathematics and Theoretical Computer Science*, ed. R. J. Lipton and E. D. Baum, 75–120. Providence: American Mathematical Society.

Roweis, S., E. Winfree, R. Burgoyne, N. Y. Chelyapov, M. R. Goodman, P. W. K. Rothemund, and L. M. Adleman. 1996. A sticker-based architecture for DNA computation. In *DNA Based Computers II*. Vol. 44 of *DIMACS: Series in Discrete Mathematics and Theoretical Computer Scierce*, ed. L. F. Landweber and E. B. Baum, 1–30. Providence: American Mathematical Society.

Rubin, H., and D. H. Wood, eds. 1999. *DNA Based Computers III*. Vol. 48 of *DIMACS: Series in Discrete Mathematics and Theoretical Computer Science*. Providence: American Mathematical Society.

Sakamoto, K., D. Kiga, K. Komiya, H. Gouzu, S. Yokoyama, S. Ikeda, H. Sugiyama, and M. Hagiya. 2000. State transitions by molecules. In *Preliminary Proceedings of the Fourth DIMACS Workshop on DNA Based Computers*, ed. L. Kari, 87–99.

Santoro, S. W., and G. F. Joyce. 1997. A general purpose RNA-cleaving DNA enzyme. *Proc. Natl. Acad. Sci. USA* 94: 4262–4266.

Sassanfar, M., and J. W. Szostak. 1993. An RNA motif that binds ATP. *Nature* 364: 550–553.

Seeman, N. S., H. Wang, X. Yang, F. Liu, C. Mao, W. Sun, L. Wenzler, Z. Shen, R. Sha, H. Yan, M. H. Wong, P. Sa-Ardyen, B. Liu, H. Qiu, X. Li, J. Qi, S. M. Du, Y. Zhang, J. E. Mueller, T.-J. Fu, Y. Wang, and J. Chen. 1998. New motifs in DNA nanotechnology. *Nanotechnology* 9: 257–273.

Smith, W. D. 1995. DNA computers in vitro and vivo. Technical report, NEC Research Institute. Presented at DIMACS Workshop on DNA Based Computing, Princeton, 4 April.

Stemmer, W. P. C. 1994. Rapid evolution of a protein in vitro by DNA shuffling. *Nature* 370: 389–391.

Vahey, M. T., M. T. Wong, and N. L. Michael. 1995. A standard PCR protocol: Rapid isolation of DNA and PCR assay for β-globin. In *PCR Primer*, ed. C. W. Dieffenbach and G. S. Dveksler, 17–22. Plainview, N.Y.: Cold Spring Harbor Laboratory Press.

Wang, L., Q. Liu, A. G. Frutos, S. D. Gillmor, A. J. Thiel, T. C. Strother, A. E. Condon, R. M. Corn, M. G. Lagally, and L. M. Smith. 2000. Surface-based DNA computing operations: DESTROY and READOUT. In *Preliminary Proceedings of the Fourth DIMACS Workshop on DNA Based Computers*, ed. L. Kari, 247 (poster).

Winfree, E. 1996. On the computational power of DNA annealing and ligation. In *DNA Based Computers*. Vol. 27 of *DIMACS: Series in Discrete Mathematics and Theoretical Computer Science*, ed. R. J. Lipton and E. D. Baum, 199–221. Providence: American Mathematical Society.

Winfree, E. 2000. Whiplash PCR for $O(1)$ computing. In *Preliminary Proceedings of the Fourth DIMACS Workshop on DNA Based Computers*, ed. L. Kari, 175–188.

Winfree, E., and D. K. Gifford, eds. 2000. *DNA Based Computers V*, Vol. 54 of *DIMACS: Series in Discrete Mathematics and Theoretical Computer Science*. Providence: American Mathematical Society.

Winfree, E., F. Lin, L. Wenzler, and N. C. Seeman. 1998. Design and self-assembly of two-dimensional DNA crystals. *Nature* 394: 539–545.

Winfree, E., X. Yang, and N. C. Seeman. 1998. Universal computation via self-assembly of DNA: Some theory and experiments. In *DNA Based Computers II*. Vol. 44 of *DIMACS: Series in Discrete Mathematics and Theoretical Computer Science*, ed. L. F. Landweber and E. B. Baum, 191–214. Providence: American Mathematical Society.

Yoshinobu, T., Y. Aoi, K. Tanizawa, and H. Iwasaki. 2000. Ligation errors in DNA computing. In *Preliminary Proceedings of the Fourth DIMACS Workshop on DNA Based Computers*, ed. L. Kari, 245–246.

6 Bioelectronics and Protein-Based Optical Memories and Processors

Duane L. Marcy, Bryan W. Vought, and Robert R. Birge

Molecular computing is defined as the encoding, manipulation, and retrieval of information at a molecular or macromolecular level. Bioelectronics (or biomolecular electronics) is a subfield of molecular electronics that investigates the use of native, as well as modified biological molecules (chromophores, proteins, etc.), in place of the organic molecules synthesized in the laboratory. Because natural selection processes have often solved problems of a similar nature to those that must be solved in harnessing organic compounds, and because self-assembly and genetic engineering provide sophisticated control and manipulation of large molecules, bioelectronics has shown considerable promise. The ability to explore new architectures unique to molecular-based systems has a potential equal to that provided by molecular-scale engineering and miniaturization.

Semiconductor electronics is a well-established technology for developing computing systems. Therefore one should not consider that bioelectronics could instantly replace semiconductor electronics as a tool for developing computing systems, but that it will become a more competitive technology as the trend advances toward more powerful computers. The continuing push toward miniaturization and high speed as evidenced by Moore's Law is driving the semiconductor industry toward the limits of lithographic manipulation of bulk materials and into the domain of the molecular world. Experts in the semiconductor industry predict that standard room-temperature silicon CMOS will reach its scalable limit within the next two decades and after that, new inventions, particularly new "transistors" as well as new computer architectures, will be needed to circumvent currently known material, device, and circuit limits (Meindl 1993). When the requirement to directly manipulate compounds at the molecular level is reached, technologies such as bioelectronics will become more viable. For this reason, this chapter begins by comparing bioelectronics to semiconductor electronics as the molecular limit is approached.

A bioelectronic material that has gathered considerable interest is the protein bacteriorhodopsin. The salt marsh bacterium *Halobacterium salinarium* uses the protein in a process that converts light energy to chemical energy, and therefore it has many unique optoelectronic properties. The properties important for employing bacteriorhodopsin in computing systems will be discussed. Bacteriorhodopsin has found many applications as a storage and computing material. Several systems in the field of optical memories and optical processors that have been prototyped or envisioned are described in this chapter.

Finally, the fact that bacteriorhodopsin is a biological substance opens the door for a unique method of material optimization. Although the optimization of inorganic materials requires detailed knowledge of the structure and properties of that material before modifications can be made to improve its performance in an application, a biological material can be modified simply based on its performance. Through genetic mutation, changes in a material can be tested to see if they decrease or increase the performance of the material in the application. The mutations that improve the system can then be further modified, forcing an accelerated version of evolution to take place. Evolution, which has worked so well in making the material perform its function in the living organism, is now applied to make the material work in the application of interest. This can all take place without detailed knowledge of the structure or properties of the material. Genetic engineering as applied in this manner is described in the final section of this chapter.

6.1   Bioelectronics versus Semiconductor Electronics

One of the best ways to introduce bioelectronic computing is to compare the potential advantages of this new technology with the current advantages of semiconductor electronics, as outlined in table 6.1. Many additional characteristics could have been

Table 6.1
Potential advantages of implementing bioelectronics and current advantages of semiconductor electronics

Characteristic	Potential Advantages (Bioelectronics)	Current Advantages (Semiconductor)
Size	Small size of molecular scale offers high intrinsic speed. Picosecond switching rates are common.	Already impressive minimum feature sizes are decreasing by 15%/year. However, advancement into the molecular domain will be limited by similar hurdles faced by bioelectronics.
Speed	High intrinsic speed is a result of small size. Picosecond switching rates are common.	Current clock speeds are on the order of 1 GHz and a factor of 3–5 improvement is expected before the standard technology reaches its scalable limit.
Nanoscale engineering	Synthetic organic chemistry, self-assembly and genetic engineering provide nanometer resolution.	Nanolithography provides higher scale factors and flexibility than current molecular techniques.
Architecture	Neural, associative and parallel architectures can be implemented directly.	Three terminal devices and standard logic designs offer high levels of integration.
Reliability	Ensemble averaging via optical coupling or state assignment averaging provides high reliability.	Current technology provides highly reliable systems, but advancement toward molecular realm will create reliability issues.

included, but those listed in table 6.1 were selected to provide the broadest coverage with a minimum number of categories. The first column of table 6.1 serves to represent the principal issues that not only encourage but also challenge scientists seeking to implement bioelectronics. We should also point out that many of the same challenges faced by molecular engineers to achieve the goals of miniaturization and speed will soon be faced by the semiconductor engineers as technology advances. The problems involved in developing computing systems become the same (i.e., quantum limits, interconnect issues, nanoscale engineering, and stability and reliability issues), independent of the technology used, as the molecular level is approached. We discuss each item in table 6.1 separately below.

Size

Molecules are synthesized "from the bottom up" by carrying out additive synthesis, starting with readily available organic compounds. Bulk semiconductor devices are generated "from the top down" via lithographic manipulation of bulk materials. A synthetic chemist can selectively add an oxygen atom to a chromophore with a precision that is far greater than a comparable lithographic step—facilitated using electron beams or X-rays—to pattern an oxide layer on a semiconductor surface. Molecular-based gates can be made hundreds of times smaller than their semiconductor equivalents. At the same time, such gates have yet to approach a comparable level of reliability or interconnect capacity as compared to their semiconductor counterparts.

Consider the size of transistors fabricated in production for use in computers today. A schematic diagram of such a device is shown in figure 6.1. Superimposed over this schematic is a scanning capacitance image of an experimental transistor created by Bell Labs which is near the minimum limit for the standard room temperature CMOS architecture. The Semetech semiconductor roadmap predicts that transistor fabrication of this size will be reached in approximately the year 2012 (ITRS, 1999). A small white window appears in this image, which is a scale representation of a bacteriorhodopsin molecule. The BR molecule by itself is a complete optically triggered binary switching device. Notice that the switching devices considered in bioelectronics are of an extremely small size. The key research effort in the bioelectronics field is to develop an architecture that can harness the switching capability of extremely small components such as the bacteriorhodopsin molecule.

It is also interesting to examine the trends in bit size that have characterized the last few decades of memory development. The results shown in figure 6.2 indicate that the area per bit has decreased logarithmically since the early 1970s (Keyes 1992; Birge 1994). For comparison, we also show in figure 6.2 the cross-sectional area per

Schematic layout of a 180 nm transistor in use today (year 2000)

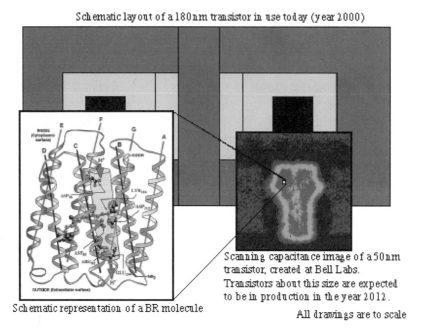

Schematic representation of a BR molecule

Scanning capacitance image of a 50 nm transistor, created at Bell Labs.
Transistors about this size are expected to be in production in the year 2012.

All drawings are to scale

Figure 6.1
A schematic representation of a semiconductor transistor currently in production (0.18-μm minimum dimension). A scanning capacitance image of a 0.05-μm transistor fabricated at Bell Labs (© 2000 Lucent Technology) is superimposed over this schematic with the same scale factor. The 0.05-μm transistor is considered to be about the minimum dimension for room temperature CMOS device operation because the "off" state will not be separable from the "on" state due to noise in smaller devices. Transistors of this size are to be fabricated in production around the year 2012 (Sematech). Also, inset in the figure is a small white square. The square represents the relative size of a bacteriorhodopsin molecule, which by itself is a complete optically activated switching device.

bit calculated for the human brain (assuming one neuron is equivalent to one bit) and for proposed three-dimensional memories and proposed molecular memories. Although current technology has surpassed the cross-sectional density of the human brain, the major advantage of the neural system of the brain is that information is stored in three dimensions. At present, the mind of a human being can store more "information" than the disk storage allocated to the largest supercomputer. Of course, the human brain is not digital, and such comparisons are tenuous. Nevertheless, the analogy underscores the fact that current memory technology is still anemic compared to the technology that is inherent in the human brain. It also demonstrates the rationale for, and potential of, the development of three-dimensional memories as described later in this chapter. We can also conclude from

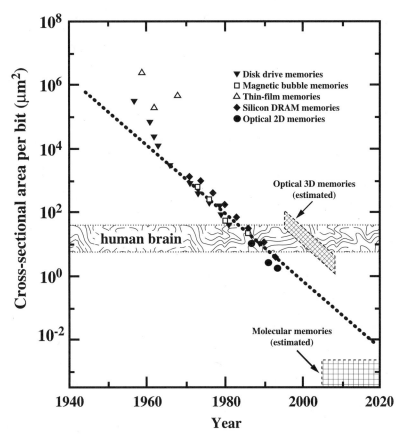

Figure 6.2
Analysis of the area in square microns required to store a single bit of information as a function of the evolution of computer technology in years. The data for magnetic disk, magnetic bubble, thin-film and silicon DRAM memories are taken from (Keyes 1992). These data are compared to the cross-sectional area per bit (neuron) for the human brain as well as anticipated areas and implementation times for optical three-dimensional memories and molecular memories (Birge 1994). Note that the optical 3D memory, the brain and the molecular memories are three-dimensional and therefore the cross-sectional area (A) per bit is plotted for comparison. The area is calculated in terms of the volume per bit, V/bit, by the formula $A = (V)^{2/3}$.

an analysis of figure 6.2 that the trend in memory densities will soon force the bulk semiconductor industry to address some of the same issues that confront scientists who seek to implement molecular electronics.

Speed

Molecular gates achieve very rapid switching speeds due in large part to their small sizes. Whether the gate is designed to operate via electron transfer, electron tunneling, or conformational photochromism, a decrease in size will yield a comparable increase in speed. The fact that all gates in use, under study, or envisioned, are activated by the shift in the position of a charge carrier and all charge carriers have mass, creates the speed-versus-size trade-off. Whether the device is classical or relativistic, the mass of the carrier places a limit on how rapidly the conformational change can take place. One can criticize this view as arbitrarily restrictive in that electrostatic changes can be generated via optical excitation, and the generation of an excited electronic state can occur within a large chromophore in less than one femtosecond (one femtosecond = 10^{-15} sec, the time it takes light to travel ~ 0.3 μm). Nevertheless, the reaction of the system to the charge shift is still a size-dependent property and the relationship between the total size of the device and the response time remains valid. A comparison of switching speeds of molecular versus some of the higher-speed semiconductor gates and switches is presented in figure 6.3.

When considering extremely small devices, the ultimate speed is determined by quantum mechanical effects. Heisenberg uncertainty limits the maximum frequency of operation, f_{max}, of a monoelectronic or monomolecular device based on the following relationship (Birge, Lawrence, and Tallent 1991):

$$f_{max} \cong \frac{0.00800801 \cdot \tilde{v}_s \cdot \pi^2}{hN\left[2\pi + 2\tan^{-1}(-2) + \ln\left(\dfrac{\tilde{v}_s^2}{4}\right) - \ln\left(\dfrac{5\tilde{v}_s^2}{4}\right)\right]} \qquad (6.1a)$$

$$f_{max}(\text{GHz}) \approx \frac{0.963\tilde{v}_s}{N} \qquad (6.1b)$$

where v_s is the energy separation of the two states of the device in wave numbers and N is the number of state assignments that must be averaged to achieve reliable state assignment. This equation only applies to monoelectronic or monomolecular devices; Heisenberg's uncertainty principle permits higher frequencies for ensemble averaged devices. For example, if a device requires 1000 state assignment averages to achieve reliability and $v_s \cong 1000$ cm^{-1}, it will have a maximum operating frequency of ~ 960 MHz. (The concept of state assignment averaging is defined and quantita-

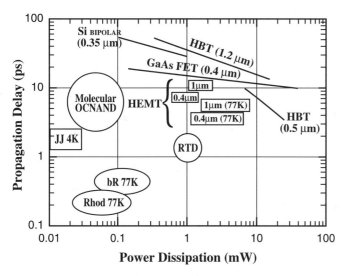

Figure 6.3
The propagation delay and power dissipation of selected molecular systems and semiconductor devices. HBT, hetero-junction bipolar transistor; HEMT, high electron mobility transistor; RTD, resonant tunneling device; OCNAND, optically coupled NAND gate; JJ, Josephson junction; bR, bacteriorhodopsin primary photochemical event; Rhod, visual rhodopsin primary photochemical event. Feature sizes of the semiconductor devices are indicated in parentheses. Propagation delay of photonic molecular devices are defined in terms of the time necessary for the absorption spectrum to reach $1/e$ of the final photoproduct absorption maximum.

tively examined in Birge, Lawrence, and Tallent 1991.) Virtually all monomolecular or monoelectronic devices require $N > 500$ at ambient temperature, but cryogenic devices operating at 1.2 K can approach $N = 1$. Thus, although molecular devices have an inherent advantage with respect to speed, quantum mechanics places constraints on the maximum operating frequency, and these constraints are significant at ambient temperatures.

Nanoscale Engineering
As indicated in figure 6.2, continued improvement in computer processing power requires a decrease in feature size. Driven by the demand for higher speeds and densities, submicron feature sizes are now commonplace. Ultraviolet lithography must eventually be replaced by higher resolution techniques such as electron beam or X-ray lithography. Although such lithography is well understood, it is very expensive to implement. As we have noted above, organic synthesis provides a "bottom-up" approach that offers a 10- to 100-fold improvement in resolution relative to the best

lithographic methods. Organic synthesis has been developed to a high level of sophistication, due in large part to the efforts of natural product synthetic chemists to re-create a priori the complex molecules that nature has developed via billions of years of natural selection. There is already a sophisticated synthetic effort within the drug industry, and thus a commercially viable molecular electronic device could likely be generated in large quantities using present commercial facilities.

There are two alternatives to organic synthesis that have had a significant impact on current efforts in molecular electronics; self-assembly and genetic engineering. The use of the Langmuir-Blodgett technique to prepare organized structures is the best known example of self-assembly (Birge 1994b; Ratner and Jortner 1997). But self-assembly can also be used in the generation of membrane-based devices, micro-tubule-based devices, and liquid crystal holographic films (Birge 1994b; Ratner and Jortner 1997). Genetic engineering offers a unique approach to the generation and manipulation of large biological molecules. We discuss this unique element of bio-electronics below. Thus molecular electronics provides at least three discrete methods of generating nanoscale devices: organic synthesis, self-assembly, and mutagenesis. The fact that the latter two methods currently offer access to larger and often more complicated structures has been responsible in part for the early success of bio-molecular electronics. All three techniques offer resolutions significantly better than those possible via bulk lithography.

Architecture
The fundamental building block of current computer systems and signal processing circuitry is the three-terminal transistor. Lithography offers an advantage that none of the techniques available to bioelectronics can duplicate. Lithography can be used to construct ultra large scale integrated (ULSI) devices involving from 10^7 to 10^9 discrete components with complex interconnections. The true power of the integrated circuit does not come from the fact that many millions of devices can be fabricated on a chip, but stems from the ability to interconnect the devices in a complex circuit. This particular architecture is difficult to implement using molecules, although it should be recognized that it is even becoming difficult to implement with semi-conductor materials. As an example, one can cite the need to switch to copper from aluminum for the interconnection material because aluminum has become suscepti-ble to electromigration at the wire size in use today. It is not clear how interconnect technology would be implemented with molecular-sized semiconductor transistors.

Bioelectronics offers significant potential for exploring new architectures and rep-resents one of the key features prompting the enthusiasm of researchers. The need for new architectures as devices approach the molecular level could encourage the investigation and development of new designs based on neural, associative, or parallel architectures and lead to hybrid systems with enhanced capabilities relative to current technology. For example, as described later in this chapter, optical associative memories and three-dimensional memories can be implemented with unique capabilities based on molecular electronics (Birge et al. 1997). Implementation of these memories within hybrid systems is anticipated to have near-term application. Furthermore, the human brain, a computer with capabilities that far exceed the most advanced supercomputer, is a prime example of the potential of molecular electronics (Kandel, Schwartz, and Jessell 1991). Although the development of an artificial neural computer is beyond our current technology, it would be illogical to assume that such an accomplishment is impossible. Thus we should view molecular electronics as opening new architectural opportunities that will lead to advances in computer and signal processing systems.

Reliability

The issue of reliability has been invoked repeatedly by semiconductor scientists and engineers as a reason to view molecular electronics as impractical. Some believe that the need to use ensemble averaging in optically coupled molecular gates and switches is symptomatic of the inherent unreliability of molecular electronic devices. This point of view is comparable to suggesting that transistors are inherently unreliable because more than one charge carrier must be used to provide satisfactory performance. The majority of ambient-temperature molecular and bulk semiconductor devices use more than one molecule or charge carrier to represent a bit for two reasons: ensemble averaging improves reliability and it permits higher speeds. The nominal use of ensemble averaging does not, however, rule out reliable monomolecular or monoelectronic devices.

The probability of correctly assigning the state of a single molecule, p_1, is never exactly unity. This less-than-perfect assignment capability is due to quantum effects as well as inherent limitations in the state assignment process. The probability of an error in state assignment, P_{error}, is a function of p_1 and the number of molecules, n, within the ensemble used to represent a single bit of information. P_{error} can be approximated by the following formula (Birge, Lawrence, and Tallent 1991):

$$P_{error}(n, p_1) \cong -erf\left[\frac{(2p_1 + 1)\sqrt{n}}{4\sqrt{2p_1(1 - p_1)}} \cdot \frac{(2p_1 - 1)\sqrt{n}}{4\sqrt{2p_1(1 - p_1)}}\right] \qquad (6.2)$$

where $erf[Z_0; Z_1]$ is the differential error function defined by:

$$erf[Z_0; Z_1] = Erf[Z_1] - Erf[Z_0] \qquad (6.3)$$

where

$$erf[Z] = \frac{2}{(\pi)^{1/2}} \int_0^Z \exp(-t^2)\, dt \tag{6.4}$$

Equation 6.2 is approximate and neglects error associated with the probability that the number of molecules in the correct conformation can stray from their expectation values based on statistical considerations. Nevertheless, it is sufficient to demonstrate the issue of reliability and ensemble size. First, we define a logarithmic reliability parameter, ξ, which is related to the probability of error in the measurement of the state of the ensemble (device) by the function, $P_{error} = 10^{-\xi}$. A value of $\xi = 10$ is considered a minimal requirement for reliability in non-error-correcting digital architectures.

If we assume that the state of a single molecule can be assigned correctly with a probability of 90 percent ($p_1 = 0.9$), then equation 6.2 indicates that 95 molecules must collectively represent a single bit to yield $\xi > 10$ [$P_{error}(95, 0.9) \cong 8 \times 10^{-11}$]. We must recognize that a value of $p_1 = 0.9$ is larger than is normally observed—some examples of reliability analyses for specific molecular-based devices are given in Birge, Lawrence, and Tallent (1991). In general, ensembles larger than 10^3 are required for reliability unless fault-tolerant or fault-correcting architectures can be implemented.

The question then arises as to whether or not we can design a reliable computer or memory that uses a single molecule to represent a bit of information. The answer is "yes," provided one of two conditions apply. The first condition is architectural. It is possible to design fault-tolerant architectures that either recover from digital errors or simply operate reliably with occasional error due to analog or analog-type environments. An example of digital error correction is the use of additional bits beyond the number required to represent a number. This approach is common in semiconductor memories, and under most implementations these additional bits provide for single bit error correction and multiple bit error detection. Such architectures lower the required value of ε to values less than 4. An example of analog error tolerance is embodied in many optical computer designs that use holographic and/or Fourier architectures to carry out complex functions.

The second condition is more subtle. It is possible to design molecular architectures that can undergo a state reading process that does not disturb the state of the molecule. For example, an electrostatic switch could be designed that can be "read" without changing the state of the switch. Alternatively, an optically coupled device can be read by using a wavelength that is absorbed or diffracted but that does not initiate state conversion. Under these conditions, the variable n (which appears in equation 6.2) can be defined as the number of read "operations" rather than the ensemble size. Thus our previous example, indicating that 95 molecules must be included in the ensemble to achieve reliability, can be restated as follows: A single molecule can be used, provided we can carry out 95 nondestructive measurements to define the state. Multiple-state measurements are equivalent to integrated measurements, and should not be interpreted as a start-read-stop cycle repeated n number of times. A continuous read with digital or analog averaging can achieve the same level of reliability.

6.2 Bioelectronic Devices Based on Bacteriorhodopsin

Bacteriorhodopsin is the light-transducing protein in the cell membrane of an archae bacterium called *Halobacterium salinarium*, an organism originally called *Halobacterium halobium* (Oesterhelt and Stockenius 1971; Balashov, Litvin, and Sineshchekov 1988; Mathies et al. 1991; El-Sayed 1992; Lanyi 1992; Ebrey 1993; Luecke et al. 1999). Upon absorption of light, a covalently attached chromophore (light-absorbing group) initiates a complex series of molecular events that converts light energy to chemical energy. Bacteriorhodopsin-based devices exploit this complex series of spectrally distinct thermal intermediates (Zimanyi and Lanyi 1993; Lanyi and Varo 1995). The excellent holographic properties of the protein derive from the large change in refractive index that occurs following light activation. Furthermore, bacteriorhodopsin converts light into a refractive index change with remarkable efficiency (approximately 65%). The protein is ten times smaller than the wavelength of the stimulating light. Therefore the diffraction limit of the optical geometry, rather than the "graininess" of the film, determines the resolution of the thin film. Because the protein can absorb two photons simultaneously with an efficiency that far exceeds other materials, it can store information in three dimensions using two-photon architectures. Finally, the protein was designed by nature to function under conditions of high temperature and intense light (Shen et al. 1993; Lukashev and Robertson 1995), a necessary requirement for a salt marsh bacterial protein and a significant advantage for photonic device applications.

Photonic Properties of Bacteriorhodopsin
When the protein absorbs light in the native organism, it undergoes a complex photocycle, which generates intermediates with absorption maxima spanning the entire visible region of the spectrum (figure 6.4). Most current devices operate at ambient or

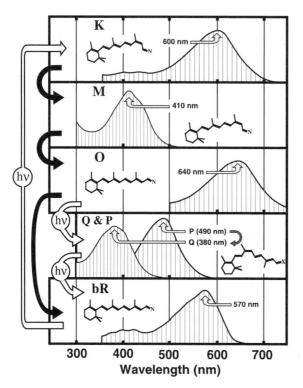

Figure 6.4
Spectra of select intermediates during the bacteriorhodopsin photocycle. The outlined arrows indicate photochemical transitions, and the solid arrow represent thermal transitions. The insets represent the conformation of the retinal in that state. N, nitrogen; X, Schiff base nitrogen (in P) or carbonyl oxygen (in Q).

near-ambient temperature and utilize the following two states: the initial green-red absorbing state (bR) and the long-lived blue absorbing state (M). The forward reaction only takes place via light activation and is complete in ~50 μsec. In contrast, the reverse reaction can be either light activated or can occur thermally. The light-activated $M \rightarrow bR$ transition is a direct photochemical transformation. The thermal $M \rightarrow bR$ transition is highly sensitive to temperature, environment, genetic modification, and chromophore substitution. This sensitivity is exploited in many optical devices based on bacteriorhodopsin. Another reaction of importance is a photochemical branching reaction from the O intermediate to form P. This intermediate subsequently decays to form Q, a species that is unique in that the chromophore breaks the bond with the protein but is trapped inside the binding site. The Q intermediate is stable for extended periods of time (many years) but can be photochemically converted back to *bR*. This branching reaction provides for long-term data storage, as discussed below (Birge et al. 1994).

Associative Memories

Associative memories take an input data block (or image) and, independently of the central processor, "scan" the entire memory for the data block that matches the input. In some implementations, the memory will find the closest match if it cannot find a perfect match. Finally, the memory will return the data block in memory that satisfies the matching criteria or it will return the address of the data block to permit access of contiguous data. Some memories will simply return a binary bit indicating whether the input data are present or not present. Because the human brain operates in a neural, associative mode, many computer scientists believe that the implementation of large capacity, high-speed associative memories will be required if we are to achieve genuine artificial intelligence. We have implemented the design proposed by Paek and Psaltis (1987) by using thin films of bacteriorhodopsin as the photoactive components in holographic associative memories (Birge et al. 1997). The memory is shown schematically in figure 6.5.

Both the reference and input images are entered into the system via a spatial light modulator (input SLM) and are focused via Fourier lenses (FL) onto the two holographic films, H1 and H2. Fourier association at H1 results in preferential illumination of the pinhole corresponding to the reference image that has the highest correlation (similarity) to the input image, or partial image. The radiation passing through that pinhole illuminates the selected image on H2, which is then transferred out of the associative loop onto a CCD detector. Thresholding is handled electronically, rather than optically in this implementation; however, optical thresholding can improve performance (Paek and Psaltis 1987; Gross, Izgi, and Birge 1992; Birge et al. 1997). As the example in figure 6.5 shows, only a partial input image is required to generate a complete output image.

The utility of the associative memory regarding a data search can be greatly enhanced by rapidly changing the holographic reference pattern via the single optical input while maintaining both feedback and thresholding. In conjunction with solid-state hardware, a search engine of this type can be integrated into hybrid computer architectures. The diffraction limited performance of the protein films, coupled with high write/erase speeds associated with the excellent quantum efficiencies of these films, represents a key element in the potential of this memory. The ability to modify the protein by selectively replacing one amino acid with another (see discussion below) provides significant flexibility in enhancing the properties of the protein (Hampp et al. 1994).

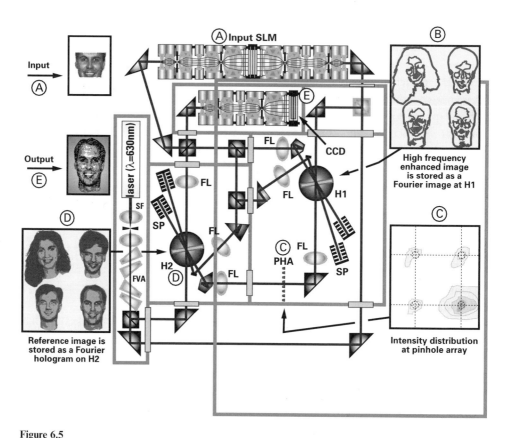

Figure 6.5
Schematic diagram of a Fourier transform holographic (FTH) associative memory with read/write FTH reference planes using thin polymer films of bacteriorhodopsin to provide real-time storage of the holograms. Note that a partial input image can select and regenerate the entire associated image stored on the reference hologram. Although only four reference images are shown, an optical associative memory can store many hundreds or thousands of images simultaneously. This memory can also work on binary data by using redundant binary representation logic, and a small segment of data can be used to find which page has the largest association with the input segment. Selected components are labeled as follows: FL, Fourier lens; FVA, Fresnel variable attenuator; H1,H2, holographic films; PHA, pin-hole array; SF, spatial filter; SP, beam stop.

Three-Dimensional Memories

Many scientists and engineers believe that the major impact of molecular electronics on computer hardware will be in the area of volumetric memory. There are three different types of protein-based volumetric memories currently under investigation: holographic (d'Auria et al. 1974; Birge 1990; Heanue, Bashaw, and Hesselink 1994; Psaltis and Pu 1996), simultaneous two-photon (Parthenopoulos and Rentzepis 1989; Chen et al. 1995; Dvornikov and Rentzepis 1996) and sequential one-photon (Birge et al. 1994; Stuart et al. 1996; Birge et al. 1999). We have already described a holographic memory based on bacteriorhodopsin. Thus we will confine our discussion to the latter two architectures. These memories read and write information by using two orthogonal laser beams to address an irradiated volume (10–200 μm^3) within a much larger volume of a photochromic material. Either a simultaneous two-photon or a sequential one-photon process is used to initiate the photochemistry. The former process involves the unusual capability of some molecules to capture two photons simultaneously. The sequential one-photon process requires a material that undergoes a branching reaction, where the first photon activates a cyclical process and the second photon activates a branching reaction to form a stable photoproduct. The three-dimensional addressing capability of both memories derives from the ability to adjust the location of the irradiated volume in three dimensions. In principle, an optical three-dimensional memory can store roughly three orders of magnitude more information in the same size enclosure relative to a two-dimensional optical disk memory. In practice, optical limitations and issues of reliability lower the above ratio to values closer to 300. Nevertheless, a 300-fold improvement in storage capacity is significant. Furthermore, the two-photon or sequential one-photon approach makes parallel addressing of data possible, which enhances data read/write speeds and system bandwidth.

The simultaneous two-photon memory architecture has received a great deal of attention in the past few years, and because bacteriorhodopsin exhibits both high efficiency in capturing two-photons and a high yield of producing photoproduct after excitation (Birge and Zhang 1990), this material has been a popular memory medium. But more recent studies suggest that the branched-photocycle memory architecture may have greater potential. This sequential one-photon architecture minimizes unwanted photochemistry outside of the irradiated volume and provides for a particularly straightforward parallel architecture. Above, we discussed the use of the P and Q states for long-term data storage. The fact that these states can only be generated via a temporally separated pulse sequence provides a convenient method of storing data in three dimensions by using orthogonal laser excitation. The process is based on the sequence shown in figure 6.6, where $K, L, M, N,$ and O are all

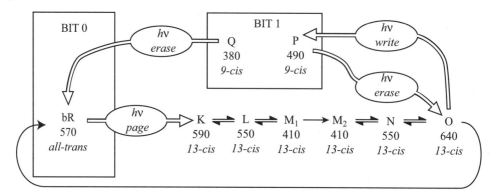

Figure 6.6
Data storage based on the branched photocycle reactions of bacteriorhodopsin.

intermediates within the main photocycle, and *P* and *Q* are intermediates in the branching cycle. The numbers underneath the letters give the wavelengths of the absorption maxima of the intermediates in nanometers (e.g., *bR* has a maximum absorbance at 570 nm, or yellow-green region; *O* absorbs at 640 nm, in the red). The terms all-trans, 13-cis, and 9-cis below the letters refer to the isomerization state of the chromophore while the protein is in the particular intermediate form. Figure 6.7 shows a schematic representation of the operations required for implementing the branched-memory architecture, which are described in detail below.

The reading and writing process starts by selecting a very thin region ($\sim$15 microns) inside the data cuvette by a process called "paging." In this process, the paging lasers (there are two, one on each side of the data cuvette, but only one is shown for clarity), with a wavelength in the region 550–640 nm, initiates the photocycle within a $\sim$15 micron slice of the memory medium. The photocycle will return to the resting state (*bR*) in about 10 msec, the time window during which subsequent writing or reading must take place. In the absence of secondary laser stimulation, the protein within the paged region will simply return to the resting state. Thus a page operation by itself is nondestructive.

A parallel write is accomplished by using the sequential one-photon optical protocol. The paging beam activates the photocycle of bacteriorhodopsin and after a few milliseconds, the *O* intermediate approaches maximal concentration. The data laser and the SLM are now activated ($\lambda = 680$ nm, $at \approx 3$ msec) to irradiate those volume elements ("voxels") into which 1 bits are to be written. This process converts *O* to *P* in only the simultaneously activated and irradiated locations within the memory

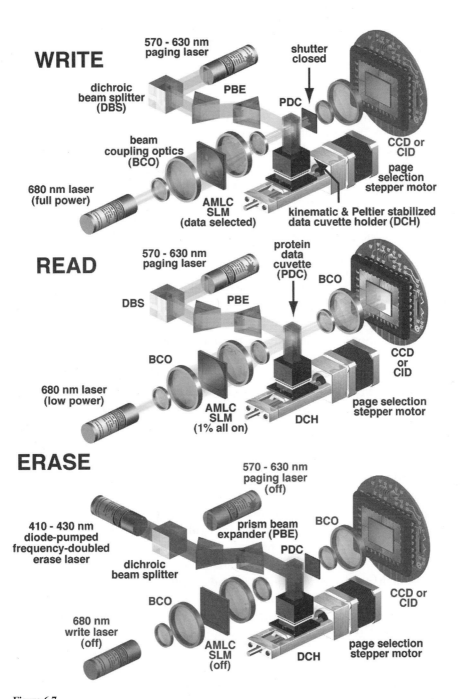

Figure 6.7
Schematic diagram of the branched-photocycle three-dimensional memory. The top diagram shows the write process, which is based on a page operation followed a few milliseconds later by an orthogonal write operation.

cuvette. After many minutes, the P state thermally decays to form the Q state (the $P \rightarrow Q$ decay time, τ_P, is highly dependent upon temperature and polymer matrix). The write process is accomplished in ~ 10 msec, the time it takes the protein to complete the photocycle. Because the decay time of the P state is variable, our memory architecture must treat both P and Q as bit 1, and have the capability to erase both of these species simultaneously when the voxel is to be reset to bit 0.

The read process takes advantage of the fact that light around 680 nm is absorbed by only two intermediates in the photocycle of light-adapted bacteriorhodopsin, the primary photoproduct K and the relatively long-lived O intermediate (see figure 6.4). The read sequence starts out in a fashion identical to that of the write process by activating the 568 nm paging beam. After two milliseconds, the data timing (DTS) and the data read (DRS) shutters are opened for 1 msec, but the SLM is left off, allowing only 0.1 percent of the total laser power through. A CCD array (clocked to clear all charges prior to reading) images the light passing through the data cuvette. Those elements in binary state 1 (P or Q) do not absorb the 680 nm light, but those volumetric elements that started out in the binary 0 state (bR) absorb the 680 nm light, because these elements have cycled into the O state. Noting that all of the volumetric elements outside of the paged area are restricted to the bR, P, or Q states, the only significant absorption of the beam is associated with O states within the paged region. The CCD detector array therefore observes the differential absorptivity of the paged region, and the paged region alone. This selectivity is the key to the read operation, and it allows a reasonable signal-to-noise ratio even with thick (1–1.6 cm) memory media containing $>10^3$ pages. Because the absorptivity of the O state within the paged region is more than one thousand times larger than the absorptivity of the remaining volume elements combined, a very weak beam can be used to generate a large differential signal. The read process is complete in ~ 10 msec, which gives a rate of 10 MB/sec. Each read operation must be monitored for each page, and a refresh operation performed after ~ 1000 reads. Although data refresh slows the memory slightly, page caching can minimize the impact.

Data erasure can be accomplished a single page at a time by using a blue laser with output near 410 nm or globally by using incoherent light in the 360–450 nm range. The former method has the advantage of selectivity. The first commercially available blue diode lasers at 405 nm can soon be implemented to perform this type of erasure process. The current prototype uses the global erasure process, which is an acceptable alternative, and is certainly much less expensive. These and other issues are more clearly understood with reference to an actual prototype, as discussed below.

Prototyping and Reliability Studies

The 3-D volumetric memory based on the branched photocycle is in a second generation of prototyping, and the current prototype is shown in figure 6.8. The prototype has been designed in a modular fashion so that individual components can be rapidly replaced and new component subsections can be tested quickly. The key features are discussed below.

Dual paging lasers are used to provide homogeneous page activation. Although 570 nm lasers would be optimal, we are using two 60 mW, 630–635 nm lasers because relatively inexpensive diode lasers are available with this wavelength. We hope to convert ~ 25 percent of the molecules within the irradiated page to O state, in preparation for either writing or reading.

Holographically coupled dual data lasers are implemented to deal with an interesting problem associated with small, pixel-sized active matrix liquid crystal spatial light modulators (AMLC SLMs). The use of such SLMs to control coherent light sources generates pixel aperture interference that is otherwise absent with incoherent sources. This problem has been reduced to acceptable levels by using two data lasers that are coupled via a pair of lenses to a holographic diffuser, as shown in figure 6.8. The coupling of two lasers removes the coherence inherent in single laser sources, and the holographic diffuser provides an even intensity distribution across the surface of the modulator. We use two 50 mW 680 nm diode lasers. The high power is required because of the low quantum efficiency of the $O \rightarrow P$ photochemistry (see discussion above). If the native protein is used, only a very small amount of protein can be converted from bR to Q. We can repeat the write process as many times as we wish until the necessary amount of Q state is present for the read operation. Organic cation analogs or Glu-194/Glu-204 mutants yield conversions that are 5–10-fold higher, and approach the conversion levels that are necessary for reliable and efficient operation in one write sequence.

Although it may appear inefficient to move the data cuvette rather than the optics, paging through cuvette translation is the preferred method when speed and reliability are taken into account. The data cuvettes are light (4.5 g plastic, 9.1 g BK-7) and the kinematic mount and the Peltier device dominate the inertial weight. The prototype uses a high-speed linear actuator (Newport 850F-HS) to locate the cuvette. This device allows the cuvette to be positioned, on average, in 60 msec, a value sufficient for the present testing purposes. Ultimately, we will use linear magnetic motors to achieve 10 msec latencies.

Global erasure of the entire data cuvette is achieved via activation of a pair of cylindrical UV lamps (All Electronics, UV-325 + BXA 12576), which have outputs

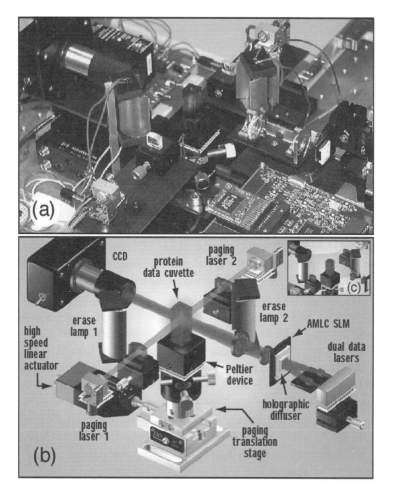

Figure 6.8
A close-up picture (*a*) and a schematic (*b*) of the current Level II prototype of the branched-photocycle volumetric memory. Key components of the prototype are shown and labeled in the schematic (*b*). This prototype uses a global erasure of the entire data cuvette via activation of a pair of cylindrical UV lamps. The lamps are located at the focus of two cylindrical hyperbolic mirrors positioned so that the entire memory cuvette can be irradiated (insert *c*). Dual data lasers coupled to the active matrix liquid crystal spatial light modulator (AMLC SLM) via a holographic diffuser are used to generate non-coherent light so that the imaged data beam does not contain diffracted artifacts (see text). (Reproduced from Birge et al. 1999.)

of 463 ± 40 nm. This soft UV light couples adequately to the absorption spectra of both P and Q, and sets all the bits within the entire memory cuvette to state zero (bR) in a few minutes. The lamps are located at the focus of two cylindrical hyperbolic mirrors and are collimated, as shown in the inset (c), so that the entire memory cuvette is irradiated when properly positioned.

Multiplexing of the data to achieve higher storage density can be implemented by using gray-scale multiplexing. This scheme stores 5 bits per voxel. (If we included polarization, we could store ten bits per voxel; Birge et al. 1999.)

Multiplexing is an important component of 3-D data storage, as it achieves viable storage densities without the need to operate at or near the diffraction limit. The spatial light modulator (Kopin, 320C) and the CCD detector (Cohu 1100) are designed to provide 8-bit gray-scale capability, which yields the potential of multiplexing 16 bits into each voxel via polarization doubling. In practice, reliability limits the writing and reading processes to 5 bits per polarization, leading to a current best-case scenario of 10 bits/voxel. In addition, a number of bits along the edges must be allocated to alignment and checksum information. With these features fully implemented, a standard $1 \times 1 \times 3$ cm^3 data storage cuvette can store approximately ten gigabytes. This storage capacity translates to the use of between 10^4 and 10^5 protein molecules per bit for typical protein concentrations utilized here, and provides an adequate number of molecules per bit to yield a statistically relevant ensemble, as required to maintain reliability (see below) (Birge, Lawrence, and Tallent 1991; Birge et al. 1999).

Error analysis can be carried out by measuring read histograms (Lawrence et al. 1998; Birge et al. 1999). A detailed discussion of error sources and error analysis for 3-D memories is beyond the scope of this chapter (we direct the reader to Lawrence et al. 1998 for a more comprehensive discussion). Briefly, we note that a read operation carried out via differential absorption is measured on a normalized scale where 0 is low intensity reaching the detector (bit 0, O state absorption), and 1 is high intensity reaching the detector (bit 1, P and Q present and less O state absorption). By using a differential read process, the detector and associated circuitry normalize the signals across the detector array so that when no gray scaling is done, you get peaks at only two locations, 0 and 1. When gray scaling is used to increase bit density, you get peaks corresponding to each of the allowed levels, which correspond to bit assignments (see discussion in Birge et al. 1999). Read errors invariably increase the width of these peaks, and can even cause the peaks to overlap. The error rate is proportional to the overlap, and the goal is to keep such error at a level that can be handled via error-correcting codes.

6.3   Genetic Engineering of Proteins for Device Applications

Genetic engineering is the systematic manipulation of the genetic code (i.e., DNA) of an organism to modify the traits of that organism. Material scientists and molecular electronic engineers view genetic engineering primarily as a tool for changing the properties of biological molecules, like proteins, for potential device applications. For example, although the quantum efficiency of the $O \rightarrow P$ photo conversion in wild-type bacteriorhodopsin is approximately 10^{-6}, the ideal quantum efficiency for the volumetric memory is on the order of 10^{-3}. Like chemical modification and organic cation replacement, as discussed above, mutagenesis is a powerful technique for modifying the properties of proteins. Genetic engineering has long been a standard technique in the fields of biochemistry, pharmaceuticals, and agriculture, but it has only recently become a standard method in bioelectronics. Although a comprehensive review of the techniques and theory of genetic engineering is beyond the scope of this work, a brief discussion is provided below. Our goal is to provide the reader with an appreciation for the basic methods and procedures as well as the inherent capabilities of these techniques.

Deoxyribonucleic acid (DNA) is the molecule that carries the genetic code for all organisms. DNA is a double-stranded helix biopolymer made up of four nucleotides: adenine (A), guanine (G), thymine (T), and cytosine (C). A region of DNA that encodes for a protein is called a gene. A gene can be isolated and transferred to a circular piece of DNA, called a plasmid, which contains only that gene and the genetic machinery required to express that gene. The average protein is 400 amino acids long, and the average gene is 1200 nucleotides long (Watson, Gilman, and Witkowski 1992). This relationship is due to the fact that three consecutive nucleotides make a codon, and each codon is ultimately translated to a single amino acid. More than one codon exists for most amino acids. For example, GGG codes for a glycine amino acid, but GGT, GGC, and GGA are synonymous. The amino acids are then constructed in the order of the codons on the DNA. Proteins are biopolymers of 20 different amino acid building blocks. A mutant protein has had the amino acid sequence modified from the naturally occurring (wild type) sequence. Mutations can take the form of site-specific or random replacements, additions of new amino acids (insertions), or deletions of amino acids within the primary structure. (For a review of mutagenesis, see Botstein and Shortle 1985; Smith 1985; Reidhaar-Olson and Sauer 1988.) Mutagenesis is routinely used to study structure-function relationships existing in different proteins by biochemists and biophysicists.

Two common strategies used in the construction of site-specific mutations employ DNA "cassettes" or mismatched primers and the polymerase chain reaction (PCR).

Restriction enzymes will cut DNA only at sites within a specific sequence. To perform cassette mutagenesis, two restriction sites unique to the plasmid must flank the location of the desired mutant, and the distance between the two restriction sites must be not more than 80 nucleotides. The sites must be unique in the plasmid because the DNA should be cut into no more than two pieces—a large fragment and a small fragment (figure 6.9). The synthetic fragments are limited to a length of about 80 nucleotides because this is the practical length limit of oligomeric synthesis. Once the small fragment is removed, a new synthetic oligonucleotide with the desired mutant is attached into place with an enzyme (ligase). Interestingly, Khorana and coworkers reported one of the first examples of cassette mutagenesis done on the bacteriorhodopsin gene (Lo et al. 1984).

Cassette mutagenesis is not always possible, because unique restriction sites usually do not flank a desired mutation location. If many mutations are going to be performed on a gene (protein), a synthetic gene can be constructed with a unique restriction site placed approximately every 70 nucleotides throughout the gene. Incorporating silent (also called synonymous) mutations—that is, mutations that change the DNA sequence (to introduce a restriction site, for example) but leave the translated amino acid sequence unchanged—is facilitated with redundant codons (Feretti et al. 1986). Because producing synthetic genes is both labor intensive and expensive, PCR-based mutagenesis methodologies are more commonly used in the laboratory.

PCR-based mutational strategies using mismatched primers are generally applicable to any sequence (figure 6.10). Thermocyclers and polymerases required for PCR have gotten more accurate, robust, and inexpensive, so almost every protein biochemistry laboratory now uses PCR regularly. Many different techniques (and many commercially available kits) take advantage of the flexibility of this method. This alternative strategy is based on the fact that double-stranded DNA can be denatured (i.e., made single stranded) and renatured as a function of temperature. A 20–30 oligonucleotide primer is designed to complement the template DNA, except for the introduced mutation. A reaction mixture contains a relatively small amount (tens of nanograms) of template DNA and a larger amount (120 ng) of primer and nucleotides. The mixture is first heated to 95 °C to melt the template DNA (making it single stranded). Upon cooling to 62 °C, the primer anneals to the template DNA. A polymerase enzyme then elongates the primer with the complement to the template DNA at 72 °C. Now two strands of DNA exist, the original (template DNA) and the new mutant extended primer. This process is repeated 20–30 more times, exponentially amplifying the mutant DNA (approximately by $2^{number\ of\ cycles}$). After 30 cycles, the reaction mixture will contain more than 268,400,000 times more mutant DNA

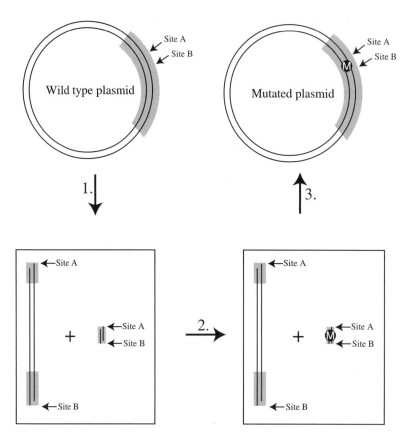

Figure 6.9
General scheme for cassette mutagenesis. The double circles represent a double-stranded plasmid, and the gray region indicates a gene. Restriction sites unique to the plasmid flank the region to be mutated. The distance from site A to site B should not be more than 80 nucleotides. In step 1, enzymes A and B are added to digest the plasmid at Sites A and B only, producing two linear pieces of DNA. The large fragment is then purified by gel electrophoresis, and added to a synthetic piece of DNA which contains the desired mutation (denoted by a M in a circle) (step 2). In the final step (step 3), the small synthetic fragment (containing the desired mutation) is ligated onto the large fragment. One end of the fragment then ligates with the other end to produce a circular mutant plasmid. The plasmid can then be expressed in bacteria to produce protein.

In the first step, template DNA is amplified by PCR. One of the primers contains a mismatch (mutation) so that all of the amplified DNA will have the new mutation.

Two forms of DNA are now present, template (wild type) and the amplified mutant. Because the DNA has been amplified, there is a lot more of the mutant DNA than there is template.In the next step, an enzyme selectively

digests only the template DNA, leaving the mutant form untouched.

Another enzyme then fixes the gaps left by the PCR reaction in the mutant DNA. The DNA is finally transformed into bacteria for amplification and protein expression.

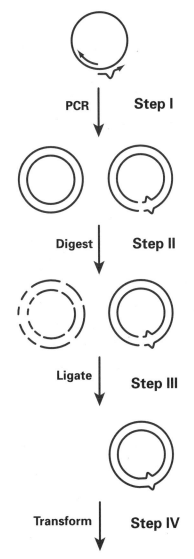

PCR | **Step I**

Digest | **Step II**

Ligate | **Step III**

Transform | **Step IV**

Figure 6.10
General schematic for mismatched primer mutagenesis. Although figure 6.9 is based on the ExSite™ Mutagenesis kit (Stratagene, LaJolla, CA), the overall strategy used by this kit is similar to many PCR-based methods. In the first step, primers are designed to copy the wild type, template DNA. One of the primers is the complement to the wild type DNA, while the second primer contains the mutation. The example shown here is for a point mutation, but in fact, insertions and deletions can also be done with this method. In the first step, the template DNA is amplified with the new mutation incorporated. An enzyme that recognizes the template DNA cuts it into multiple fragments. In step III, another enzyme, ligase, circularizes the new, mutant DNA allowing it to transform into bacteria efficiently in step IV. Once in bacteria, the gene can be amplified or expressed (resulting in the production of mutant protein).

molecules than template. The original template DNA is selectively digested (i.e., discarded) with enzymes, and the mutant DNA is transformed into a bacterium like *Escherichia coli* and expressed to obtain the mutant protein.

Evolution has optimized each protein for a specialized task in the cell. Some of these properties may be less than ideal for commercial applications. For example, proteins may not be stable at elevated temperatures. They may not be active in organic solvents, or their products may inhibit activity. As mentioned above, rationally modifying these properties in even the most studied and well-understood proteins would be nearly impossible to do—in part, because of the complexity of proteins. With 20 naturally occurring amino acids, there are 20^N possible combinations of N amino acids in a protein—20^{248} potential combinations for a protein the length of bacteriorhodopsin. Directed evolution, sometimes referred to as in vitro evolution, mimics the methods used in nature during evolution (for general reviews of directed evolution see Arnold 1998; Arnold and Volkov 1999; Schmidt-Dannert and Arnold 1999). Conceptually, directed evolution is a combinatorial approach to genetic engineering (Zhao and Arnold 1997). The gene of interest is first modified by random mutagenesis, saturation mutagenesis, or combined with other homologous genes (homologous recombination). Then, from a sampling of hundreds of these DNAs, the proteins that provide the best properties are screened or selected for another round of mutagenesis or homologous recombination. These iterations continue until the protein has the desired function. Notable successes of directed evolution have modified an enzyme's substrate (Yano, Oue, and Kagamiyama 1998), introduced thermal stability (Miyazaki et al. 2000), and made an enzyme functional in organic solvent (Moore and Arnold 1996; Spiller et al. 1999).

The first step in directed evolution is to generate a sampling of random point mutations. Because some mutations may improve the desired function while others may be deleterious or silent, the optimum mutation rate is one mutation per gene per round of evolution (Miyazaki and Arnold 1999). The most common method for mutagenesis is to use error-prone PCR to randomly mutate sites within a gene (Zhao et al. 1999). If specific amino acids are known to be important, saturation mutagenesis works with degenerate primers to modify that site to every possible combination (Hayashi et al. 1994). Another way to modify a gene is by homologous recombination, the mixing of two or more similar genes (Giver and Arnold 1998). The genes may be related to one another by homology. Homologous cephalosporinases from four different species were recombined to make a protein 270–540-fold more active than the original enzyme (Crameri et al. 1998). The genes may also be different mutants derived from a common parent. By randomly combining these genes and then screening or selecting the best products, better proteins are produced. Stemmer first introduced homologous recombination by using a DNAse to cut DNA into fragments and then randomly recombining them (Stemmer 1994, 1994b). A simpler and more efficient method has been developed. The staggered extension process (StEP) uses short bursts of extension times followed by denaturation during PCR of several genes (Shao et al. 1998; Zhao et al. 1998). A DNA primer is extended briefly on one template, denatured, bound to another template, elongated again, denatured, and so on. The result is a random recombination of the original templates (Michnick and Arnold 1999; Ness et al. 1999).

Once the modified gene is produced, the resulting proteins have to be tested by a screen or selection. Selection can be used when the protein of interest confers a growth advantage to the host organism (for a review of using selection in directed evolution see Kast and Hilvert 1997). Screens are used in all other cases (for a review of implementing screens for directed evolution, see Zhao and Arnold 1997). Choosing the most successful product from a large library of mutations is usually the most difficult step in directed evolution. New technologies like inexpensive microfabricated fluorescence-activated cell sorters (Fu et al. 1999) will make screening promising mutations cheaper and easier in the future.

Site-directed mutagenesis has been used to create rationally designed bacteriorhodopsin mutants with enhanced materials properties (Miercke et al. 1991; Hampp et al. 1992; Zeisel and Hampp 1992; Gergely et al 1993; Misra et al. 1997). For example, some mutants have enhanced the holographic properties of the protein by producing an M state with an extended lifetime (Gergely et al. 1993; Miercke et al. 1991; Hampp et al. 1992; Zeisel and Hampp 1992), while others improve the branched-photocycle memory by enhancing the yield of the O state (Misra et al. 1997). The challenge for material scientists is to predict a priori what amino acid sequence will create or enhance a specific protein property. At present, the vast majority of genetic engineering for materials applications is a trial-and-error process, due to the complexity of protein structure and function and the lack of satisfactory molecular modeling tools. However, directed evolution promises to provide new methods to solve previously limiting problems associated with available proteins. It is hoped that continued theoretical work will yield computer programs with the predictive capabilities comparable to the SPICE packages that are the cornerstone of electrical engineering. In this regard, bioelectronics is many years if not decades behind computer engineering.

References

Arnold, F. H. 1998. Design by directed evolution. *Accts. Chem. Res.* 31: 125–131.

Arnold, F. H., and A. A. Volkov. 1999. Directed evolution of biocatalysts. *Curr. Opin. Chem. Biol.* 3: 54–59.

Balashov, S. P., F. F. Litvin, and V. A. Sineshchekov. 1988. Photochemical processes of light energy transformation in bacteriorhodopsin. *Physiochem. Biol. Rev.* 8: 1–61.

Birge, R. R. 1990. Photophysics and molecular electronic applications of the rhodopsins. *Annu. Rev. Phys. Chem.* 41: 683–733.

Birge, R. R. 1994. Introduction to molecular and biomolecular electronics. *Adv. Chem.* 240: 1–14.

Birge, R. R. 1994b. Molecular and Biomolecular Electronics. *Adv. Chem.* 240: 596.

Birge, R. R., and C. F. Zhang. 1990. Two-photon spectroscopy of light adapted bacteriorhodopsin. *J. Chem. Phys.* 92: 7178–7195.

Birge, R. R., A. F. Lawrence, and J. A. Tallent. 1991. Quantum effects, thermal statistics, and reliability of nanoscale molecular and semiconductor devices. *Nanotechnology* 2: 73–87.

Birge, R. R., D. S. K. Govender, R. B. Gross, A. F. Lawrence, J. A. Stuart, J. R. Tallent, E. Tan, and B. W. Vought. 1994. Bioelectronics, three-dimensional memories, and hybrid computers. *IEEE IEDM Tech. Digest* 94: 3–6.

Birge, R. R., B. Parsons, Q. W. Song, and J. R. Tallent. 1997. Protein-based three-dimensional memories and associative processors. In *Molecular Electronics*, eds. M. A. Ratner and J. Jortner, eds. 439–471. Oxford: Blackwell Science.

Birge, R. R., N. B. Gillespie, E. W. Izaguirre, A. Kusnetzow, A. F. Lawrence, D. Singh, Q. W. Song, E. Schmidt, J. A. Stuart, S. Seetharaman, and K. J. Wise. 1999. Biomolecular electronics: Protein-based associative processors and volumetric memories. *J. Phys. Chem. B.* 103: 10746–10766.

Botstein, D., and D. Shortle. 1985. Strategies and applications of in vitro mutagenesis. *Science* 229: 1193–1201.

Chen, Z., D. Govender, R. Gross, and R. Birge. 1995. Advances in protein-based three-dimensional optical memories. *BioSystems* 35: 145–151.

Crameri, A., S. Raillart, E. Bermudez, and W. P. C. Stemmer. 1998. DNA shuffling of a family of genes from diverse species accelerates directed evolution. *Nature* 391: 288–291.

d'Auria, L., J. P. Huignard, C. Slezak, and C. Spitz. 1974. Experimental holographic read-write memory using 3-D storage. *Appl. Opt.* 13: 808–818.

Dvornikov, A. S., and P. M. Rentzepis. 1996. 3D Optical Memory Devices. System and Materials Characteristics. *Proc. IEEE Nonvol. Mem. Tech. (INVMTC)* 6: 40–44.

Ebrey, T. G. 1993. Light energy transduction in bacteriorhodopsin. In *Thermodynamics of Membrane Receptors and Channels.*, 353–387. ed. M. Jackson Boca Raton, Fla: CRC Press.

El-Sayed, M. A. 1992. On the molecular mechanisms of the solar to electric energy conversion by the other photosynthetic system in nature, bacteriorhodopsin. *Accts. Chem. Res.* 25: 279–286.

Ferretti, L., S. S. Karnik, G. Khorana, M. Nassal, and D. D. Oprian. 1986. Total synthesis of a gene for bovine rhodopsin. *Proc. Natl. Acad. Sci. USA* 83: 599–603.

Fu, A. Y., C. Spence, A. Scherer, F. H. Arnold, and S. R. Quake. 1999. A microfabricated fluorescence-activated cell sorter. *Nat. Biotechnol.* 17: 1109–1111.

Gergely, C., C. Ganea, G. Groma, and G. Varo. 1993. Study of the photocycle and charge motions of the bacteriorhodopsin mutant D96N. *Biophys. J.* 65: 2478–2483.

Giver, L., and F. H. Arnold. 1998. Combinatorial protein design by in vitro recombination. *Curr. Opin. Chem. Biol.* 2: 335–338.

Gross, R. B., K. C. Izgi, and R. R. Birge. 1992. Holographic thin films, spatial light modulators, and optical associative memories based on bacteriorhodopsin. *Proc. SPIE* 1662: 186–196.

Hampp, N., A. Popp, C. Bräuchle, and D. Oesterhelt. 1992. Diffraction efficiency of bacteriorhodopsin films for holography containing bacteriorhodopsin wildtype BR_{wt} and its variants BR_{D85E} and BR_{D96N}. *J. Phys. Chem.* 96: 4679–4685.

Hampp, N., R. Thoma, D. Zeisel, and C. Bräuchle. 1994. Bacteriorhodopsin variants for holographic pattern recognition. *Adv. Chem.* 240: 511–526.

Hayashi, N., M. Welschof, M. Zewe, M. Braunagel, S. Dubel, F. Breitling, and M. Little. 1994. Simultaneous mutagenesis of antibody CDR regions by overlap extension and PCR. *Biotechniques* 17: 310–315.

Heanue, J. F., M. C. Bashaw, and L. Hesselink. 1994. Volume holographic storage and retrieval of digital data. *Science* 265: 749–752.

International Technology Roadmap for Semiconductors (ITRS). 1999. San Jose: Semiconductor Assocition.

Kandel, E. R., J. H. Schwartz, and T. M. Jessell. 1991. *Principles of Neural Science*. 3d ed., 1135. New York: Mcgraw-Hill.

Kast, P., and D. Hilvert. 1997. 3D structural information as a guide to protein engineering using genetic selection. *Curr. Opin. Struct. Biol.* 7: 470–479.

Keyes, R. W. 1992. Electronic devices in large systems. *AIP Conf. Proc.* 262: 285–297.

Lanyi, J. K. 1992. Proton transfer and energy coupling in the bacteriorhodopsin photocycle. *J. Bioenerg. Biomembr.* 24: 169.

Lanyi, J. K., and G. Varo. 1995. The photocycles of bacteriorhodopsin. *Isr. J. Chem.* 35: 365–385.

Lawrence, A. F., J. A. Stuart, D. L. Singh, and R. R. Birge. 1998. Bit-error sources in 3D optical memory: Experiments and models. *Proc. SPIE* 3468: 258–268.

Lo, K. M., S. S. Jones, N. R. Hackett, and H. G. Khorana. 1984. Specific amino acid substitutions in bacterioopsin: Replacement of a restriction fragment in the structural gene by synthetic DNA fragments containing altered codons. *Proc. Natl. Acad. Sci. USA* 81: 2285–2289.

Luecke, H., B. Schobert, H. T. Richter, J. P. Cartailler, and J. K. Lanyi. 1999. Structure of bacteriorhodopsin at 1.55 A resolution. *J. Mol. Biol.* 291: 899–911.

Lukashev, E. P., and B. Robertson. 1995. Bacteriorhodopsin retains its light-induced proton-pumping function after being heated to 140 °C. *Bioelectrochem. Bioenerg.* 37: 157–160.

Mathies, R. A., S. W. Lin, J. B. Ames, and W. T. Pollard. 1991. From femtoseconds to biology: Mechanism of bacteriorhdopsin's light-driven proton pump. *Annu. Rev. Biophys. Chem.* 20: 491–518.

Meindl, J. D. 1993. Evolution of Solid-State Circuits: 1958-1992-20??. *IEEE ISSCC* Commemorative Supplement, 23–26.

Michnick, S. W., and F. H. Arnold. 1999. "Itching" for new strategies in protein engineering. *Nat. Biotechnol.* 17: 1159–1160.

Miercke, L. J. W., M. C. Betlach, A. K. Mitra, R. F. Shand, S. K. Fong, and R. M. Stroud. 1991. Wildtype and mutant bacteriorhodopsins D85N, D96N, and R82Q: Purification to homogeneity, pH dependence of pumping and electron diffraction. *Biochemistry* 30: 3088–3098.

Misra, S., R. Govindjee, T. G. Ebrey, N. Chen, J. X. Ma, and R. K. Crouch. 1997. Proton uptake and release are rate-limiting steps in the photocycle of the bacteriorhodopsin mutant E204Q. *Biochemistry* 36: 4875–4883.

Miyazaki, K., and F. H. Arnold. 1999. Exploring nonnatural evolutionary pathways by saturation mutagenesis: Rapid improvement of protein function. *J. Mol. Evol.* 49: 716–720.

Miyazaki, K., P. L. Wintrode, R. A. Grayling, D. N. Rubingh, and F. H. Arnold. 2000. Directed evolution study of temperature adaptation in a psychrophilic enzyme. *J. Mol. Biol.* 297: 1015–1026.

Moore, J. C., and F. H. Arnold. 1996. Directed evolution of a para-nitrobenzyl esterase for aqueousorganic solvents. *Nat. Biotechnol.* 14: 458–467.

Ness, J. E., M. Welch, L. Giver, M. Bueno, J. R. Cherry, T. V. Borchert, W. P. C. Stemmer, and J. Minshull. 1999. DNA shuffling of subgenomic sequences of subtilisin. *Nat. Biotech.* 17: 893–896.

Oesterhelt, D., and W. Stockenius. 1971. Rhodopsin-like protein from the purple membrane of Halobacterium halobium. *Nature (London), New Biol.* 233: 149–152.

Paek, E. G., and D. Psaltis. 1987. Optical associative memory using Fourier transform holograms. *Opt. Eng.* 26: 428–433.

Parthenopoulos, D. A., and P. M. Rentzepis. 1989. Three-dimensional optical storage memory. *Science* 245: 843–845.

Psaltis, D., and A. Pu. 1996. Holographic 3-D disks. *Proc. IEEE Nonvol. Mem. Tech. (INVMTC)* 6: 34–39.

Ratner, M. A., and J. Jortner. 1997. *Molecular Electronics.* Oxford: Blackwell Science.

Reidhaar-Olson, J. F., and R. T. Sauer. 1988. Combinatorial cassette mutagenesis as a probe of the informational content of protein sequences. *Science* 241: 53–57.

Schmidt-Dannert, C., and F. H. Arnold. 1999. Directed evolution of industrial enzymes. *Trends Biotechnol.* 17: 135–136.

Shao, Z., H. Zhao, L. Giver, and F. H. Arnold. 1998. Random-priming *in vitro* recombination: An effective tool for directed evolution. *Nucleic Acids Res.* 26: 681–683.

Shen, Y., C. R. Safinya, K. S. Liang, A. F. Ruppert, and K. J. Rothschild. 1993. Stabilization of the membrane protein bacteriorhodopsin to 140 °C in two-dimensional films. *Nature* 366: 48–50.

Smith, M. 1985. In vitro mutagenesis. *Ann. Rev. Genet.* 19: 423–462.

Spiller, B., A. Gershenson, F. H. Arnold, and R. C. Stevens. 1999. A structural view of evolutionary divergence. *Proc. Natl. Acad. Sci. USA* 96: 12305–12310.

Stemmer, W. P. C. 1994. Rapid evolution of a protein *in vitro* by DNA shuffling. *Nature* 370: 389–391.

Stemmer, W. P. C. 1994b. DNA shuffling by random fragmentation and reassembly: *In vitro* recombination for molecular evolution. *Proc. Natl. Acad. Sci. USA* 91: 10747–10751.

Stuart, J. A., J. R. Tallent, E. H. L. Tan, and R. R. Birge. 1996. Protein-based volumetric memory. *Proc. IEEE Nonvol. Mem. Tech. (INVMTC)* 6: 45–51.

Watson, J. D., M. Gilman, and J. Witkowski. 1992. *Recombinant DNA.* New York: Scientific American Books.

Yano, T., S. Oue, and H. Kagamiyama. 1998. Directed evolution of an aspartate aminotransferase with new substrate specificities. *Proc. Natl. Acad. Sci. USA* 95: 5511–5515.

Zeisel, D., and N. Hampp. 1992. Spectral relationship of light-induced refractive index and absorption changes in bacteriorhodopsin films containing wildtype BR_{wt} and the variant BRD_{96N}. *J. Phys. Chem.* 96: 7788–7792.

Zhao, H., and F. H. Arnold. 1997. Combinatorial protein design: Strategies for screening protein libraries. *Curr. Opin. Struct. Biol.* 7: 480–485.

Zhao, H., L. Giver, Z. Shao, J. A. Affholter, and F. H. Arnold. 1998. Molecular evolution by staggered extension process (StEP) *in vitro* recombination. *Nat. Biotech.* 16: 258–261.

Zhao, H., J. C. Moore, A. A. Volkov, and F. H. Arnold. 1999. Methods for optimizing industrial enzymes by directed evolution. In *Manual of industrial microbiology and biotechnology.* A. L. Demain and J. E. Davies eds. 597–604. Washington, D.C.: American Society for Microbiology.

Zimanyi, L., and J. K. Lanyi. 1993. Deriving the intermediate spectra and photocycle kinetics from time-resolved difference spectra of bacteriorhodopsin. The simpler case of the recombinant D96N protein. *Biophys. J.* 64: 240–251.

7 Bioelectronics and Biocomputers

Satoshi Sasaki and Isao Karube

The past ten years has seen remarkable progress in the development of biotechnology in various fields such as genetic engineering, cell engineering, and protein engineering. As the technology advances, the fields to which such technologies can be applied are becoming wider and borderless. Two fields, electronics and biotechnology, have now been mixed to produce a field called *bioelectronics*. One of the great successes in this field has been the creation of the biosensor, a device that can perform quantitative analysis on certain materials by mimicking processes found in biological organisms. This concept of mimicking is now thought to be applicable to the field of biocomputers. Present semiconductor chips are now running up against the limitation of how much more integration of semiconducter-based computers can actually be carried out. This has stimulated researchers to look for new ways to integrate circuits in a limited area. Much attention has therefore been paid to how electrons (and information) are transferred in living systems. If we could tailor the system to work down at the molecular level, an ultra-super-scale integrated circuit could be realized. In this chapter, a history of bioelectronics, the principles and examples of biosensors, and the idea and feasibility of a future biocomputer is briefly described.

7.1 Electron Transfer in Living Systems

Many living things carry out respiration to live. From the biochemical point of view, this process is called *oxidative phosphorylation*, because through this process, molecules called adenosine triphosphate (ATP) are synthesized. ATP has a very high chemical energy and acts as the mechanism of energy storage in most living systems. In reverse, a large amount of free energy is liberated when ATP is hydrolyzed to produce adenosine diphosphate (ADP) and orthophosphate (P_i), or when ATP is hydrolyzed to produce adenosine monophosphate (AMP) and pyrophosphate (PP_i) (Streyer 1988).

$$ATP + H_2O \rightarrow ADP + P_i + H^+ \qquad \Delta G^{\circ\prime} = -7.3 \text{ kcal/mol}$$

$$ATP + H_2O \rightarrow AMP + PP_i + H^+ \qquad \Delta G^{\circ\prime} = -7.3 \text{ kcal/mol}$$

ATP is used as the currency of energy in living things, using fuel molecules such as fatty acids and glucose for its synthesis. Energy liberated through the oxidation of these fuels can then be used. In such oxidation, the final electron acceptor is oxygen (O_2). O_2 cannot accept oxygen directly. Instead, electron carrier molecules such as flavins or pyridine nucleotides transfer electrons from the fuel to O_2. This process is

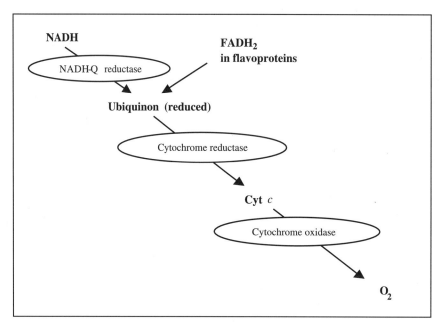

Figure 7.1
Electron transport path in a respiratory chain reaction.

performed in a chain located in the inner membrane of mitochondria. Mitochondria are organelles with an oval shape, and are 2 μm in length and 0.5 μm in diameter. Molecules such as nichotinamide adenine dinucleotide (NADH), flavin adenine dinucleotide (FADH$_2$) and cytochrome c (Cyt c) transfer electrons finally to O$_2$ (figure 7.1). Enzymes such as NADH-Q reductase, cytochrome reductase, and cytochrome oxidase help them carry electrons from one to the other.

Through this electron transfer, a proton (H$^+$) is also transmitted through the inner mitochondrial membrane (figures 7.2, 7.3). Thus a difference in the pH appears between the matrix (inner side of the membrane) and the intermembrane space (outer side). This proton gradient causes a proton-motive force Δp of ∼0.224 V, as calculated below.

$$\Delta p = \text{membrane potential} - 2.3 \, RT\Delta p/F = \text{membrane potential} - 0.06\Delta p$$

$$= 0.14 - 0.06 \times (-1.4) = 0.224 \text{ (V)}$$

In this case, the membrane potential is thought to be 0.14 V, and the pH outside is regarded as being 1.4 units lower than that on the inside. This electric energy poten-

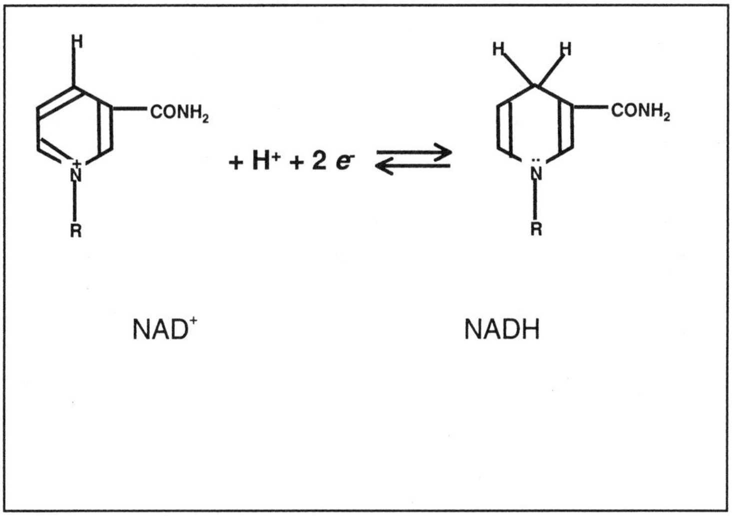

Figure 7.2
Reaction of NAD$^+$ (reactive part) with electrons. R$^-$ represents the other nonreactive part of the molecule.

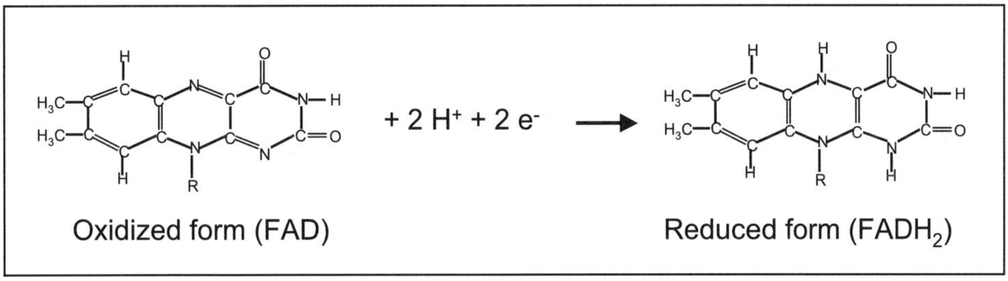

Figure 7.3
Reaction mechanism of the reactive parts of FAD and FADH$_2$.

tial is used for the synthesis of ATP. The respiratory chain is one example of electron transfer in living systems. What is interesting for us is that the enzyme specifically recognizes the molecule it has to attach to, as well as "knowing" where the electron comes from, and also where it must be donated. This is all done at the molecular level—that is, on the order of several tens of nanometers (ca. the size of the enzyme). Otherwise, oxidation or reduction in a cell would proceed in a small, limited cell space and the reaction would stop in a very short time. This means the death of the cell. Today, many projects are attempting to understand the mechanism of electron transfer among proteins (Zhang et al. 2000; Pletneva et al. 2000; Hu et al. 2000).

7.2 Biosensors

In the previous section, we saw that the molecules in living systems transport electrons to keep the metabolism working. It is therefore possible to observe the electrochemical behavior of those molecules using electrochemistry. Biosensors are the most well-studied devices that use biomolecules. Biosensors realized today do not use single molecules. They use molecules as a whole. Various kinds of biomolecules are now used for biosensors, including enzymes, antibodies, receptor proteins, and even microorganisms themselves (Karube and Yokoyama 1993). Each of these can recognize a particular target molecule with the result that some change can occur. For example, a glucose sensor is used to evaluate the glucose concentration in human blood. An enzyme called glucose oxidase is used for the glucose recognition. Glucose is "recognized" by glucose oxidase and is oxidized to gluconolactone. This recognition occurs in the same manner as in most enzymes. Glucose molecules are bound to enzymes by multiple weak attractions, while the active sites of the enzymes are in the shape of clefts or crevices. The specificity of binding depends on the very particular arrangement of atoms at an active site (see chapter 2 of this book). In this case, oxygen is consumed and hydrogen peroxide is produced simultaneously.

$$C_6H_{12}O_6 + O_2 \xrightarrow{\text{Glucose oxidase}} C_6H_{10}O_6 + H_2O_2$$

If we measure the change in dissolved oxygen or hydrogen peroxide concentration using an electrochemical device, it is possible to measure the glucose concentration— if we know the relationship between the change and the glucose concentration before measurement. As we can see in the above formula, dissolved oxygen concentration decreases and hydrogen peroxide increases with the increase of glucose. These changes are proportional to the glucose concentration.

Figure 7.4 describes the main structure of this glucose sensor. For typical oxygen electrodes, both the anode (Pb) and the cathode (Pt) are structured so they are

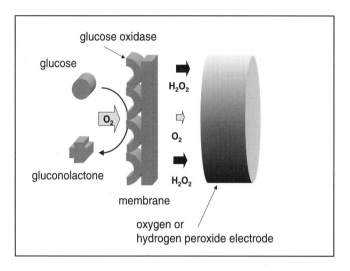

Figure 7.4
Scheme of a glucose sensor. Glucose is oxidized into gluconolactone at the membrane and O_2 is consumed. H_2O_2 is produced at the same time. Both O_2 and H_2O_2 can be measured by the electrode.

dipped in an electrolyte (30% NaOH or KOH). At the cathode end, the tip is constructed with a gas-permeable membrane such that oxygen molecules can get to the cathode layer from the outside and the electrolyte does not leak out. Pb is used as the anode material at a suitable electrochemical potential for the regeneration of oxygen. The top of the gas-permeable membrane is shielded with a membrane containing affixiated oxygen. The enzyme is a protein easily dissolved in water, so the enzyme glucose oxidase must be immobilized in a membrane to prevent its quick outflow in repeated use.

After washing, the substrate is removed from the membrane and the sensor is regenerated. If the outflow or the denaturation of the enzyme is controlled to be at a minimum, the lifetime of the sensor increases. In measurement testing, glucose is present and the above-given reaction occurs due to the activity of the enzyme immobilized in the membrane—thus the concentration of oxygen near the membrane drops. This results in a change of the electric current signal received from the oxygen electrodes. From this change in magnitude, the glucose concentration can be swiftly calculated. This type of instrument, where the result of a reaction is linked to the change in an electrical signal, is called a *transducer*. Using a suitable recognition molecule and a transducer bound together in one unit, a biosensor for a target molecule or reaction can be created. The reaction response of a curved-electrode glucose sensor is given in figure 7.5.

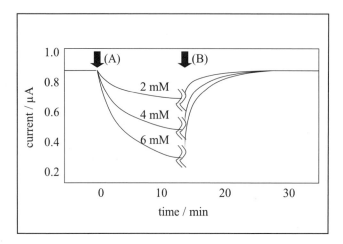

Figure 7.5
Typical response curve of a glucose sensor. Sensor is placed in a buffer solution and stirred using a magnetic stirrer. (*A*) Standard glucose solution is dropped into the solution. (*B*) Sensor is washed using a buffer solution. Enough of the buffer solution is added so that the glucose is totally washed away.

Background of Biosensors and Their Present Use

The very first biosensor created was a version of the above-outlined glucose sensor, following which various other types of biosensors were developed. The most important aspect of biosensor development has been the development of immobilizing the recognition element in a membrane. More details will be given below, but the first ever reported was that of using electric immobilization of enzymes into a collagen membrane (Karube et al. 1971; Karube and Suzuki 1972a, 1972b; Suzuki et al. Suzuki, Karube, and Watanabe 1972; 1974). Following this, biosensors using various types of recognition elements have been developed. For instance, biosensors can use various materials such as enzymes, antibodies, binding proteins, receptors, organella, organs, microorganisms, or animal/plant cells for the molecular recognition elements. Transducers such as electrodes, thermister, field effect transistor (FIT), a surface acoustic wave (SAW) device, or a quartz crystal microbalance (QCM) can be used to transduce molecular recognition into an electric signal (figure 7.6). Electrodes can receive/give electrons from/to the product molecule. H_2O_2 is oxidized at the Pt electrode and becomes H^+ and O_2. Through this oxidization, electrons are taken up by the electrode. When the electrode is connected to a device such as a potentiostat, a current change can be observed. The change in current contains information about the number of electrons transferred during the reaction.

Molecular recognition membranes can be categorized into two kinds. One is a membrane incorporating a catalyst, the other is a membrane incorporating a bio-

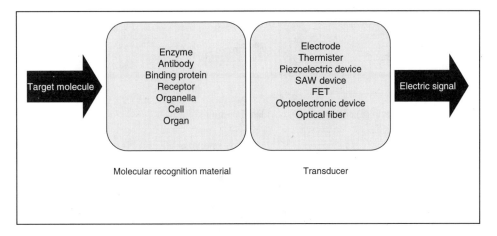

Figure 7.6
Scheme of biosensor. A target molecule is recognized by a molecular recognition element and then the result of recognition is detected by the transducer. Finally, an electric signal is produced from the transducer.

affinity compound. In the latter case, an enzyme, organella, or microorganism is used for the molecular recognition. In the catalyst-based biosensor, the change due to the catalytic reaction is measured. Dissolved oxygen, hydrogen peroxide, or hydrogen ions are measured by the transducer—in most cases by electrochemical devices. Changes in heat or optical phenomena can also be used. When glucose is oxidized into gluconolactone, energy is released and this results in an increase of the solution temperature. An enzyme-embodied thermistor or optical enzyme sensor is used as a transducer in this case. Careful design of the enzyme membrane is very important in order to have effective transduction of the physical change (optical, heat, chemical) into an electric signal. Molecular permeability, membrane thickness, and the immobilized amount of the enzyme are the main factors in determining this effectiveness.

Glucose sensors using oxygen electrodes or hydrogen peroxide electrodes have now been commercialized and are widely used in the clinical field. Several problems are now being addressed that hold back widespread applications of biosensors, such as the limited lifetime of the enzyme, or the effect of the matrix on the signal.

One solution for these problems is microfabricating the sensor device. Microfabrication of a biosensor requires two techniques—a technique for fabricating the transducer and one to fabricate the enzyme membrane. Immobilizing the enzyme into the membrane can be done in three different ways: binding to resin, cross-linking, and encapsulation (figure 7.7). In the case of binding to resin, either covalent bonding or adsorption of the enzyme onto the resin is performed. Enzymes have

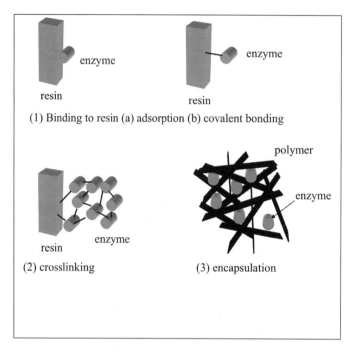

Figure 7.7
Enzyme immobilization methods.

amino groups or carboxyl groups on their surfaces, which will form covalent bonds
to chemical groups such as amino-, carboxyl-, hydroxyl-, and thiol- groups on the
resin surface.

In the second case, the cross-linking method, a multifunctional compound such as
glutaraldehyde is used. Glutaraldehyde has two aldehyde groups in one molecule and
will easily form covalent bonds with amino groups of the enzyme. Afterward, an
insoluble membrane is formed where the glutaraldehyde is cross-linked with the
enzyme. Glutaraldehyde can be mixed with the enzyme solution, or glutaraldehyde
vapor can react with enzyme already encapsulated in a polymer matrix. In the
third method, the enzyme is encapsulated in a matrix of insoluble polymer. A photo-
cross-linkable polymer such as a derivative of polyvinyl alcohol is used for this purpose. In this method, the enzyme is surrounded by the polymer so that the diffusion
of the substrate sometimes can be the determining factor in the rate of reaction.
Fabrication of a thinner membrane is therefore desired. It used to be difficult to immobilize enzymes with high spatial resolution because the methods mentioned above

are basically manual procedures. At present, electropolymerization of enzymes on the electrode surface can be performed to solve this problem (Shinohara, Chiba, and Aizawa 1988). When a platinum or gold electrode is inserted into a solution of aniline and enzyme, followed by electro-oxidization, a polyaniline membrane containing the enzyme is formed on the electrode surface. Oxygen or hydrogen peroxide can permeate through this membrane, but larger ions or molecules cannot.

Karube and Colleagues have demonstrated the usefulness of a microfabricated glucose sensor (Hiratsuka et al. 1999). This development was triggered by the aging population in Japan and the rapid increase in the number of people potentially susceptible to diabetes. The need for constant monitoring called for a procedure involving less pain. This could be done by requiring a much smaller amount of blood to be drawn from the patient. Moreover, any device used should be disposable to prevent infection of viral disease from one patient to another. A very small, disposable glucose sensor was therefore needed. Of most importance was being able to immobilize the enzyme in a very small area with good reproducibility. Plasma polymerized membrane (PPM) is known as a homogeneous, pinhole-free membrane that can load the desired functional chemical groups (Nakanishi, Muguruma, and Karube 1996; Nakanishi et al. 1996a; Nakamura et al. 1997b; Muguruma and Karube 1999). The advantage of this immobilization is that the whole process, from etching to loading of the functional groups, can be performed under vacuum. With this method, several biosensors have been fabricated and have showed good responses to the level of blood glucose. Techniques such as enzyme immobilization using PPM will help create future ultramicrobiosensor devices. Noninvasive techniques using biosensors have also been reported (Ito et al. 1995, 1996).

Enzyme Sensors for Saccharide Detection
The first attempt to fabricate an enzyme sensor was performed for the detection of glucose. Glucose oxidase, an enzyme that catalyzes the oxidation of glucose into gluconolactone, was immobilized in a polyacrylamide gel and was attached on the surface of an oxygen electrode (figure 7.8). The mechanism of this glucose measurement system was described in the preceding section. Oxygen consumed or hydrogen peroxide produced in the membrane is measured using several electrodes. For the measurement of oxygen, usually a Galvanic-type or a Clark-type electrode is used. A platinum working electrode with an applied potential of -700 mV versus Ag/AgCl reference electrode works for this purpose. For the detection of hydrogen peroxide, a platinum electrode with an applied potential of ~ 700 mV against Ag/AgCl reference electrode is often used.

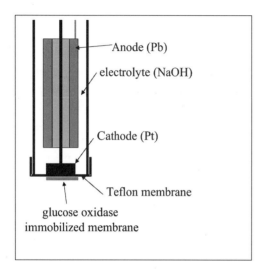

Figure 7.8
Glucose sensor using an enzyme and oxygen electrode.

The mixture of three enzymes—invertase, mutarotase, and glucose oxidase—enables an enzyme sensor for sucrose (Satoh, Karube, and Suzuki 1976). Sucrose is hydrolyzed into α-D-glucose and D-fructose with the activity of invertase. α-D-glucose will then be transformed into β-D-glucose with the function of mutarotase. The final product, β-D-glucose, is then oxidized by glucose oxidase and gluconolactone is produced. Oxygen consumed or hydrogen peroxide produced will be measured electrochemically, and the starting compound, sucrose, is measured.

Other sensors, such as maltose sensor using glucoamirase and glucose oxidase; galactose sensor using galactose oxidase (Yokoyama et al. 1989); and lactose sensor using galactosidase and glucose oxidase are developed. Among these sensors for saccharides, glucose sensor has been the most well studied (Gotoh, Chen, and Karube 1993; Murakami et al. 1994a, 1994b) because of the large number of diabetes patients in the world. Biosensors for sucrose or lactose are used for food analysis (Karube and Takeuchi 1993).

Alcohol Sensor
Measuring alcohols is often necessary in areas of medicine, industrial processes, or food preparation processes. Using an enzyme called alcohol oxidase, a biosensor for alcohol can be fabricated. This enzyme oxidizes primary alcohols with low molecular weights, producing aldehyde. Combining this enzyme and a hydrogen peroxide elec-

trode enables one to fabricate an alcohol sensor. The performance of this sensor was tested and ethanol was measured with good reproducibility (relative standard deviation of 3.2%).

A problem with the original sensor was its poor selectivity. The enzyme oxidizes methanol, allylalcohol, n-propanol, and n-butanol, with the sensor reacting with organic acids and aldehydes as well as the target substances. This problem was solved by the use of alcohol dehydrogenase, which is an enzyme that reacts only with alcohols (Kitagawa et al. 1989, 1991). This enzyme requires NAD as coenzyme, with a reduced type of NADH being produced through the reaction. If we measure NADH or a mediator reduced by NADH, an alcohol sensor can be fabricated. This system, however, is a bit complicated and is still at the development stage.

Amino Acid Sensor
The measurement of amino acids is important in the fields of clinical analysis, food processing, and fermentation procedure. In the detection of L-amino acids, L-amino-acid oxidase is used. The combination of this enzyme and an oxygen/ hydrogen peroxide electrode will enable the measurement of L-amino acids. This system, however, lacks selectivity, and the use of other enzymes for amino acid detection is necessary for selective measurement (Matsunaga et al. 1980; Karube and Suzuki 1986; Suzuki 1994).

Nucleic Acid Sensor
Nucleic acid–related compounds are found in living cells or in industrial processes. Measurement of them is therefore important. Among them, hypoxanthine can be measured using immobilized xanthine oxidase and an oxygen electrode. An inosine sensor can be fabricated using nucleoside phosphorylase and a xanthine oxidase immobilized membrane; 5′-nucleotidase, nucleoside phosphorylase, and xanthine oxidase are used for inosine 5′ monophosphate measurement. The combination of adenosine deaminase with an ammonium electrode can measure adenosine. Adenosine deaminase catalyses the decomposition of adenosine into inosine and ammonia, the latter being measured using an ammonium electrode. Other sensors such as guanine sensor using guanidine deaminase and an ammonium electrode, xanthine sensor using xanthine oxidase and a graphite electrode, or ATP (adenosine triphosphate) sensor using glucose oxidase/hexokinase and an oxygen electrode have been reported.

Recently, there has arisen a need to be able to determine the chromosomes of various bacterial strains linked with food poisoning. Because of this, sensors sensitive to special characteristics of particular bacteria have been developed. The material to test will contain exceedingly small amounts of particular DNA, which first must be amplified through PCR (see chapter 5 of this volume for details) to a measurable amount. Combining this with sensors for other DNA in the target chromosome has allowed a biosensor to be developed. By this method, bacteria linked with food poisoning can be monitored in foodstuffs and a measurement can be given in a few hours (Kai et al. 1997). The use of a completely new recognition element—PNA (peptide nucleic acid)—has proven successful in the lab for chromosomal measurement (Sawata et al. 1999).

Urea Sensor

Measurement of urea concentration in the human body is quite useful for the evaluation of kidney function. The conventional method for urea measurement is quite tedious, and therefore a fast and simple method for its measurement was desired. Urea is hydrolyzed by urease and changes into ammonium ion and carbonate ion. Combining this enzyme with an ammonium electrode or a carbon dioxide electrode produces a urea sensor (Hirose et al. 1983; Miyahara et al. 1983).

Fish-Freshness Sensor

The enzyme sensors mentioned above were designed for the measurement of a single compound. If the measurement of several compounds is possible, biosensors could be applied to a wider field. Measurement of, for example, odor or a complicated taste will be possible. Measurement of the freshness of fish can be done using a fish-freshness sensor. ATP (adenosine triphosphate) in fish flesh decomposes after the death of the fish and will change into ADP (adenosine diphosphate), AMP (adenosine monophosphate), inosinic acid, inosine, hypoxanthine, and finally uric acid. Uric acid is ultimately wasted in urine. Fish freshness was already known to be measurable using the ratio of ATP and these related compounds. Freshness value, K_I, was defined as

$$K_I = ([\text{inosine}] + [\text{hypoxanthine}])/([\text{inosinc acid}] + [\text{inosine}] + [\text{hypoxanthine}])$$

where [A] represents the concentration of compound A. As mentioned before, concentration of each compound can be measured using inosine, inosinic acid, and hypoxanthine sensors. Using a system with those three sensors, concentrations of the three compounds can be recorded as the pattern of three values, and K_I value is automatically recorded as well. By this indication of freshness as a pattern, a novel identification of freshness was performed (figure 7.9) (Karube et al. 1980; Watanabe et al. 1984a, 1984b; Karube et al. 1984a, 1984b; Suzuki et al. 1989; Chemnitius et al. 1992; Karube and Shimohigoshi 1996).

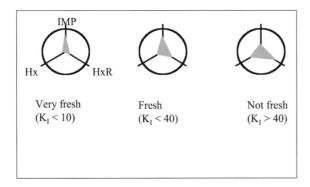

Figure 7.9
Response pattern obtained using a fish-freshness sensor. Fish freshness can be evaluated from the pattern obtained from the concentration pattern of three compounds.

Microfabricated Enzyme Sensor

Work on an enzyme sensor is now on the way to being miniaturized. Small biosensors can be implanted into the human body for clinical analysis, or they can be integrated on one chip. A lot of work has been done using microelectrodes. Anisotropic etching of a silicon wafer enables a microstructure for the device (Karube et al. 1994). A groove formed via this etching is used as a microchannel in which the sample flows. In this groove, electrodes are formed using a sputtering technique. Recently, a three-electrode system—having a platinum working electrode, an Ag/AgC reference electrode, and a platinum reference electrode—was fabricated on one silicon chip (Suzuki et al. 1999a, 1999b, 1999c). The enzyme was immobilized via γ-aminopropyl triethoxysilane or plasma polymerized film (Hiratsuka et al. 1999; Muguruma, Hiratsuka, and Karube 2000). The latter method in particular enables mass fabrication of the sensor in one vacuum chamber.

Enzyme Sensor Using a Transistor

Another transducer suitable for miniaturization is a transistor. Mass production processes for this device are already very well established. An ion-selective field effect transistor (ISFET) is so far the only silicon device that functions stably under solution. An ISFET has several advantages as a transducer for microbiosensors. First, the smaller impedance compared to that of a glass electrode makes it more suitable for miniaturization (because miniaturization of glass electrodes is accompanied by increasing impedance). Second, ISFETs are produced through a mass production procedure, so quality is consistent; cost is low as well. Third, selective measurement is possible using an ion-selective membrane formed on the device surface. ISFETs were originally developed using an insulator layer, so the addition of a high-impedance membrane does not affect the response speed. Any enzyme that catalyzes a reaction with pH change or ion concentration change can be used in combination with ISFET. For example, lipoprotein lipase hydrolyzes neutral fat in lipoprotein and produces glycerol and long-chain fatty acids. Part of these fatty acids are dissociated, so detecting the accompanying hydrogen ion enables the analysis of the original neutral fat. A urea sensor can be fabricated using the same principle (Gotoh, Tamiya, and Karube 1986; Gotoh et al. 1987, 1988, 1989a, 1989b). In practical measurements, the response of the urea sensor was not stable. When two ISFETs were used, one having urease and the other not, a stable response was obtained regardless of pH, temperature, drift of the baseline, or the disturbance at the injection of the sample. Several other enzyme sensors using ISFET have been reported (Miyahara et al. 1982; Murakami et al. 1986): for example, a glucose sensor using glucose oxidase, a lactate sensor using lactate dehydrogenase, an acetylcholine sensor using acetylcholine esterase, an L-glutamate sensor using L-glutamate decarboxylase, a tributylene sensor using lipase, and an ATP sensor using proton-dependent ATPase.

Enzyme Sensor Using a Thermistor
Most enzymatic reactions are accompanied by an enthalpy change of 5–100 kJ/mol. Measurement of the resulting temperature change of the solution will enable the measurement of substrate concentration. An enzyme thermistor, based on this principle, can be applied to all enzymatic reactions, and its field is very wide. The use of two thermistors, one with an immobilized enzyme and the other with a deactivated enzyme, resulted in the higher performance of the system. This two-thermistor system showed no effects from pH, temperature, and disturbance from the injection of the sample solution (figure 7.10) (Karube and Shimohigoshi 1996).

Enzyme Sensor Using an Optical Device
Chemiluminescence-based measurements are generally more sensitive compared to electrode-based methods because of their high S/N value. The technique is as follows: Several biochemical and chemical reactions are accompanied by optical irradiation. A typical example is the light emission of a firefly. Luciferin is the source of the irradiation, and the reaction is catalyzed by an enzyme called luciferase. Measurement of the light intensity is used to measure the strength of the reaction (Tamiya et al. 1989, 1990; Lee et al. 1992). Chemical luminescence (or chemiluminescence) is often used for measurements rather than biochemical luminescence (Ikebukuro et al. 1996; Nakamura et al. 1997a). For example, luminol (5-amino-2,3-

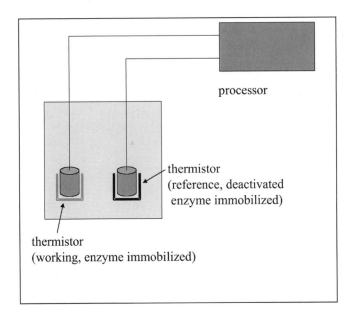

Figure 7.10
Enzyme sensor using thermistors. Two thermistors are used for the measurement.

dihydro-1,4-naphthalazinedione) is known to irradiate after the addition of hydrogen peroxide and a metal complex. Hydrogen peroxide is produced from various reactions catalyzed by oxidases, so combining the oxidase and luminol reactions will enable the measurement of substrate concentration or enzyme activity. Glucose, uric acid, cholesterol, L-amino acid, or hypoxanthine were measured using this system (figure 7.11). Luminol (C_6H_7-N_3O_2) emits purple light ($v = 460$ nm) through the following mechanism:

$$LH^- + O_2^- + H^+ \rightarrow L\cdot^- + H_2O_2$$

$$2\,L\cdot^- + O_2^- \rightarrow L + LO_2^{2-}$$

$$LO_2^{2-} \rightarrow AP\cdot^{2-} + N_2$$

$$AP\cdot^{2-} \rightarrow AP^{2-} + light$$

where L = luminol, LH^- = monoanionic form of luminol, $L\cdot^-$ = radical state of luminol, $AP\cdot^{2-}$ = excited state of aminophthalic acid, and $AP\cdot^{2-}$ = ground state of aminophthalic acid.

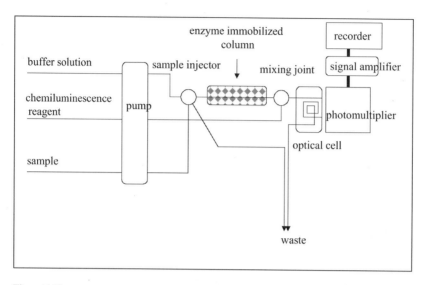

Figure 7.11
Schematic diagram of an enzyme sensor using chemiluminescence.

Immunosensor

Enzyme sensors are applied to measuring small molecules that can be "recognized" by the enzyme. For molecules that cannot be recognized by them, an immunosensor is useful. An immunoreaction is characterized by the interaction between an antibody and an antigen. Analyses using this interaction, *immunoassay*, are used in clinical analysis, where a protein, antibody, hormone, or drug is measured in blood. Conventional immunoassay requires labeling using radio isotopes, a fluorescent probe, or enzymes. In radio immunoassay using radio isotope, a picogram-level measurement is possible. This highly sensitive method has a disadvantage of safety. Other immunoassays are accompanied with the disadvantages of complex handling and take a long time. The idea came about of developing an immunosensor. The advantage of using a biosensor is the short measuring time required, because recognition and signal transduction take place at the same time.

Several attempts to fabricate an immunosensor were reported. Electrode-based immunosensors, for example, use the principle of enzyme immunoassay. An electrode with an immobilized antibody is used. A mixture of target antigen and catalase-labeled antigen is then added to the system. Finally, hydrogen peroxide is added. Oxygen is produced from the reaction catalyzed by catalase-labeled antigen, and is measured by the electrode. Competition between target antigen and catalase-

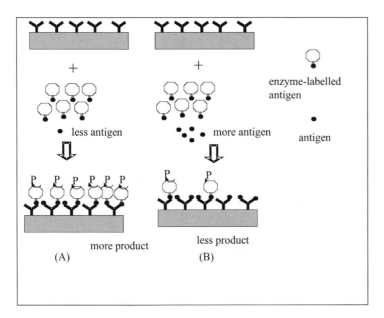

Figure 7.12
Schematic of an immunosensor. Antigen and an enzyme-labeled antigen (fixed concentration) are added to an antibody-immobilized substrate. If the concentration of antigen is low, the enzyme reaction product is high. Conversely, if the concentration of antigen is high, the amount of enzyme reaction product is low. Due to this, measuring the amount of the product gives the amount of antigen. The validity of this measurement depends on whether or not nonspecific protein adsorption occurs, i.e., adsorption of other non-desired proteins to the sensor surface. Some sticky materials in the sample often stick to the metal surface or antibody or enzyme of the sensor. Such interaction occurs due to electrostatic interaction. As a result, the antibody or enzyme on the sensor surface will be blocked.

labeled antigen result in a change of the electric current from the electrode; said change being dependent on the antigen concentration. The same method of competition can be used in a system based on luminescence. As mentioned above, luminol produces chemiluminescence under the existence of hydrogen peroxide and a metal complex such as peroxidase. The use of a peroxidase-labeled antigen competing with the target antigen will produce a luminescence dependent upon antigen concentration. Measurement of the luminescence intensity using a photon counter or photomultiplier is the foundation of this system. The attempts made were, unfortunately, still far from real use—problems have been caused by the nonspecific adsorption of other protein over the electrode, or the steric hindrance caused by the peroxidase resulting in the inhibition of the reaction (figure 7.12) (Karube and Gotoh 1988; Karube, Seki, and Sode 1990).

Immunosensor Using QCM

QCM (quartz crystal microbalance) sensors are based on the measurement of mass change of the surface of a piezoelectric crystal (= QCM). When a certain electric field is applied between two electrodes, sandwiching an AT-cut quartz crystal, a resonant frequency (F) is observed. F changes with the adsorption of compounds on the surface. The relationship is reported as follows:

$$\Delta F = (-2.3 \times 10^6)F^2 \Delta M / A$$

Where ΔF (Hz) is the change in the fundamental frequency of the crystal, F (Hz) is the resonant frequency, ΔM (g) is the change of mass, and A is the area of the device. When an antibody is immobilized on the surface of QCM, the interaction of antigen with antibody can be measured using this device. Anti-atrazine (herbicide) antibody was immobilized on a QCM and was used as an atrazine sensor. Because the mass change after the interaction of atrazine and anti-atrazine antibody is small, due to the molecular weight of the atrazine molecule, a competitive method was used. Horseradish-peroxidase-labeled atrazine was added to the system with the target atrazine. Mass change on the surface decreased with the increase of atrazine concentration, enough to allow measurments to be carried out. QCM systems have been used for several other purposes such as measurement of odorants or cells (Nakanishi et al. 1996b) (figure 7.13). One example is the following: Using an antibody that recognizes the chemical structure of the surrounding membrane, a sensor has been developed to detect the plankton causing red tide. An antibody is immobilized on the surface of the QCM, which links up with the surface chemical structure of the

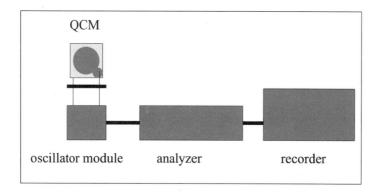

Figure 7.13
Scheme of a QCM sensor system. The antibody is immobilized on the gold electrode surface of a QCM chip.

plankton. The resultant change in mass will change the frequency of the crystal and thus can be observed (Nakanishi, Muguruma, and Karube 1996).

Immunosensor Using an SPR Device
Highly sensitive immunosensors have been developed using an SPR (surface plasmon resonance) device. The principle of SPR is based on the fact that the intensity of reflected light at glass-gold interface becomes minimum at a certain incident angle (θr). θr changes as the optical index of the media facing gold changes. When an antibody is immobilized on the gold surface, the surface optical index changes after the antigen-antibody interaction, resulting in the change in θr. A proportional relationship between θr and antigen concentration can be observed. Such a system can be used in an immunosensor (figure 7.14) (Nakamura et al. 1997b; Sasaki et al. 1998).

Microbial Sensor
Enzyme sensors, as mentioned above, are applicable for many purposes but have disadvantages, such as their relatively higher cost and shorter lifetimes. Enzymes are

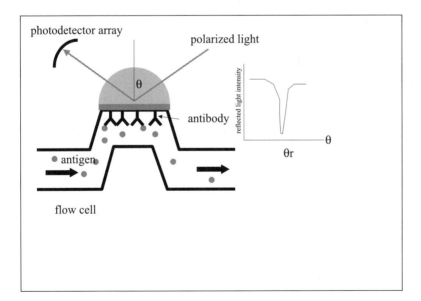

Figure 7.14
Principle of an immunosensor using an SPR device. Interaction between antibody and antigen results in a change in θr.

usually extracted from microorganisms; microorganisms contain various enzymes, allowing them to be used directly as the target recognition device. Microbial sensors using microorganisms for recognition are used in the fields of industrial processing and environmental monitoring. The difference between various types of sensors can be quite large. For instance, a microbial-based BOD sensor is limited by the lifetime of the immobilized microbes—which is about one month even when used intermittently. (Karube and Sode 1988, 1990; Karube and Chang 1991). Conversely, a chemical sensor would have a lifetime of several months.

Electrode-Based Microbial Sensor

Microorganisms carry out functions such as respiration or metabolism. Using these functions enables the selective measurement of chemical compounds. A microbial sensor consists of microorganisms immobilized in a membrane and an electrode. A microrganism that is alive in the immobilization matrix is used and the biochemical reaction inside is generally complicated. A microbial sensor using respiration activity is called a *respiration-type microbial sensor*. Aerobic microorganisms consume oxygen through respiration; the use of an oxygen electrode equipped with a gas-permeable membrane enables measurement of this activity. When an electrode with a microbial membrane attached is placed into a sample solution, the concentration of the target compound can be measured.

A typical example would be the measurement of an organic compound, which is performed in two steps. First, the microbial electrode is placed in a solution of saturated dissolved oxygen (DO). The response from the electrode is recorded. Second, the electrode is placed in the sample solution saturated with DO. Organic compound diffuses into the membrane and is decomposed by the microorganism. Respiration activity then becomes larger and the amount of oxygen diffusing to the electrode becomes smaller. The concentration of the organic compound and the decrease of oxygen are in a certain relationship, and the measurement of the compound is thus possible via the electrode signal.

Microorganisms also take up organic compounds and produce several metabolites. Among them exist electroactive materials. Metabolites measurable amperometrically are hydrogen, formic acid, or several reduced-type coenzymes. On the other hand, carbon dioxide and organic acids are potentiometrically measurable metabolites. Combining together a microbe-immobilized membrane and electrode will thus enable the fabrication of a microbial sensor (Karube et al. 1976, 1977; Karube, Matsunaga, and Suzuki 1977; Suzuki and Karube 1978).

Alcohol Sensor

Trichosporon blassicae, a type of yeast, is known as an alcohol-assimilating micro-organism. This microorganism was immobilized in a porous acetylcellulose membrane and affixed to an oxygen electrode. Finally, the tip of the device was covered with a gas-permeable Teflon membrane. In a neutral pH buffer solution, ethanol evaporated and permeated through the gas-permeable membrane, reaching the microbe-immobilized membrane, and was finally assimilated by the microorganism. Change in the oxygen concentration is observed, resulting in a change in the response. Both the enzymatic saccharide and alcohol sensors are based on oxidation and were developed subsequently to the microbial versions. The stability and capabilities are equivalent to the microbial-based sensors (Hikuma, Kubo, and Yasuda 1979; Kubo and Karube 1988).

Biochemical Oxygen Demand Sensor

BOD (biochemical oxygen demand) is an international index for river water quality. The conventional method of BOD measurement is time consuming (5 days) and is not suitable for real-time monitoring. The authors invented a biosensor for BOD a quarter century ago and this sensor has now been commercialized. This sensor is mainly used for the BOD measurement of wastewater from food factories, which usually contains many organic compounds. Sensor response shows a very good match with the results of conventional method-based BOD monitoring. Trichosporon cutaneum, a yeast used in the wastewater plant, was immobilized in a membrane and was placed on an oxygen electrode. The decrease in current from the electrode was proportionally related to the BOD of the sample. Measurement of BOD can now be performed using this sensor; the time for measurement was reduced to only 20 minutes (Karube et al. 1989). Actual cases of measuring in the middle of a river need to detect a BOD on the scale of parts per million, and the sensor described above was not able to detect down to this level. Because of this, a high-sensitivity microbial-based biosensor was developed (using ozone pretreatment to make the sample more digestable for the microbes; Nomura, Chee, and Karube 1998; Chee et al. 1999). Testing is ongoing to make this available for practical use. Separate from this, there has been work on a BOD sensor using an embedded oxygen-based transducer by incorporating semiconductor production techniques (Yang et al. 1997).

7.3 Molecular Electronic Devices

The attempts to realize a *molecular electronic device* arose from the needs to develop a next-generation electronic device. Conventional electronic devices are based on semiconductor technology. Very narrow lines are drawn on the silicon wafer that function as electric circuits. The magnitude of integration depends on how narrow the lines are. Present technology using photolithography allows lines narrower than a submicrometer, but with this size, the flow of electrons cannot be expected to work correctly. As long as we rely on a silicon-photolithography "style," growth of integration will reach a limit.

In 1974, Aviram and Colleagues (Aviram and Ratner 1974) proposed the idea of a molecular electronic device, as did Carter in 1982 (Carter 1982). Their idea was to synthesize molecules that show electronic functions. Electro-rich molecules are ready to give electrons to other molecules when conditions allow, and these molecules will play the role of electron donor. Some molecules are poor in electrons and tend to accept electrons from their environment. When the two kinds of molecules are separated with an insulating molecule, forming a donor-insulator-acceptor structure, this could theoretically function as a rectifier when sandwiched by two electrodes. This idea was not, unfortunately, followed by experimental proofs until now. The main barrier to this concept has been the difficulty of measuring a signal from only one molecule. The key to opening the gate is to mimic biomolecules.

As mentioned earlier, proteins recognize their counterpart specifically inside the cell, and they make a very narrow but safe passway for electrons in a molecular size (several tens of nanometers). If we succeed in inventing a good method to come in contact with each molecule, and also a good method to assemble them as we want, the development of a biomolecular electronic device (biochip) will proceed. With a scanning tunneling microscope, the electrical characteristics of individual atoms can be measured. The transposition of individual atoms to desired locations is also possible. Theoretically, a device based on the electrical characteristic of only one molecule could be possible, but the problem is that such a device would be extremely large. A current topic of discussion is how to miniaturize STM technology down to the point that it could be used with high consistency.

Some biomolecules work as a rectifier. For example, an accumulated Langmuir-Blodgett membrane of flavin-porphiline prepared on an electrode showed the behavior of a rectifier. Ueyama, Isoda, and Maeda (1989) used six layers of LB membrane of ruthenium complex prepared on a gold electrode; two layers of organic compounds were formed over it. With this system, the electron transfer rates between each layer and electrodes were measured. The rate of one direction was much larger than the opposite way. With this result, the system acted as a rectifier.

Aizawa and coworkers (Aizawa et al, 1989) reported a system using a conductive polymer-enzyme conjugation that showed a molecular switch property. Enzyme activity was controlled by the potential of an electrode on which the conjugation was prepared.

Our technology level is now sufficient to create several submillimeter biosensors. This will be a key for the realization of future biocomputers. The combination of the work on microbiosensors and that of molecular electronic devices will be the only way to reach the goal.

7.4 Biocomputers

The integration of various electronic devices has led to the invention of the present-day computer. In this sense, if we can integrate biomolecular electronic devices as we wish, a new computer will be developed. We can call it a *biocomputer*. But what will a biocomputer look like? How will it work, and what will it do? Comparison between a brain and a computer will help us illustrate. You can easily recognize your wife or husband, your daughter or son among many people walking in the airport or a station. You can also easily imagine what kind of present will be good for your parents. Our brain is very good at recognition and imagination. Computers cannot defeat us in these respects. On the other hand, you will easily forget the name or the face of the person you met at a business party. When it comes to memorization, we are very poor compared to a computer. A biocomputer will be, and should be, one that can function like our brain. If we define a biocomputer that is very good at a certain performance (like recognition of images, of sounds, or imagination) as a single-function biocomputer (SFB), future biocomputers will be used by connecting SFBs in a web. Biomaterials such as enzymes or antibodies are not as stable as silicon-based LSI. We have started work on synthesizing a 100 percent artificial enzyme or antibody (Rachkov et al. 2000). In this way, a biocomputer could be used without "getting tired." Up to now, artificial antibodies have much lower susceptibilities and activities than natural antibodies. Natural antibodies/elements are extremely flexible, which is thought to contribute to their good discrimination. If more flexible (but long-lived) artificial antibodies and elements can be created, this should result in a striking improvement in materials made from them.

Such biocomputers will play an important role, for example, in an aging society. If a machine can recognize what it saw or heard, it will help the development of a nursing robot. Soon we will have the whole information on our genome, and part of our tendencies toward diseases will be predicted by the result of genetic diagnosis. Biocomputers will be a good interface between patients and the medical care system. Furthermore, the development of a biocomputer itself is an act of elucidation of our brain. It is, in a sense, the act of understanding ourselves.

Recently, a trial was carried out to solve a mathematical problem using DNA molecules (Adleman 1994). In this work, the high selectivity of DNA molecules was used for calculation. In a method of calculation using DNA, one parameter is addressed to a DNA molecule of a certain thirty-base sequence (Sakamoto et al., 2000). A DNA sequence that is complemental to the other sequence was defined as a negation of the parameter expressed with the counterpart DNA sequence. These two parts, the original and its counterpart, would make a complemental binding and make a hairpin structure. DNAs that have hairpin structures can be regarded as "false" solutions. In such a way, DNA computation is performed. This is just a very beginning of the molecular computation, and its future image is now just becoming manifest.

References

Adleman, L. M. 1994. Molecular computation of solutions to combinatorial problems. *Science* 266: 1021–1024.

Aizawa, M., S. Yabuki, H. Shinohara, and Y. Ikariyama. 1989. In *Molecular Electronics-Science and Technology*, ed. A.Aviram, 301. New York: Eng. Foundation.

Aviram, A., and M. A. Ratner. 1974. Molecular rectifiers. *Chem. Phys. Lett.* 29: 277–283.

Carter, F., ed. 1987. *Molecular Electronic Devices*. (Proceedings of the Workshop on Molecular Electronic Devices held at NRL, Washington, D.C. 1981.) New York: Marcel Dekker.

Chee, G-J., Y. Nomura, K. Ikebukuro, and I. Karube. 1999. Development of highly sensitive BOD sensor and its evaluation using preozonation. *Anal. Chimica Acta.* 394: 65–71.

Chemnitius, G.C., M. Suzuki, K. Isobe, J. Kimura, I. Karube, and R. D. Schmid. 1992. Thin-film polyamine biosensor: Substrte specificity and application to fish freshness determination. *Anal. Chem. Acta* 263: 93–100.

Gotoh, M., E. Tamiya, and I. Karube. 1986. Polyvinylbutyral resin membrane for enzyme immobilization of an ISFET microbiosensor. *J. Mol. Catalysis* 37: 133–139.

Gotoh, M., A. Seki, E. Tamiya, and I. Karube. 1987. Biosensor using amorphous silicon ISFET. *Proc. Chem. Sensors* 285–291.

Gotoh, M., E. Tamiya, A. Seki, I. Shimizu, and I. Karube. 1988. Inosine sensor based on amorphous silicon ISFET. *Anal. Lett.* 21: 1785–1800.

Gotoh, M., S. Oda, I. Shimizu, A. Seki, E. Tamiya, and I. Karube. 1989a. Construction of amorphous silicon ISFET. *Sensors Actuators* 16: 55–65.

Gotoh, M., E. Tamiya, A. Seki, I. Shimizu, and I. Karube. 1989b. Glucose sensor based on amorphous silicon ISFET. *Anal. Lett.* 22: 309–322.

Goto, M., C.-Y. Chen, and I. Karube. 1993. Glucose biosensor using chitosan membrane. *Sensors Materials* 4: 187–193.

Hikuma, M., T. Kubo, and T. Yasuda. 1979. Microbial electrode sensor for alcohols. *Biotechnol. Bioeng.* 21: 1845–1853.

Hiratsuka, A., H. Muguruma, S. Sasaki, K. Ikebukuro, and I. Karube. 1999. A glucose sensor with a plasma-polymerised thin film fabricated by dry processes. *Electroanalysis* 11: 1098–1100.

Hirose, S., M. Hayashi, N. Tamura, T. Kamidate, I. Karube, and S. Suzuki. 1983. Determination of urea in blood serum with use of immobilized urease and a microware cavity ammonia monitor. *Anal. Chim. Acta* 151: 377–382.

Hu. Y. Z., S. Tsukiji, S. Shinkai, S. Oishi, and I. Hamachi. 2000. Construction of artificial photosynthetic reaction centers on a protein surface: Vectorial, multistep, and proton-coupled electron transfer for long-lived charge separation. *J. Am. Chem. Soc.* 122: 241–253.

Ikebukuro, K., M. Shimomura, N. Onuma, A. Watanabe, Y. Nomura, K. Nakanishi, Y. Arikawa, and I. Karube. 1996. A novel biosensor system for cynanide based on a chemiluminescence reaction. *Anal. Chim. Acta* 329: 111–116.

Ito, N., T. Matsumoto, H. Fujiwara, Y. Matsumoto, S. Kayashima, T. Arai, M. Kikuchi, and I. Karube. 1995. Transcutantous lactate monitoring based on a micro-planar amperometric biosensor. *Anal. Chim. Acta* 312: 323–328.

Ito, N., S. Miyamoto, J. Kimura, and I. Karube. 1996. The detection of lactate using the repeated application of stepped potentials to a micro-planar gold electrode. *Biosensors Bioelectronics* 320: 269–276.

Kai, E., S. Sawata, K. Ikebukuro, T. Iida, T. Honda, and I. Karube. 1997. Novel DNA detection system of flow injection analysis(z). The distinctive properties of a novel system employing PNA (peptide nucleic acid) as a probe for specific DNA detection. *Nucleic Acids Symposium Series* 37: 321–322.

Karube, I., and S. M. Chang. 1991. In *Handbook of Biosensors*, eds. L. J. Blum and P. R. Coulet, 267–302. New York: Marcel Dekker.

Karube, I., and M. Gotoh, 1988. Immunosensors. In *Analytical Uses of Immobilized Biological Compounds for Detection, Medical and Industrial Uses*, eds. G. G. Guibault, M. Massine, 267–279. Dordrecht: D. Reidel.

Karube, I., and M. Shimohigoshi. 1996. Development of uric acid and oxalic sensors using a bio-thermo-chip. *Sensors Actuators B* 30: 17–21.

Karube, I., and K. Sode. 1988. Enzyme and microbial sensor. In *Analytical Uses of Immobilized Biological Compounds for Detection, Medical and Industrial Uses*, NATO ASI Series, eds. G. G. Guilbault and M. Mascini, 115–130. Dordrecht: D. Reidel.

Karube, I., and K. Sode. 1990. Microbial sensors for process and environmental control. In *Biosensors and Bioinstrumentation*, ed. Donald L. Wise, 1–18. New York: Marcel Dekker.

Karube, I., and S. Suzuki. 1972a. Electrochemical preparation of urease-collagen membrane. *Biochem. Biophys. Res. Commun.* 47: 51–54.

Karube I., and S. Suzuki. 1972b. Electrochemical aggregation of tropocollagen. *Biochem. Biophys. Res. Commun.* 48: 320–325.

Karube, I., and S. Suzuki. 1986. Automatic analysis of amino acid using biosensors. In *Biotechnology of Amino Acid Production*, eds. K. Aida, I. Chibata, and K. Nakayama, 81–89. Tokyo: Kodansha Elsevier.

Karube, I., and T. Takeuchi. 1993. Biosensors for food analysis. *Sensors Biosensors for Food Analysis Process*. Italy.

Karube, I., and K. Yokoyama. 1993. Trends in biosensor research and development. *Sensors and Actuators B* 13: 12–15.

Karube, I., S. Suzuki, S. Kinoshita, and J. Mizuguchi. 1971. *Ind. Eng. Chem.* 10: 160–163.

Karube, I., S. Mitsuda, T. Matsunaga, and S. Suzuki. 1976. A rapid method for estimation of BOD by using immobilized microbial cells. *J. Ferment. Technol.* 55: 243–248.

Karube, I., T. Matsunaga, and S. Suzuki. 1977. A new microbial electrode for BOD estimation. *J. Solid-Phase Biochem.* 2: 97–104.

Karube, I., T. Matsunaga, S. Mitsuda, and S. Suzuki. 1977. Microbial Electrode BOD sensors. *Biotechnol. Bioeng.* 19: 1535–1547.

Karube, I., I. Satoh, Y. Araki, S. Suzuki, and H. Yamada. 1980. Monoamine oxidase electrode in freshness testing of meat. *Enzyme Microb. Technol.* 2: 117–120.

Karube, I., H. Matsuoka, S. Suzuki, E. Watanabe, and K. Toyama. 1984a. Determination of fish freshness with an enzyme sensor system. *J. Agric. Food Chem.* 32: 314–319.

Karube, I., H. Matsuoka, E. Watanabe, and S. Suzuki. 1984b. Measurement of freshness with a multi-functional enzyme sensor using multienzyme membrane. *Kobunshi Ronbunshu* 41: 233–248 (in Japanese).

Karube, I., K. Yokoyama, K. Sode, and E. Tamiya. 1989. Microbial BOD sensor using thermophilic bacteria. *Anal. Lett.* 22: 791–801.

Karube, I., A. Seki, and K. Sode. 1990. Microbiosensors and immunosensors. In *Microbial Enzyme and Biotechnology*, eds. W. Fogarty and C. Kelly, 425–431. Amsterdam: Elsevier Science.

Karube, I., K. Ikebukuro, Y. Murakami, and K. Yokoyama. 1994. Micromachining technology and bio-sensors. Enzyme Engineering XII. *Ann. NY Acad. Sci.* 750: 101–108.

Kitagawa, Y., K. Kitabatake, I. Kubo, E. Tamiya, and I. Karube. 1989. Alcohol sensor based on membrane-bound alcohol dehydrogenase. *Anal. Chim. Acta* 218: 61–68.

Kitagawa, Y., K. Kitabatake, M. Suda, H. Muramatsu, T. Ataka, A. Mori, E. Tamiya, and I. Karube. 1991. Amperometric detection of alcohol in beer using a flow cell and immobilized alcohol dehydrogenase. *Anal. Chem.* 63: 2391–2393.

Kubo, I., and I. Karube. 1988. *Bunseki Kagaku* 37: 628–632 (in Japanese).

Lee, S. M., M. Suzuki, M. Kumagai, H. Ikeda, E. Tamiya, and I. Karube. 1992. Bioluminescence detection system of mutagen using firefly luciferase introduced in *Escherichia coli* lysogenic strain. *Anal. Chem.* 64: 1755–1759.

Matsunaga, T., I. Karube, N. Teraoka, and S. Suzuki. 1980. Microbioassay of amino acid with a lactate sensor. *J. Chem. Soc. Japan* (Special Articles on Sensors in Chemistry) 10: 1537–1541 (in Japanese).

Miyahara, Y., T. Moriizumi, S. Shiokawa, H. Matsuoka, I. Karube, and S. Suzuki. 1983. Micro urea sensor using semiconductor and enxyme-immobilizing technology. *J. Chem. Soc. Japan* 6: 823–830 (in Japanese).

Miyahara, Y., S. Shiokawa, T. Moriizumi, H. Matsuoka, I. Karube, and S. Suzuki. 1982. Biosensors using ISFET with immobilized enzyme membrane. *Proceeding of the 2nd Sensor Symposium*, 91–95. Tokyo: IEEJ.

Muguruma, H., A. Hiratsuka, and I. Karube. 2000. Thin-film glucose biosensor based on plasma-polymerized film: Simple design for mass production. *Anal. Chem.* 72: 2671–2675.

Muguruma, H., and I. Karube. 1999. Plasma-polymerized films for biosensors. *Trends Anal. Chem.* 18: 62–68.

Murakami, Y., T. Takeuchi, K. Yokoyama, E. Tamiya, I. Karube, and M. Suda. 1994a. Integration of enzyme-immobilized column with electrochemical flow cell using micromachining techniques for a glucose detection system. *Anal. Chem.* 65: 2731–2735.

Murakami, T., S. Nakamoto, J. Kimura, T. Kuriyama, and I. Karube. 1986. A micro-planar ampero-metric glucose sensor using an ISFET as a reference electrode. *Anal. Lett.* 19: 1973–1986.

Murakami, Y., M. Suda, K. Yokoyama, T. Takeuchi, E. Tamiya, and I. Karube. 1994b. Micromachined enzyme reactor for FIA system. *Microchem. J.* 49: 319–325.

Nakamura, H., K. Ikebukuro, S. McNiven, I. Karube, H. Yamamoto, K. Hayshi, M. Suzuki, and I. Kubo. 1997a. A chemiluminescent FIA biosensor for phosphate ion monitoring using pyruvate oxidase. *Biosensors Bioelectronics* 12: 959–966.

Nakamura, R., H. Muguruma, K. Ikebukuro, S. Sasaki, R. Nagata, I. Karube, and H. Pedersen. 1997. A plasma-polymerized film for surface plasmon resonance immunosensing. *Anal. Chem.* 69: 4649–4652.

Nakanishi, K., M. Adachi, Y. Sako, Y. Ishida, H. Muguruma, and I. Karube, 1996. Detection of the red tide-causing plankton *Alexandrium affine* by a piezoelectric immunosensor using a novel method of immobilizing antibodies. Analytical Letters 29: 1247-1258.

Nakanishi, K., I. Karube, S. Hiroshi, A. Uchida, and Y. Ishida. 1996b. Detection of the red tide-causing plankton *Chattonella marina* using a piezoelectric immunosensor. *Anal. Chim. Acta* 325: 73–80.

Nakanishi, K., H. Muguruma, and I. Karube. 1996. A novel method of immobilizing antibodies on a quartz crystal microbalance using plasma-polymerized films for immunosensors. *Anal. Chem.* 68: 1695–1700.

Nomura, Y., G. Chee, and I. Karube. 1998. Biosensor technology for determination of BOD. *Field Anal. Chem. Technol.* 2–6: 333–340.

Pletneva, E. V., D. B. Fulton, T. Kohzuma, and N. M. Kostic. 2000. Direct kinetic evidence for multiple binary complexes. *J. Am. Chem. Soc.* 122: 1034–1046.

Rachkov, A., S. McNiven, A. El'-skaya, K. Yano, and I. Karube. 2000. Fluorescence detection of β-estradiol using a molecularly imprinted polymer. *Anal. Chim. Acta* 405: 23–29.

Sakamoto, D., H. Gouzu, K. Komiya, D. Kiga, S. Yokoyama, T. Yokomori, and M. Hagiya. 2000. Molecular computation by DNA hairpin formation. *Science* 288: 1223–1226.

Sasaki, S., E. Kai, H. Miyachi, H. Muguruma, K. Ikebukuro, H. Ohkawa, and I. Karube. 1998. Direct determination of etofenprox using surface plasmon resonance. *Anal. Chim. Acta* 363: 229–233.

Satoh, I., I. Karube, and S. Suzuki. 1976. Enzyme electrode for saccharose. *Biotechnol. Bioeng.* 18: 269–272.

Sawata, S., E. Kai, K. Ikebukuro, T. Iida, T. Honda, and I. Karube. 1999. Application of peptide nucleic acid to the direct detection of deoxyribonucleic acid amplified by polymerase chain reaction. *Biosensors Bioelectronics* 14: 397–404.

Shinohara, H., T. Chiba, and M. Aizawa. 1988. Enzyme microsensor for glucose with an electrochemically synthesized enzyme-polyaniline film. *Sensors Actuators B* 13: 79–86.

Streyer, L. 1988. *Biochemistry*, third edition, New York: W. H. Freeman and Company.

Suzuki, S., I. Karube, and Y. Watanabe. 1972. Electrolytic preparation of enzyme-collagen films. *Proc. IV IFS: Ferment. Technol. Today* 375–377.

Suzuki, S., N. Sonobe, I. Karube, and M. Aizawa. 1974. Electrochemical preparation of uricase-collagen membrane. *Chem. Lett.* 1: 9–10.

Suzuki, M., H. Suzuki, I. Karube, and R. D. Schmid. 1989. Disposable micro hypoxanthine sensors for freshness estimation. In *Biosensors: Applications in medicine, environmental protection and process control*, eds. R. D. Schmid, F. Scheller, 107–111. Proceedings of the second International Workshop on Biosensors, held in Braunschweig, FRG, May 1989, published as GBF Monograph 13.

Suzuki, H. 1994. Integrated amino acid sensors for detection of L-glutamate, L-lysine, L-arginine, and L-histidine. *Electroanalysis* 6: 299–304.

Suzuki, H., H. Shiroishi, S. Sasaki, and I. Karube. 1999. Microfabricated liquid junction Ag/AgCl reference electrode and its application to a one-chip potentiometric sensor. *Anal. Chem.* 71: 5069–5075.

Suzuki, H., T. Hirakawa, S. Sasaki, and I. Karube. 1999b. An integrated three-electrode system with a micromachined liquid-junction Ag/AgCl reference electrode. *Anal. Chim. Acta* 387: 103–112.

Suzuki, H., H. Ozawa, S. Sasaki, and I. Karube. 1999c. A novel thin-film Ag/AgCl anode structure for microfabricated Clark-type oxygen electrodes. *Sensors Actuators B* 53: 140–146.

Suzuki, S., and I. Karube. 1978. Microbial electrode: BOD sensor. *Enzyme Eng.* 4: 329–333.

Tamiya, E., K. Masaki, T. Sugiyama, and I. Karube. 1989. Highly selective detection system for luciferase gene in transgenic fish. *Proc. 1st Int. Marine Biotechnology Conference*, 281–284. Held 3–6 September 1989, Toranomon Pastral, Tokyo, Japan. Published as *Current Topics in Marine Biotechnology*, eds. Miyachi, S., I. Karube, and Y. Ishida, 1990. Tokyo: Japan Society of Marine Biotechnology.

Tamiya, E., T. Sugiyama, K. Masaki, A. Hirose, T. Okoshi, and I. Karube. 1990. Spatial imaging of luciferase gene expression in transgenic fish. *Nucleic Acids Res.* 18: 1072.

Ueyama, S., S. Isoda, and M. Maeda. 1989. Electrochemical behavior of a flavin Langmuir-Blodgett monolayer on gold electrodes. *J. Electroanal. Chem.* 364: 149–156.

Watanabe, E., K. Toyama, I. Karube, H. Matsuoka, and S. Suzuki. 1984a. Determination of Inosine-5-monophosphate in fish tissue with an enzyme sensor. *J. Food Sci.* 49: 114–116.

Watanabe, E., T. Ogura, K. Toyama, I. Karube, H. Matsuoka, and S. Suzuki. 1984b. Determination of adenosine 5′-monophosphate in fish and shellfish using an enzyme sensor. *Enzyme Microbiol. Technol.* 6: 207–211.

Yang, Z., H. Suzuki, S. Sasaki, S. McNiven, and I. Karube. 1997. Comparison of dynamic transient and steady state measuring measuring methods in a batch type BOD sensing system. *Sensors Actuators B* 45: 217–222.

Yokoyama, K., K. Sode, E. Tamiya, and I. Karube. 1989. Integrated biosensor for glucose and galactose. *Anal. Chim. Acta* 218: 137–142.

Zhang, L., C. H. Tai, L. Yu, and C.A. Yu. 2000. pH induced electron transfer between iron-sulfur clusters and heme c1 in the bovine cyloctrane bc1 complex. *J. Biol. Chem.* 275: 7656–7661.

Contributors

Andrew Adamatzky
Computing, Engineering, and
Mathematical Sciences
University of the West of England
Bristol, England

Robert R. Birge
W. M. Keck Center for Molecular
Electronics and Department of
Chemistry
Syracuse University
Syracuse, New York
and:
Departments of Chemistry and
Molecular and Cell Biology
University of Connecticut
Storrs, Connecticut

Michael Conrad (deceased)
Department of Computer Science
Wayne State University
Detroit, Michigan

Isao Karube
School of Bionics
Tokyo Institute of Technology
Hachioji, Tokyo

Jean-Marie Lehn
College de France
Strasbourg, France

Carlo C. Maley
Fred Hutchinson Cancer Research
Center
Seattle, Washington

Duane L. Marcy
W. M. Keck Center for Molecular
Electronics and Department of
Chemistry
Syracuse University
Syracuse, New York

Nicholas G. Rambidi
International Research Institute for
Management Sciences
and Physics Department
Moscow State University
Moscow, Russia

Satoshi Sasaki
Katayanagi Advanced Research
Laboratories
Tokyo University of Technology
Hachioji, Tokyo

Tanya Sienko
Institute of Computer Science
Friedrich-Schiller-University
Jena, Germany

Bryan W. Vought
W. M. Keck Center for Molecular
Electronics and Department of
Chemistry
Syracuse University
Syracuse, New York
and
Department of Biological Chemistry
and Molecular Pharmacology
Harvard Medical School
Boston, Massachusetts

Klaus-Peter Zauner
Institute of Computer Science
Friedrich-Schiller-University
Jena, Germany

Index